DAVID LYNCH
INTERVIEWS

CONVERSATIONS WITH FILMMAKERS SERIES
PETER BRUNETTE, GENERAL EDITOR

DAVID LYNCH
INTERVIEWS

EDITED BY RICHARD A. BARNEY

UNIVERSITY PRESS OF MISSISSIPPI / JACKSON

www.upress.state.ms.us

The University Press of Mississippi is a member of the Association of American University Presses.

Copyright © 2009 by University Press of Mississippi

All rights reserved

First printing 2009

Library of Congress Cataloging-in-Publication Data

David Lynch : interviews / edited by Richard A. Barney.
    p. cm. — (Conversations with filmmakers series)
  Includes index.
  ISBN 978-1-60473-236-8 (cloth : alk. paper) — ISBN 978-1-60473-237-5 (pbk. : alk. paper) 1. Lynch, David, 1946—Interviews. 2. Motion picture producers and directors—United States—Interviews. I. Barney, Richard A., 1955–
  PN1998.3.L96D48 2009
  791.4302'33092—dc22

2009014227

British Library Cataloging-in-Publication Data available

CONTENTS

Introduction   vii

Chronology   xvii

Filmography   xxi

Eraserhead: Is There Life after Birth?   3
    STEPHEN SABAN AND SARAH LONGACRE

Good Eraserhead: Indiana   9
    GARY INDIANA

Director David Lynch—From Cult Film to *Elephant Man*   19
    JIMMY SUMMERS

You Can Have Any Colour So Long as It's Black   22
    STUART DOLLIN

Is There Life after *Dune*?   29
    TIM HEWITT

Out to Lynch   34
    DAVID CHUTE

Blue Movie   41
    JEFFREY FERRY

A Dark Lens on America   49
    RICHARD B. WOODWARD

David Lynch   60
    DAVID BRESKIN

Interview with David Lynch 106
MICHEL CIMENT AND HUBERT NIOGRET

An Interview with David Lynch 125
KRISTINE MCKENNA

Twin Peaks: Fire Walk with Me: The Press Conference at Cannes 1992 134
S. MURRAY

Naked Lynch 145
GEOFF ANDREW

Interview 150
CHRIS DOURIDAS

The World Reveals Itself 163
KATHRIN SPOHR

Highway to Hell 170
STEPHEN PIZZELLO

The *Icon* Profile: David Lynch 180
CHRIS RODLEY

The Road to Hell 194
DOMINIC WELLS

I Want a Dream When I Go to a Film 200
MICHAEL SRAGOW

David Lynch: A 180-Degree Turnaround 213
MICHAEL HENRY

Getting Lost Is Beautiful 222
JOHN POWERS

Mulholland Drive, Dreams, and Wrangling with the Hollywood Corral 232
RICHARD A. BARNEY

David Lynch and Laura Dern: *Inland Empire* 246
JOHN ESTHER

Inland Empire, Transcendental Meditation, and the "Swim" of Ideas 251
RICHARD A. BARNEY

Index 267

INTRODUCTION

IT COMES CLOSE to the homespun expressions for which David Lynch is famous to say that interviewing him can be a lot like trying to pin down a very talkative sidewinder—and a darn friendly one at that. This feature of his personality and career explains why the frequent characterizations of him as "elusive" do not quite get it right, because Lynch loves to converse: he genuinely enjoys telling stories, swapping jokes, philosophizing off the cuff, and the like. For him it is quite another thing, however, to reveal aspects of his personal life or to expound on what his movies may mean, even to remark pointedly on what they mean to him individually as an artist. And so, *elusive*, he may not be, but *enigmatic*, an interviewer's moving target, a canny conversationalist who often says more in an interview by what he does not say than by what he does—those things certainly are his trademark.

There are several reasons why interviewing Lynch can be an experience of sinuous indirection, and the first is his oft-cited lack of skill with language. Both Lynch and his former wives or partners have frequently referred to his so-called "preverbal stage" during the 1970s and early 1980s, when otherwise relatively straightforward moments for communication would break down under his seeming inability to use words. Isabella Rossellini, for instance, has described numerous times when in response to a question or remark, Lynch would gesture unpredictably with his arms or create whooshing sounds with his lips rather than produce coherent sentences. Among his own comments on this state of affairs, Lynch has remarked to me in a conversation included in this volume (from 2008) that in his earliest interviews, especially those about *Eraserhead*, "for a long time, I didn't understand the concept, really, of speaking about a thing. So I didn't say very much. And I didn't say very much for a long time."

Needless to say, as the interviews in this collection illustrate, Lynch made a concerted effort from the 1980s into the 1990s toward becoming more and more adept at talking about his films. Putting aside, for the moment, the question of how much interviewers may try to polish his unique parlance, there is a clear difference, for instance, between his rough and halting locutions in the early interviews in the *Soho Weekly News* or the *East Village Eye* and the much more composed, articulate conversations he had later with interviewers for the *New York Times Magazine* in 1990 or *Salon Magazine* in 1999. Still, Lynch remains a director with a somewhat vexed relationship to language: his sentences—always powered with immense enthusiasm—continue to be propelled by herky-jerky rhythms that are alternately arresting and puzzling. And the folksy or street-casual expressions that pepper his statements—ranging from "peachy keen" to "very cool" to "fantastic!"—are frequently pressed into service to help explain one of the most difficult aspects of his films: what he calls their "abstraction," a quality of atmospheric suggestiveness that, for him, should not be reduced to an intellectual formula or definitive description.

This brings us to the second reason for Lynch's oblique relationship to talking about his work, since he has been committed from the very beginning of his career to a cinematic aesthetic that is based on the essential value of the unidentified and the unsaid. As a proponent of the ability of movies to make audiences dream, Lynch aims to produce work that is vividly concrete but also evocatively mysterious, and since his very first interview in 1977 with Stephen Saban and Sarah Longacre, "mystery" is therefore not surprisingly one of the words he frequently uses. This is not, however, the generic sort of "mystery" that in the course of a particular narrative will eventually be resolved or dissipated. On the contrary, the point for Lynch is to create films that will remain *perpetually* mysterious, in the sense of inducing a sense of wonder that both provokes and resists—in a potentially endless cycle—viewers' desire to make sense of the images and stories he offers them. Among other things, that priority means that in interviews, Lynch sees his job as avoiding anything that will dispel that aura by providing what he perceives as superficial "solutions" for the puzzles that his movies create. When in 2001, for instance, after I put a question to him about *Mulholland Drive* that produced an extremely long pause, he responded bluntly to my query whether the question was a difficult one with: "No, I don't want to say too much."

Elsewhere, in an interview with Chris Hodenfield (not included in this volume), he has remarked more expansively, "It's a very dangerous thing, this movie business. Because no one will ever know what film *could* be when a filmmaker has to talk about it and convince people with words."[1] For Lynch, then, it is absolutely necessary, in a very literal-minded sense, to talk *around* his films. Circumlocution is thus not about being cagey or coy, but about leaving the real work of making meaning to his viewers.

The combination of developing his linguistic facility and sticking to his aesthetic principles has produced a sometimes idiosyncratic and always intriguing thing that is *the Lynch interview*. In terms of content, Lynch is most ready to talk about the process of making his movies, rather than what particular elements may mean, although there are notable exceptions to this rule, such as his steadfast refusal over the years, beginning in 1977, to reveal how he created the "baby" in *Eraserhead*. Moreover, as both Lynch and his interviewers have recognized in other cases, discussing how he may have come up with particular characters or plot elements can readily become coded as an authoritative "guide" for how to interpret his work—another temptation Lynch always vigilantly guards against.

Over time, a vocabulary with special meaning has evolved for Lynch, and precisely because he has worked so hard over the years to create it, he repeatedly relies on its terms to talk about his films—again, in an act of explanation that goes only so far. He frequently describes aspects of his films, for example, as "beautiful," "thrilling," or "magical," as being constructed on the basis of "harmony," "contrast," or "balance," where the generated "mood" or "feeling" helps create a "world" that you "fall in love with" and that can "give you room to dream." The inspiration that comes to him for particular images, as well as the feeling that he aims to invoke by them, is often "in the air," a "gift" that arrives from a source that cannot be completely pinpointed. These terms are more than stock formulas for Lynch, since they can gain nuance in the context of particular situations or conversations, and, more importantly, although he rarely defines them, they gather a sense of meaning by his insistence on repeatedly employing them. And thus, like Lynch, who claims that the "texture" of words can be as important as their literal meaning, readers of his interviews must be willing to be patient, to accumulate an understanding of things intuitively rather than only analytically.

While it is inevitable, then, that both interviewers and readers will have the constant sense that Lynch knows a lot more than he is saying, it also becomes clear from the pieces in this volume that in the process of filmmaking itself, Lynch often prefers not knowing too much about what may be transpiring. As he remarks to Michel Ciment and Hubert Niogret, rather than reducing a project to an oversimplified concept, "it's good not to know too much about what you're going to do." This approach is captured vividly in the metaphor Lynch probably uses most often to describe the process of making a film, in which he "fishes" for "ideas" that arrive piecemeal and in their own timing from the "ocean" of possibilities. By this way of doing things, Lynch claims, he never has the full picture about his moving pictures until almost the very end of post-production. Moreover, he imagines his task mainly as one of being true to those ideas, which he contrasts strongly with something like a "theme," which for him would impose a reductive scheme onto a film's ability to develop in more organic fashion (see, for instance, his comments to me about *Mulholland Drive* in 2001). In interviews, when describing how he has gathered ideas for particular films, Lynch typically avoids specifying what those ideas actually were—again, fearful that they might dictate viewers' opinions—and he is particularly keen not to disclose the very first one, since it could pose as the putative foundation or origin explaining everything else. The enigmatic quality of "ideas" thus applies both to Lynch as filmmaker and to his viewer-readers. As Lynch remarks to Stuart Dollin, "I think that for me everything is feelings or intuition. There's not too much intellectualising."

A third reason why interviews with Lynch can be snakelike, slipping in all kinds of diverting directions, is that he has a legion of roles and artistic abilities that have all converged at one time or another on how he has made films from *Six Men Getting Sick* to *Inland Empire*. While he is no doubt best known as a director, he has regularly worked on his films—both officially, as noted in the credits, and unofficially, when not—as producer, cinematographer, camera man, sound man, screenwriter, editor, soundtrack designer and engineer, animator, and set designer. And that is the short list. In addition to being one of the most intuitive filmmakers alive today, Lynch has been close to being the most complete one, with a hands-on approach that exceeds that of most directors who are his contemporaries. What is more, Lynch's projects and interests outside of film have strongly shaped his films as well: his active interest in painting, for instance, has influenced what is sometimes described as his "painterly" approach to shot composition; his furniture design and building projects have contributed to film sets such as the home of Fred and Renée Madison (played by Bill Pullman and Patricia Arquette) in *Lost Highway*; and his well-known passion for music and, most recently, for singing, has found its way into a number of soundtracks from *Blue Velvet* to *Inland Empire*. The result is that Lynch can talk with considerable expertise about a host of topics more or less close to the process of filmmaking. This volume aims to suggest that diversity by collecting interviews that include Lynch's observations on camerawork and film stock (see, for instance, Stuart Dollin and Stephen Pizzello); his quasi-philosophical musings on painting, nature, and his representation of the American family (Kristine McKenna); his comments about the importance of sound and music (Chris Douridas, Michel Ciment and Hubert Niogret, and Michael Henry); and his discussion of how furniture design and architecture relate to the way he imagines the spatial dimensions of his films (Kathrin Spohr).

Taken as a whole, the arc of Lynch's career has tracked a steadily increasing appreciation for the peculiar way that Lynch makes films and talks about them, although it has also been punctuated by moments of enthused public response—recall, for example, the huge popularity of the television series, *Twin Peaks*—and by equally bracing lows characterized by a critical and box-office thrashing, such as the harshly negative reaction to the "prequel" feature, *Twin Peaks: Fire Walk with Me*. Overall, Lynch's efforts to engage viewers more articulately, as well as a greater familiarity with his work in the U.S. from the mid-1980s into the early 1990s, have had their effect: moviegoers have come to know more and more what to expect, and the term *Lynchian* has entered the vocabulary of both critics and the general public as a kind of counterpart, in the world of film, to the earlier adjective inspired by Woody Allen: *Kafkaesque*.

Within that general trend, the interviews in this book also suggest that the range of responses to Lynch's personal style and work has been strikingly divergent. Some interviews, such as the one in *The Face*, thrill at the subversiveness they find in a film like *Blue Velvet*; other interviews, like those by David Chute, Tim Hewitt, or Richard Woodward, highlight the strange or bizarre in Lynch's work. This latter element seems to provoke an especially zany reflex of alliterative, punning formulations: "Out to Lynch," "Wizard of Weird," "Czar of the Bizarre," "Naked Lynch," and so on. Here, several of the collected interviews reflect a broader pattern of characterizing Lynch or his movies, especially in the U.S. In some cases, those kinds of monikers have been delivered with genuine fondness, as Lynch himself acknowledges, such as when Mel Brooks famously called him "Jimmy Stewart from Mars" while working with him on *The Elephant Man*. But even genuine fondness can have a double edge: at the

Independent Spirit Awards in 2007, with an off-kilter affection that only Frank Booth could muster, Dennis Hopper announced that Lynch and Laura Dern were being given a Special Distinction Award with the remark: "You know, at the core of every Lynch film is a fundamental mystery that is best summed up this way: 'What the fuck was *that* about?'" The tone of amused exasperation in Hopper's one-liner is escalated in several interviews I have included, represented particularly by the press conference for *Fire Walk with Me* at the Cannes Film Festival and Dominic Wells's piece for *Time Out*, which register an aggressive frustration with Lynch's oblique explanations, if not also some sarcastic skepticism about whether he really knows what he is talking about. It is worth noting that in both these cases, the interviewers were no strangers to the parameters of Lynch's films or to his usual approach to discussing them.

To be sure, there are also substantive issues that sometimes provoke interviewers to press Lynch harder for better explanations. To take only a few examples, several of the questioners at the Cannes press conference want him to reflect seriously on the implications of his representation of violence and sadomasochism in films like *Blue Velvet* or *Wild at Heart*. Kristine McKenna asks Lynch to clarify his apparent double vision of a world filled with fearful elements and of one that also can be construed as genuinely benevolent for human existence. David Breskin practically urges Lynch to explore the issue of how he represents women—their ostensible passivity and need to suffer for a seemingly greater good—a topic that, in interviews elsewhere, Lynch has never addressed to the same degree of detail. In my own interview with him about *Inland Empire*, I find several ways to ask him to explain how an apparent similarity between his films and transcendental meditation—a delving down into levels beyond everyday human understanding—produces such drastically different consequences: in his films, a terrifying encounter with a dimension of life whose danger must usually be vanquished, by contrast with meditation, which proves to be a tranquil exploration of a larger, invariably edifying, consciousness. I leave to the volume's readers to decide to what extent Lynch may have successfully responded to any of these promptings.

In retrospect, the topic of transcendental meditation turns out to highlight another thread that runs throughout Lynch's interviews from 1977 until the present: his interest in altered, distended, or enhanced states of consciousness. As Lynch has told many interviewers, he began transcendental meditation in 1973, and he has described practicing it daily ever since, characterizing its effects as personally and artistically transforming. Although he does not explicitly mention TM to Stephen Saban and Sarah Longacre in 1977, it is intriguing to note that in attempting to work out the symbolic twists and turns of identity in *Eraserhead*, they draw on another Eastern spiritual system, Tibetan Buddhism. Overall, however, until at least the early 1990s, Lynch remained somewhat cautious about discussing TM in any detail. When David Breskin asks about it in 1990, for instance, Lynch responds that "I don't really talk about meditation. A lot of people are against it. It's just something I like." Still, in that same interview, Lynch talks about his interest in an evolutionary process of "different levels of human growth. Degrees of awareness or consciousness . . . being totally aware and totally conscious at the end of the evolutionary trail." Similarly, in 1992, Lynch remarks to Kristine McKenna that the ultimate proof of life's meaningfulness would be "Total bliss consciousness."

This does not mean, of course, that there is a direct, one-to-one correlation between Lynch's commitment to TM and the experience his films' protagonists often undergo, in which their normal sense of self or awareness is shaken by dark, often threatening states of feeling or mind—the examples that come to mind include Henry in *Eraserhead*, Fred Madison in *Lost Highway*, and Nikki Grace in *Inland Empire*. Instead, as Lynch explained to me in 2008, he perceives a big difference between the genuine enlightenment of consciousness and the less spiritual traumas of characters who remain tangled in what he describes as the material world of "the marketplace." Still, since Lynch has functioned more or less as a public spokesperson for TM since 2005, founding the David Lynch Foundation for Consciousness-Based Education and Peace and, more recently, traveling across the U.S. for months at a time on lecture tours, he has demonstrated an increasing willingness not only to talk about his relation to meditation, but also to contemplate possible connections between the world of meditation and that of his films. As his remarks to me about *Inland Empire* indicate, those connections remain tenuous, but clearly the single, unifying element of both worlds is Lynch's unwavering commitment to exploring the radical transformation of ego-based identity, whether or not that venture may lead to profound serenity or harrowing distress.

Finally, I have aimed to capture in this volume at least a glimpse of the strong international interest in Lynch's films that has grown markedly since the mid-1980s. Four of the interviews here—by Christine McKenna, Kathrin Spohr, Michel Ciment and Hubert Niogret, and Michael Henry—come from three European publications in Spain, Switzerland, and France. I have made a particular point of representing the French response to

Lynch's work, since the French have had such an important role not only as an influential audience for his films, but also as financial sponsors for Lynch's various projects. In 1990, *Wild at Heart* received the Palme d'Or at Cannes, and since then, in 2002, he served as Président of the Cannes Official Selection Jury, as well as being awarded the title "Chevalier" in the Legion of Honor. Lynch himself has quipped with complete sincerity, "Thank God for the French," and for good reason, since the companies Canal Plus and StudioCanal, for instance, were crucial in producing films such as *Lost Highway*, *Mulholland Drive*, and *Inland Empire*. In fact, given the notorious difficulty Lynch has frequently had obtaining American funding for his projects—perhaps most dramatically, the abrupt decision of ABC to cancel *Mulholland Drive* as a television series before it had even started—it is hard to imagine that Lynch's films during the past decade would have had the same impact without the substantial French assistance they received.

For the interviews by McKenna and Spohr, the original English versions were available, but in the case of the interviews in French, the original recordings had been lost, and therefore I have translated them back into English (since Lynch always conducts his interviews with international publications in English). This means that the interviews by Ciment, Niogret, and Henry have suffered the process of double translation, and while I have done my best to replicate Lynch's voice in them, it is inevitable that, given their intermediary stage in the French language, those interviews make him sound at certain moments more formal than he does elsewhere in the collection. That relative drawback, however, is worth the larger gain of American readers learning more about what French audiences have wanted to know regarding Lynch's perspective on his work.

In following the standard procedure of the Conversations with Filmmakers series, the interviews collected in this volume are reprinted without any significant editing. Although this may result in some repetition in Lynch's remarks, it does offer more integrity for the scholarly reader. More importantly, these repetitions mark not only the topics that have preoccupied Lynch over the years, but also the very specific vocabulary he has persisted in using when discussing his projects.

Many thanks to the people who have helped with this book along the way, including Jay Aaseng, Aaron Cerny, Michel Ciment, Dominic Kulcsar, Mindy Ramaker, Anna Skarbek, Mary Sweeney, and Michael Henry Wilson. Special thanks to Mike Lee for brainstorming sessions;

Ted Augustyn and Robert Keasler for their hospitality; and Jaclyn Ippolito for her unflagging energy in organizing things. Thanks as well to Seetha Srinivasan and Walter Biggins for their near-infinite patience in getting this done. And I am grateful to John Ireland for checking my French translations; any errors, or moments when Lynch may sound like a Frenchman not quite getting the American idiom right, are entirely my own doing.

RAB

Note

1. Chris Hodenfield, "Daring *Dune*," *Rolling Stone*, December 6, 1984, p. 28.

CHRONOLOGY

1946	Born David Keith Lynch on January 20 in Missoula, Montana, to Donald and Sunny Lynch.
1963–64	Attends the Corcoran School of Art in Washington, D.C.
1964–65	Attends the Boston Museum School.
1966	Enters the Pennsylvania Academy of the Fine Arts in Philadelphia.
1967	*Six Men Getting Sick*, Lynch's first "moving picture," awarded the second annual Dr. William S. Biddle Cadwalader Memorial Prize, Pennsylvania Academy of the Fine Arts.
1968	*The Alphabet*, a four-minute animated film financed by a grant from the American Film Institute.
1970	*The Grandmother*, a short film combining live action and animation. Attends the American Film Institute's Center for Advanced Film Studies in Los Angeles.
1972	Begins filming *Eraserhead*, his first full-length film.
1977	*Eraserhead* premieres at Filmex, the annual film festival in Los Angeles; thereafter, the film gains notable cult status on the midnight movie circuit.
1980	*The Elephant Man*, nominated for Academy Awards for best director, best writing, screenplay from another medium; and for BAFTA awards for best direction and best screenplay; wins a César award (France) for Best Foreign Film.
1982	Launches his weekly cartoon, "The Angriest Dog in the World."
1984	The release of *Dune*, based on Frank Herbert's popular novels, but a critical and box-office failure.
1986	*Blue Velvet* released; voted best film of 1986 by the National Society of Film Critics and nominated for Academy Awards for best film and best director.

1988	*The Cowboy and the Frenchman*, a whimsical treatment of the American West meeting haute culture, in the French television series *France As Seen by Others*.
1989	Coproduces with Angelo Badalamenti *Industrial Symphony No. 1*, based on their concert at the New Wave Festival, Brooklyn Academy of Music.
1990	First season of *Twin Peaks* on ABC generates wide-ranging critical and viewer enthusiasm; receives five Emmy nominations. *Wild at Heart* has its world premiere at the Cannes Film Festival, where it receives the Palme d'Or.
1991	In its second season, *Twin Peaks* is cancelled by ABC, despite an intense campaign by viewers to extend the series. Receives the American Film Institute's first Franklin J. Schaffner Alumni Medal.
1992	Release of *Twin Peaks: Fire Walk with Me*, a film prequel to the television series, which is received harshly by most critics and audiences.
1994	Publishes *Images*, a collection of drawings, photographs, and film stills.
1995	*Lumière and Company*, a fifty-five-second film contributed as part of a celebration of the centenary of cinema, using the original cameras of Auguste and Louis Lumière.
1996	Release of *Lost Highway*, described by Lynch as a "psychogenic fugue" about "a man in trouble."
1999	*The Straight Story* is released, based on the true story of Alvin Straight traveling several hundred miles on a John Deere tractor to visit his ailing brother.
2000	Begins work on a television series titled *Mulholland Drive* with ABC, but after seeing a rough cut of the pilot, the executives cancel plans for the series.
2001	*Mulholland Drive*, based on the original pilot, is released as a feature film; Lynch receives award for best director at the Cannes Film Festival and the César award (France) for Best Foreign Film.
2002	Launches davidlynch.com, a subscription-based website featuring animation series, experimental videos, and news for fans. Serves as Président of the Official Selection Jury for competition at the Cannes Film Festival. Is made "Chevalier" (Knight) in France's Legion of Honor.
2005	Launches the David Lynch Foundation for Consciousness-Based Education and Peace.
2006	Release of *Inland Empire*, a nearly three-hour film in digital video, starring Laura Dern as "a woman in trouble." Receives Golden Lion award from the Venice Film Festival for lifetime

	achievement. Publishes *Catching the Big Fish*, a combination of memoir, filmography, and reflections on Transcendental Meditation.
2007	Receives a Special Distinction Award, along with Laura Dern, from Independent Spirit Awards for their collaborative work. Publishes *The Air Is on Fire*, a compendium of forty years of painting, drawing, photography, sculpture, and film, based on an exhibition at the Fondation Cartier pour l'art contemporain in Paris, March–May, 2007.
2008	At Cannes, it is announced that Lynch will executive produce Alejandro Jodorowsky's next film, *King Shot*, as well as Werner Herzog's project titled *My Son, My Son*. Works on postproduction of an untitled documentary film about his public lectures and other activities regarding Transcendental Meditation. Releases *The Lime Green Set*, a ten-disc DVD compilation including *The Short Films of David Lynch*, the remastered *Eraserhead*, *The Elephant Man* with second-disc extras, *Wild at Heart* with over thirty outtakes, *Industrial Symphony No. 1*, the web series *Dumbland* and *Rabbits*, and 16mm experimental films from the 1960s.

FILMOGRAPHY

Includes films, videos, television programs, and internet-based media

1967
SIX MEN GETTING SICK
Written and animated by **David Lynch**
16 mm, projected on a sculpted screen, Color
1 minute

1968
THE ALPHABET
Producer: H. Barton Wasserman
Written, directed, and filmed by **David Lynch**
Cast: Peggy Lynch (Girl)
16 mm, Color
4 minutes

1970
THE GRANDMOTHER
Financed by an American Film Institute grant
Written, directed, filmed, and animated by **David Lynch**
Assistant Script Consultants: Margaret Lynch, C. K. Williams
Still Photography: Doug Randall
Music: Tractor
Sound Editing and Mixing: Alan Splet
Sound Effects: David Lynch, Margaret Lynch, Robert Chadwick, Alan Splet
Cast: Richard White (Boy), Dorothy McGinnis (Grandmother), Virginia Maitland (Mother), Robert Chadwick (Father)
16 mm, Color
34 minutes

1974
THE AMPUTEE
Produced, written, and directed by **David Lynch**
Photography: Herb Caldwell, Frederick Elmes
Cast: Catherine E. Coulson (Woman), **David Lynch** (Doctor)
Videotape, B & W
Version 1: 5 minutes; Version 2: 4 minutes

1977
ERASERHEAD
Columbia Pictures
Producer: **David Lynch**, with support from the American Film Institute Center for Advanced Film Studies
Written and directed by **David Lynch**
Assistant to the Director: Catherine Coulson
Camera and Lighting: Herbert Cardwell, Frederick Elmes
Special Effects Photography: Frederick Elmes
Assistant Camera: Catherine Coulson
Picture Editing: **David Lynch**
Location Sound and Recording: Alan Splet
Sound Editing: Alan Splet
Sound Effects: **David Lynch**, Alan Splet
Production Design and Special Effects: **David Lynch**
Production Manager: Doreen G. Small
Cast: Jack Nance (Henry Spencer), Charlotte Stewart (Mary X), Allen Joseph (Bill X), Jeanne Bates (Mary's Mother), Judith Anna Roberts (Beautiful Girl Across the Hall), Laurel Near (Lady in the Radiator), Jack Fisk (Man in the Planet), Jean Lange (Grandmother), Thomas Coulson (The Boy), John Monez (Bum)
35 mm, B & W
89 minutes

1980
THE ELEPHANT MAN
Paramount
Producer: Jonathan Sanger
Director: David Lynch
Assistant Directors: Anthony Waye, Gerry Cavigan
Screenplay: Christopher De Vore, Eric Bergren, **David Lynch** (based on *The Elephant Man and Other Reminiscences* by Sir Frederick Treves and *The Elephant Man: A Study in Human Dignity* by Ashley Montagu)
Photography: Freddie Francis
Editor: Anne V. Coates
Sound Design: Alan Splet

Music: John Morris
Costumes: Patricia Norris
Production Design: Stuart Craig
Art Director: Bob Cartwright
Cast: Anthony Hopkins (Frederick Treves), John Hurt (John Merrick), Anne Bancroft (Mrs. Madge Kendal), Sir John Geilgud (Carr Gomm), Wendy Miller (Mothershead), Freddie Jones (Bytes), Michael Elphick (Night Porter), Hannah Gordon (Mrs. Treves), Helen Ryan (Princess Alex), John Standing (Fox)
35 mm, B & W
124 minutes

1984
DUNE
Universal
Producer: Raffaella De Laurentiis
Director: **David Lynch**
Assistant Director and Associate Producer: José Lopez Rodero
Screenplay: **David Lynch**, based on the novel by Frank Herbert
Photography: Freddie Francis
Editor: Antony Gibbs
Sound Design: Alan R. Splet
Music: Mary Paich, Toto, Brian Eno, Daniel Lanois, Roger Eno
Costumes: Bob Ringwood
Special Effects: Kit West, Albert J. Whitlock, Charles L. Finance, Barry Nolan
Production Design: Anthony Masters
Production Coordinator: Golda Offenheim
Art Directors: Pierluigi Basile, Benjamin Fernandez
Cast: Francesca Annis (Lady Jessica), Kyle MacLachlan (Paul Atreides), Dean Stockwell (Dr. Wellington Yueh), Max Von Sydow (Dr. Keynes), Jurgen Prochnow (Duke Leto Atreides), Brad Dourif (Peter De Vries), Jose Ferrer (Padisha Emperor Shaddam IV), Freddie Jones (Thufir Hawat), Silvana Mangano (Reverend Mother Ramallo), Kenneth McMillan (Baron Vladimir Harkonnen)
70 mm, Color
137 minutes

1986
BLUE VELVET
De Laurentiis Entertainment Group
Executive Producer: Richard Roth
Direction and Screenplay: **David Lynch**
Assistant Directors: Ellen Rauch, Ian Woolf
Photography: Frederick Elmes
Editor: Duwayne Dunham
Sound Design: Alan Splet

Music: Angelo Badalamenti
Sound: Alan Splet, Ann Kroeber
Sound Effects: Richard Hyams
Special Effects: Greg Hull, George Hill
Special Effects Makeup: Dean Jones
Production Design: Patricia Norris
Production Supervisor: Gail M. Kearns
Cast: Kyle MacLachlan (Jeffrey Beaumont), Isabella Rossellini (Dorothy Vallens), Dennis Hopper (Frank Booth), Laura Dern (Sandy Williams), Hope Lange (Mrs. Williams), Dean Stockwell (Ben), George Dickerson (Detective Williams), Brad Dourif (Raymond), Jack Nance (Paul), Priscilla Pointer (Mrs. Beaumont)
35 mm, Color
120 minutes

1988
THE COWBOY AND THE FRENCHMAN
Propaganda Films
Executive Producer: Paul Cameron
Producers: Daniel Toscan du Plantier, Marcia Tenney, Julie Matheson, Scott Flor
Written and directed by **David Lynch**
Photography: Frederick Elmes
Sound: John Huck
Editor: Scott Chestnut
Art Direction and Costumes: Patricia Norris, Nancy Martinelli
Cast: Harry Dean Stanton (Slim), Frédéric Golchan (Pierre), Jack Nance (Pete), Michael Horse (Broken Feather), Rick Guillory (Howdy), Tracey Walters (Dusty), Marie Lauren (French Girl), Patrick Hauser (Gun Twirler), Eddy Dixon (Rock-a-Billy Guy), Magali Alvarado, Ann Sophie, Robin Summers (Beehive Western Gals)
35 mm, Color
26 minutes

1989
TWIN PEAKS (TV pilot for series, later released as a feature)
Lynch/Frost Productions, Propaganda Films, Spelling Entertainment
Executive Producers: Mark Frost, **David Lynch**
Producer: David J. Latt
Director: **David Lynch**
Screenplay: **David Lynch** and Mark Frost
Photography: Ron Garcia
Sound: John Wentworth
Editor: Duwayne Dunham
Music: Angelo Badalamenti

Production Design: Patricia Norris
Cast: Kyle MacLachlan (Special Agent Dale Cooper), Michael Ontkean (Sheriff Harry S. Truman), Sheryl Lee (Laura Palmer), Ray Wise (Leland Palmer), Grace Zabriskie (Sarah Palmer), Dana Ashbrook (Bobby Briggs), Phoebe Augustine (Ronette Pulaski), Catherine Coulson (Log Lady), Al Strobel (One-Armed Man), Frank Silva (Bob)
35 mm, Color
112 minutes

1989
TWIN PEAKS (TV series of twenty-nine episodes after the pilot)
Directors: **David Lynch**, Mark Frost, Tina Rathborne, Tim Hunter, Lesli Linka Glatter, Caleb Deschanel, Todd Holland, Graeme Gifford, Duwayne Dunham, Diane Keaton, James Foley, Uli Edel, Jonathan Sanger, and Stephen Gyllenhaal
Co-Writers: Harley Peyton, Robert Engels, Jerry Stahl, Barry Pullman, Scott Frost, and Tricia Brock
Cast: Kyle MacLachlan (Special Agent Dale Cooper), Michael Ontkean (Sheriff Harry S. Truman), Sheryl Lee (Laura Palmer), Ray Wise (Leland Palmer), Grace Zabriskie (Sarah Palmer), Dana Ashbrook (Bobby Briggs), Phoebe Augustine (Ronette Pulaski), Catherine Coulson (Log Lady), Al Strobel (One-Armed Man), Frank Silva (Bob)

1990
WILD AT HEART
Propaganda Films for Polygram
Executive Producer: Michael Kuhn
Producers: Monty Montgomery, Steve Golin, Sigurjon Sighvatsson
Director: **David Lynch**
Screenplay: **David Lynch**, based on the novel by Barry Gifford
Photography: Frederick Elmes
Editor: Duwayne Dunham
Music: Angelo Badalamenti
Production Design: Patricia Norris
Cast: Nicolas Cage (Sailor Ripley), Laura Dern (Lula Pace Fortune), Diane Ladd (Marietta Pace), Willem Dafoe (Bobby Peru), Isabella Rossellini (Perdida Durango), Harry Dean Stanton (Johnnie Farragut), Crispin Glover (Dell), Grace Zabriskie (Juana), J. E. Freeman (Marcello Santos), W. Morgan Shepherd (Mr. Reindeer)
35 mm, Color
124 minutes

INDUSTRIAL SYMPHONY NO. 1
Live performance filmed at the Brooklyn Academy of Music

Executive Producers: **David Lynch** and Angelo Badalamenti
Producers: Steve Golin, Monty Montgomery
Director: **David Lynch**
Music: Angelo Badalamenti
Sets: Franne Lee
Choreography: Martha Clark
Photography: John Schwartzmann
Cast: Laura Dern (Heartbroken Woman), Nicolas Cage (Heartbreaker), Julee Cruise (Dreamself of the Heartbroken Woman), Michael Anderson (Lumberjack / Twin A.), Andre Badalamenti (Clarinet Player / Twin B.), Lisa Giobbi and Felix Blaska (Solo Dancers), John Bell (Deer)
Video, Color
49 minutes

1990-91
AMERICAN CHRONICLES (TV documentary series)
Lynch / Frost Productions
Executive Producers: **David Lynch**, with others
David Lynch and Mark Frost co-directed one contribution: *Champions*

1991-92
ON THE AIR (TV series)
ABC Worldvision Entertainments
Lynch / Frost Productions and Twin Peaks Productions (for first episode only)
David Lynch directed episode one; co-wrote episode one with Mark Frost and episode six with Robert Engels
Video, Color
Seven 24-minute episodes

1992
HOTEL ROOM (TV trilogy)
Home Box Office
Asymmetrical Productions and Propaganda Films
Executive Producers: **David Lynch**, Monty Montgomery
Producer: Deepak Nayar
Directors: **David Lynch** ("Tricks" and "Blackout"), James Signorelli ("Getting Rid of Robert")
Scripts: Barry Gifford ("Tricks," "Blackout"), James McInerney ("Getting Rid of Robert")
Photography: Peter Deming
Music: Angelo Badalamenti
Cast:

"Tricks": Glenne Headly (Darlene), Freddie Jones (Lou), Harry Dean Stanton (Mo)
"Getting Rid of Robert": Griffin Dunne (Robert), Deborah Unger (Sasha), Mariska Hargitay (Diane), Chealsea Field (Tina)
"Blackout": Crispin Glover and Alicia Witt (Tulsa Couple), Clark Heathcliffe Brolly, Camilla Overbye Roos, John Solari, Carl Sundstrom
Video, Color
90 minutes

TWIN PEAKS: FIRE WALK WITH ME
Twin Peaks Productions
Executive Producers: **David Lynch** and Mark Frost
Producers: Gregg Fienberg and John Wentworth
Director: **David Lynch**
Screenplay: **David Lynch** and Robert Engels
Photography: Ron Garcia
Editor: Mary Sweeney
Sound Editor: Douglas Murray
Music: Angelo Badalamenti
Sound Design: **David Lynch**
Special Effects Coordinator: Robert E. McCarthy
Makeup: Katharina Hirsch-Smith
Production Design: Patricia Norris
Cast: Sheryl Lee (Laura Palmer), Ray Wise (Leland Palmer), Chris Isaak (Special Agent Chester Desmond), Keifer Sutherland (Sam Stanley), Grace Zabriskie (Sarah Palmer), Kyle MacLachlan (Special Agent Dale Cooper), Dana Ashbrook (Bobby Briggs), Phoebe Augustine (Ronette Pulaski), Frank Silva (Bob), Moira Kelly (Donna Harward), James Marshall (James Hurley)
35 mm, Color
134 minutes

1995
LUMIÈRE AND COMPANY
Segment later titled *Premonition Following an Evil Deed*
Producer: Neal Edelstein
Director: **David Lynch**
Photography: Peter Deming
Wardrobe: Patricia Norris
Cast: Jeff Alperi, Mark Wood, Stan Lothridge (Cops), Russ Pearlman (Dead Son), Pam Pierrocish (Mother), Clyde Small (Father), Joan Rurdlestein, Michele Carlyle, Kathleen Raymond (Women), Dawn Salcedo (Woman in Tank)
35 mm, B & W
55 seconds

1996
LOST HIGHWAY
CIBY 2000 / Asymmetrical Productions
Producers: Deepak Nayar, Tom Sternberg, and Mary Sweeney
Director: **David Lynch**
Screenplay: **David Lynch** and Barry Gifford
Photography: Peter Deming
Sound: Sasumu Tokunow
Editor: Mary Sweeney
Composer and Conductor: Angelo Badalamenti
Production and Costume Design: Patricia Norris
Cast: Bill Pullman (Fred Madison), Patricia Arquette (Renée Madison / Alice Wakefield), Balthazar Getty (Pete Dayton), Robert Blake (Mystery Man), Robert Loggia (Mr. Eddy / Dick Laurant), Michael Manssee (Andy), Natasha Gregson Wagner (Sheila), Gary Busey (Bill Dayton), Richard Pryor (Arnie), Lucy Butler (Candice Dayton), Jack Nance (Phil)
35 mm, Color
135 minutes

1999
THE STRAIGHT STORY
Picture Factory in association with Le Studio Canal+ and Film Four
Executive Producers: Pierre Edelman and Michael Polaire, in association with Alain Sarde
Producers: Mary Sweeney and Neal Edelstein
Director: **David Lynch**
Screenplay: John Roach and Mary Sweeney
Photography: Freddie Francis
Editor: Mary Sweeney
Composer and Conductor: Angelo Badalamenti
Costume Design: Patricia Norris
Production Design: Jack Fisk
Cast: Richard Farnsworth (Alvin Straight), Sissy Spacek (Rose Straight), Harry Dean Stanton (Lyle Straight), Everett McGill (Tom the John Deere Dealer), John Farley (Thorvald Olsen), Kevin Farley (Harald Olsen), Jane Galloway Heitz (Dorothy), Joseph A. Carpenter (Bud), Donald Weigert (Sig), Tracey Maloney (Nurse)
35 mm, Color
111 minutes

2001
MULHOLLAND DRIVE
Les Films Alain Sarde / Asymmetrical Productions

Executive Producer: Pierre Edelman
Producers: Mary Sweeney, Alain Sarde, Neal Edelstein, Michael Polaire, and Tony Krantz
Written and directed by **David Lynch**
Photography: Peter Deming
Sound: Susumu Tokunow, Edward Novick
Editing: Mary Sweeney
Composer and Conductor: Angelo Badalamenti
Production Design: Jack Fisk
Cast: Naomi Watts (Betty Elms / Diane Selwyn), Laura Elena Harring (Rita / Camilla Rhodes), Justin Theroux (Adam Kesher), Ann Miller (Coco Lenoix), Dan Hedaya (Vincenzo Castigliane), Angelo Badalamenti (Luigi Castigliane), Robert Forster (Detective Harry McKnight), Brent Briscoe (Detective Domgaard), Jeanne Bates (Irene), Dan Birnbaum (Irene's Companion), Michael J. Anderson (Mr. Roque), Joseph Kearney (Roque's Manservant), James Karen (Wally Brown), Monty Montgomery (Cowboy), Maya Bond (Aunt Ruth), Patrick Fischler (Dan), Michael Cooke (Herb), Bonnie Aarons (Bum), Marcus Graham (Mr. Darby), Melissa George (Camilla Rhodes), Michael des Barnes (Billy), Lori Heuring (Lorraine), Billy Ray Cyrus (Gene), Chad Everett (Jimmy Katz), Wayne Grace (Bob Booker), Rita Taggart (Linny James), Michelle Hicks (Nicki), Richard Green (The Magician), Cori Glazer (Blue-Haired Lady), Rebekah del Rio (herself)
35 mm, Color
146 minutes

2002
DUMBLAND
Produced, written, directed, and edited by **David Lynch**
Cast: all voices by **David Lynch** (Randy, Sparky, et al)
Digital Videotape, B & W
35 minutes total, eight website episodes

RABBITS
Written, directed, and edited by **David Lynch**
Cast: Scott Coffey (Jack), Rebekah Del Rio (Jane), Laura Harring (Jane), Naomi Watts (Suzie)
Digital Videotape, Color
50 minutes total, eight website episodes

DARKENED ROOM
Produced, written, directed, and photographed by **David Lynch**
Cast: Jordan Ladd (Girl #1), Etsuko Shikata (herself), Cerina Vincent (Girl #2)
Digital Videotape, Color
8 minutes

2006
INLAND EMPIRE
Studio Canal, Camerimage / Tumult Foundation, and Absurda Productions
Executive Producers (Poland): Ewa Puszczynska, Marek Zydowicz
Producers: **David Lynch**, Mary Sweeney, Jeremy Alter, Laura Dern
Producers (Poland): Kazimierz Suvala, Janusz Hetman, Michal Stopowski
Written, directed, photographed, and edited by **David Lynch**
Art Direction: Christina Ann Wilson, Wojciech Wolniak
Set Decoration: Melanie Rein, Svietlana Slawska
Costume Design: Karen Baird, Heidi Bivens
Cast: Karolina Gruszka (Lost Girl), Jan Hench (Janek), Krzysztof Majchrzak (Phantom), Grace Zabriskie (Visitor #1), Laura Dern (Nikki Grace / Susan Blue), Ian Abercrombie (Henry the Butler), Jeremy Irons (Kingsley Stewart), John Churchill (Chuck Ross, 1st Assistant Director), Justin Theroux (Devon Berk / Billy Side), Harry Dean Stanton (Freddie Howard), Diane Ladd (Marilyn Levens), William H. Macy (Announcer), Julia Ormond (Doris Side), Jeremy Alter (Stage Manager), Mary Steenburgen (Visitor #2), Jason Weinberg (Nikki Grace's Manager), Bucky Jay (Film Crew Grip; voice by **David Lynch**), Stanislaw Kazimierz Cybulski (Mr. Zydowicz), Henryka Cybulski (Mrs. Zydowicz), Emily Stofle (Lanni), Jordan Ladd (Terri), Kristen Kerr (Lori), Terryn Westbrook (Chelsi), Jamie Eifert (Sandi), Kathryn Turner (Dori), Michelle Renea (Kari), Erik Crary (Mr. K), Leon Niemczyk (Marek), Josef Zbiróg (Darek), Marian Stanislawski (Franciszek), Masuimi Max (Niko), Nastassja Kinski (Special Appearance), Scott Coffey (Jack Rabbit), Laura Harring (Jane Rabbit), Naomi Watts (Suzie Rabbit)
Digital Videotape, Color
179 minutes

2007
MORE THINGS THAT HAPPENED
Story drawn from outtakes from original footage of *Inland Empire*
Written, directed, photographed, and edited by **David Lynch**
Cast: Karolina Gruszka (Lost Girl), Peter J. Lucas (Piotrek Król), Krzysztof Majchrzak (Phantom), Laura Dern (Nikki Grace / Susan Blue)
Digital Videotape, Color
75 minutes

BALLERINA
Issued with *Inland Empire* DVD
Directed and photographed by **David Lynch**
Digital Videotape, Color
12 minutes, 19 seconds

ABSURDA
Written, photographed, and directed by **David Lynch**
Digital Videotape, Color
2 minutes, 17 seconds

BOAT
Written and directed by **David Lynch**
Editing: Hilary Schroeder, **David Lynch**
Cast: **David Lynch** (as himself); narration by Emily Stofle
Digital Videotape, Color
8 minutes

DAVID LYNCH
INTERVIEWS

Eraserhead: Is There Life after Birth?

STEPHEN SABAN AND
SARAH LONGACRE/1977

MARY LYNCH HAS THE uncertain advantage of being married to the writer/producer/director of *Eraserhead*, a film currently playing weekend midnights at the Cinema Village. "I saw one twenty-minute segment before I saw the whole film," she says, "and it was so beautiful. I had no idea of anything about it, and I was so struck by its beauty. Then I saw the whole thing, and some of the images were really disconcerting. I mean, I just couldn't look at some of them, and sometimes that bothered me so much that I didn't actually see what was going on. Now I've seen it eight or ten times, and the images have gotten less and less like that to me, and I see more of the integral part of the film. I'll tell David what I think it means and sometimes he'll laugh at me."

David Lynch, a thirty-year-old painter and filmmaker who was born in Montana, has created in his first feature-length film an experience and atmosphere that is so unlike anything that has ever appeared on the commercial screen before, that it almost defies description or interpretation. Even his wife, obviously a close part of his life, must try to understand solely for herself, from her own experience. He's not telling.

"That's the way it oughta be," he says. "The whole film is undercurrents of sort of subconscious. . . . You know, and it kind of wiggles around in there, and it's how it strikes each person. It definitely means something to me, but I don't want to talk about that. It means other things to other people, and that's great."

The story upon which the film is structured is simple. It's merely the thread that holds the images together. The protagonist, a printer named

From the *Soho Weekly News* (20 October 1977). Reprinted by permission of Stephen Saban.

Henry Spencer, has perhaps got a woman pregnant and he marries her. After the birth, she leaves him and goes back to her parents. He has a sexual encounter with a beautiful woman who lives across the hall in his apartment building. He "kills" his child out of mercy and goes "off into the sunset" with a fantasy woman in the radiator in his room. "Henry is like sort of a confused guy," Lynch says, "and he's sort of come unglued. He's trying to maintain, and there are problems."

Lynch thinks of *Eraserhead* as "A dream of dark and troubling things." The remarkable fact of the film is that, unlike other films that are dreams (*Dead of Night, Fireworks*) or have dream sequences (*Wild Strawberries*), Eraserhead actually reproduces the dream state in all its nightmarish possibilities and impossibilities. The effect is not achieved by showing someone going to sleep and/or waking up (although there are dreams within the film). The film itself is the dream, the nightmare.

The film is very personal, and because there was no deadline for its completion, it is very controlled. It took two years to finish. The time and personal attention show. The framing, the tones of black and white, the montages, the slow pacing all reveal the effort of an artist creating a work. The dialogue comes in clusters and the rest of the soundtrack is filled with heightened industrial noises, steam, and assorted natural sounds that have been distorted. "Alan Splet and I worked together in a little garage studio," Lynch says, "with a big console and two or three tape recorders, and worked with a couple of different sound libraries for organic effects. Then we fed them through the console. It's all natural sounds. No Moog synthesizers. Just changes like with a graphic equalizer, reverb, a Little Dipper filter set for peaking certain frequencies and dipping out things or reversing things or cutting things together. We had a machine to vary the pitch but not the speed. We could make the sounds the way we wanted them to be. It took several months to do it and six months to a year to edit it."

The sounds and sound effects of the movie do not work like a conventional soundtrack where the music is used to underscore or flesh out a weak scene. At times, the sound/noise changes with each shot in the same scene. It is used as atmosphere, almost as a character, and is a memorable part of the film.

The characters themselves are drab depressing figures in a wrist-slittingly cheerless environment. John Nance, who plays Henry Spencer, is in Lynch's words "just a regular guy and a real good actor." He was Henry for a long time and really got into the part, even wearing Henry's slippers at home.

The character of Mary X was played by Charlotte Stewart, who can be seen on television in *Little House on the Prairie* as the schoolteacher. With her cardigan and shapeless dress, she is the perfect "Unknown." Her scenes with Henry are painful. Her mother, Mrs. X, is Jeanne Bates, a veteran of numerous Columbia Pictures B-films and currently a soap opera actress.

Judith Anna Roberts, the Beautiful Girl Across the Hall, was married to Pernell Roberts of *Bonanza*. *Eraserhead* is her first big break, and already most people are talking about her scene in Henry's room. Although she has very little dialogue, her presence is charged with sexuality.

The black and white tone of the movie is evocative of early Polish films and some Japanese and Russian films. Greys are shot against greys, figures emerge out of grey and become translucent (especially the appearance of the Beautiful Girl Across the Hall). There is no sense of obvious lighting; the film is lit beautifully. *Eraserhead* was filmed entirely at night in Los Angeles, and subsequently the movie has a very nighttime feel to it.

Lynch disclaims any influence from foreign films, and says he hasn't seen them. "Well, people say that *Eraserhead* has a real Germanic quality to it," he admits, "but I got *Eraserhead* really from Philadelphia." Lynch went to Pennsylvania Academy of Fine Arts on Broad Street, where he studied painting and eventually made his first movie, a one-minute animated film loop projected on a sculptured screen. "I lived at 13th and Wood, right kitty-corner from the morgue. That's real industrial. At 5:00 there's nobody in that neighborhood. No one lives there. And I really do like that. It's beautiful, if you see it the right way."

Eraserhead was made with a grant from the American Film Institute, but Lynch will not say how much it cost. Mary Lynch says she did fundraising for the film before she had seen any of it. "To me," Lynch says, "the film cost a lot of money. The warehouse only cost about thirty-five or fifty dollars to build, but other things cost a lot of money. You know you can build something and work it up over some time and really make it look just the way you want it to. The most frustrating part of the whole thing was finding locations. There just isn't anything in L.A. like I wanted. Like the front of Mr. and Mrs. X's house, I'd seen a place in San Francisco that had the kind of feeling I wanted. But when we went looking in Los Angeles, we finally had to build it. In the movie, it's just a facade. In fact, the steps are Styrofoam, and there's no porch at all. When Henry walks up there, he's standing on a plank. The whole thing was barely held together."

Lynch will talk about the technical production of the film to a point.

The child that Henry and Mary Spencer have is premature. It is one of the images that is most repellent and fascinating.

Q: *Did you make that thing?*
A: "That I . . . I don't . . . I . . . Stephen, I don't wanna, uh . . . talk about that."

Q: *Can you just tell me if it's a . . . sculpture? It's so well done. Someone I saw it with thought that it might be a calf fetus.*
A: "That's what a lot of people think it is."

Q: *I thought it was made, but couldn't figure out how you got it to move. Was it battery-operated?*
A: "I really don't . . ."

Q: *Even if I don't print it? I want to know.*
A: "Stephen, come on . . ."

Q: *You credit a doctor in the film. Is that related?*
A: "Well, I was looking into different ways, you know, in the beginning . . ."

Q: *And?*
A: (silence)

Q: *And?*
A: "If I say, I'll really feel bad."

Q: *Is it because you'd be giving away a technical secret, or you'd be arrested?*
A: "You know, there's no promotional photos of the baby because people, like, uh . . . you know . . . it's like, nice to discover along in the film and not to know, like . . . much about it."

Q: *You say all the sounds are organic. Do you use the sound of a real baby crying?*
A: "No."

Q: *Then what is it? Or won't you tell that either?*
A: "I'm sorry, Stephen. Doggone it, you know, I'm not trying to, you know . . . It's just the baby stuff, I, uh. . . ."

David Lynch's background of surrealistic painting surfaces in *Eraserhead*. Surrealistic obsessions with dreams, chance, libido, and intuitive rather than logical thinking are manifest in the mood and narrative of the film. Henry Spencer decides very little about his life. He lives in a room that seems to be furnished with Salvation Army purchases, with piles of string that appear and disappear, bowls of water on drawers. Fetuses are "delivered" unceasingly in his bed, electrical malfunctioning occurs throughout and climaxes in the cataclysmic denouement. A fantasy figure, The Lady in the Radiator, smiles inanely, dances sedately on a black-and-white-tiled stage, steps on and squashes fetuses and sings: "In heaven everything is fine / In heaven everything is fine / In heaven everything is fine / You've got your good thing / and you've got mine."

The film was worked up rather like a painting. "It changed a couple of different times," Lynch says. "But it was real weird how stuff that had been shot before was ready for a change. And a few of the new things just went in naturally, and I changed emphasis. I never got locked in and said I wished it had been done like that. There were scenes that were taken out, but they were scenes where Henry went off, away from the line. They fell away pretty naturally. The Lady in the Radiator was not in the original script at all. It was a very dark film until she came along."

Women tend to react strongly to the film, to be afraid, and perhaps this is because they fear the chance of giving birth to abnormalities. Others who have seen *Eraserhead* have hated it, gone home to nightmares, or laughed. There are funny moments, but they work as releases.

"There's a guy," Lynch says, "a projectionist, who will not see this film, and he couldn't stand to see the film I made before this, *The Grandmother*. It would do something to him inside that he could not stand. It wasn't the film at all, it just triggered something. Everybody has a subconscious and they put a lid on it. There's things in there. And then along comes something, and something bobs up. I don't know if that's good."

Lynch's images have a strong emotional impact and dredge up experiences in the viewer; although the facts of the viewer's experiences may be different, the intuitive knowledge of them is similar. It's as if Lynch subscribes to the Jungian theory of the "collective unconscious." Or, as Mary Lynch says, "There's a little *Eraserhead* in everybody."

Eraserhead concerns itself with death and rebirth. Jung describes a state not unlike Limbo (called "Bardo" in the *Tibetan Book of the Dead*), an intermediate state between death and rebirth. It is broken up into three stages: 1) the psychic happenings at the time of death, 2) the dream state that follows immediately after death and is accompanied by karmic illusions, and 3) the birth instinct and prenatal events. At the very end of *Eraserhead*, Henry goes through the radiator and joins his fantasy woman and the screen becomes flooded with light so that the figures are hardly visible. In the *Book of the Dead*, it says, "The wisdom . . . will shoot forth and strike thee with a light so radiant that thou will scarcely be able to look at it."

Anyway, Lynch isn't saying. "The film's gotta make sense somehow, you know, in your own way. When you go to a mystery film and they tie it all up at the end—to me, that's a real letdown. In a mystery, somehow in the middle it's all opened up, and you can go out to infinity trying to form your own conclusions. There's so many possibilities. And that feeling is, like, real neat to me. . . . In *Eraserhead*, there are a lot of openings and you go into areas and it's all. . . . There're sort of like rules you kind of go by to keep that feeling kind of open and I don't know, it's real important to it. It's more like a poem or a . . . more abstract, even though it has a story. It's like an experience.

"I've heard people say that people who write and direct their own things sort of make the same film over and over again, but I don't know about that. I don't know where these things come from really. Ideas sort of pop up out of some different levels somewhere, and down in there that's where Henry is. So it's hard to say it's a philosophy or anything. Everything makes sense to me, you know. *Eraserhead* is real logical to me, and it has rules that were followed and it has a certain feeling that was followed all the way through. And you sort of tune into that at the beginning of the film, and you sort of know what's right. And it makes certain sense to me and it feels right."

And again, he says, "Other people seem to pick up on that, but they have different interpretations of what it all means. Because the openness has room for different interpretations."

Good Eraserhead: Indiana

GARY INDIANA/1980

ERASERHEAD IS THE story of Henry, a *schlemeil* who lives in a world of ugliness and fear. In his dreams, a hideously deformed giant on a distant black asteroid pulls the cranks and levers that control his awful life. When Henry's girlfriend becomes pregnant, she invites him to her parents' house, across town in an industrial suburb of hell. The dog snaps at him. The father rants demonically that the neighborhood's going downhill, then serves little squabs that start rattling and finally hemorrhaging on the plate. The mother shoves Henry up against the wall. "There's a baby," she hisses.

The child Henry fathers makes the extraterrestrial youngster in *Alien* look like Deanna Durbin. Its oral cravings are so developed that the entire organism functions to keep the mouth going. Worse, it comes down with the flu right after its mother walks out on Henry.

Henry can only escape this situation by dreaming about the Lady in the Radiator, a winsome, pudgy blonde *chanteuse* who sports two enormous tumors on her cheeks. As she dances daintily on the little stage inside the radiator, white, pulpy fetuses drop from the ceiling like turds from outer space. She squishes them underfoot while singing, "In Heaven, everything is fine," in a trembly falsetto. "You've got your good things, and I've got mi-ine."

Eraserhead can be read in several ways, but its real importance lies in its complete inversion of traditional aesthetics. It suggests the opposite of Wittgenstein's aphorism, "Imagine this butterfly just as it is, but ugly instead of beautiful." On an interpretive level, *Eraserhead* is the most compelling, frightening film about the nuclear family made in the past ten

---

From the *East Village Eye* (February 1980). Reprinted by permission.

years. It lacks the clammy self-consciousness and sour yearnings of soap opera, is almost totally free of cliché and dissolves every species of romanticism in a suet of gore and alienation. Other films that set out to do this usually exhibit some special reserve on the part of the filmmaker—a reverence for the aged, for instance, or a marginal unwillingness to deny the possibility of love. *Eraserhead* goes much further than the obligatory social anarchism of New Wave. In terms of human partisanship *Eraserhead* is "that rare thing" (to borrow a trope from *Newsweek*): a completely impersonal work of art.

(The following interview is an excerpt from an interview conducted in 1978 in Los Angeles. Other portions of the transcript appeared in *NO Magazine*.)

David Lynch is a stocky, blond, blandly good-looking man of medium height with the cheerful demeanor of an Eagle Scout. He is quietly anxious to please; his manner lacks the smallest trace of neuroticism. He doesn't smoke or drink, and throughout the interview he orders hot water to make Postum.

GARY INDIANA: *You worked very closely, obviously, with the sound engineer. Would you like to talk about that?*
DAVID LYNCH: Sure.

GI: *It's the best sound track on any film I've heard except* Citizen Kane, *I think.*
DL: Well, thank you. My good friend Alan Splet and I worked together before this on a film I made called *The Grandmother*. And, I met Alan in Philadelphia. The film I made before that, I worked on the sound with another guy at the same lab where Alan worked. And I was going back with the idea of working with the first guy on *The Grandmother*. And I was sort of disappointed when he told me no, he couldn't do it, but he was going to turn me over to this guy Alan. So Alan's this real tall skinny guy. And I shook his hand and I felt his bones rattle. And he's a great . . . the guy is packed with energy, and we hit it off fantastically. It was really fun. And the way we worked is, the picture dictates the sound, and the sounds have got to build a mood, and we started off with just raw organic sounds. We didn't use a Moog synthesizer in either film. For instance, we'd have a lot of electronic material, but we'd start off with a regular sound and start altering it in lots of different ways and trying different things, until we got something that was right for one little thing.

First of all, in a lot of films they have like fifty sound track rolls. But really, on one reel they might have only one gunshot, see. And it might be fifty for one battle scene. But on one reel they only have one gunshot. So we had ten or fifteen reels, but they were like dense, densely packed . . . I guess up to . . . well, at some points we maybe had fifteen sounds going at one time, and some places we only had a presence. But the presences we worked with were very strange, Very, very little of the sound was real, at all. We concocted and made every single sound. One sound we made, for the love scene, was, we took a bathtub, and floated a Sparklettes bottle in the bathtub; we had a microphone down inside the Sparklettes bottle. Then we had a garden hose inside the Sparklettes bottle, and at the other end of the hose, someone blew air into the bottle while, I don't know, Alan was probably doing it, but I was moving the bottle around in the tub like this, and it would make like a little ringing, very subtle, a dreamy ringing, and this air moving in there had a tone to it, and it would change as it moved around. It's the greatest sort of ethereal sound you can . . . And we would just, we would record everything and anything, and we had hundreds of effects we never used. And we built these sound-deadening blankets, Alan designed them and we built them and hung them on the walls, and the place was dead as a doornail. So the sound that we got for dialogue was very, very, very dead and very, very, very clean, and that's the only natural sounds, you know, from the scenes that we used. Every single thing else was added in, and none of it was real, at all.

GI: *The actors obviously had to be available for a long time. How was that for them?*
DL: Well, it was rough. It was roughest for Jack Nance, John Nance as he wants to be called; he started, he got his hair cut for Henry in about, I guess May of 1972, and pretty much had to have it cut that way, but it wasn't standing up, you know, all the time; and he wore a little hat . . . but he had to be around for several years, and that was the worst of it, because who knows what would happen to him, and holding the whole thing together, and trying to hold together that mood or feeling of it all when it's so fragmented was a real, real difficult thing. For instance, in one scene, Henry walks down the hall and opens the door, and the next shot is a year and a half earlier. Things like that.

GI: *Well the actors obviously believed very strongly in the film.*
DL: We really got into it, yeah. When we were ready to shoot again,

when we got money together and were ready to go, we got right back into it. There was no cutting corners at all. But at the same time it's like building a bridge out of little glass strands, and you get out there building it and at any moment it can all come down. It's not until it's all finished that it all turns to steel.

GI: *I think in five years it'll be recognized as a classic. It's just going to take time.*

DL: It's gonna take time; a lot of people though are real turned off by the film, and it's definitely a specialized audience film. Although the word of mouth is real good on it, and people are talking about it. So I think, as you say, over a period of time, people will finally go see it. And another thing is it's hard for a lot of people to go out at midnight to see a film.

GI: *But I think one of the things that's so impressive about* Eraserhead— *you may not agree with me, but I think it's a very revolutionary way of perceiving things. You show things that people have never seen before in a movie, and I think the film expands what's acceptable to show and what it's acceptable to be interested in, and people will catch up with that. A lot of what is in* Eraserhead *I think reflects the world we live in, completely. The fact that he lives in so much ugliness and squalor, he takes for granted . . . you know that he doesn't take it totally for granted, because for example he's repulsed by the baby, even though he smiles at it and everything you know he's really freaked out . . . but quite a lot of it is just the background of his life. And, you know, ugliness is the background of a lot of our lives.*

DL: I really . . . see, I came into filmmaking from being a painter. But that ugliness I find really beautiful. See, that's my problem.

GI: *Maybe I shouldn't use that word.*

DL: That's okay. It is ugliness on one level, but I see it as textures and shapes, and fast areas and slow areas, and stuff like that. So I guess I'm really interested in the whole thing, the whole image, and the whole sounds . . .

GI: *Well, everything in it has a really beautiful composition. And what I noticed—for me, what my own reaction was, when I first saw it, and it hasn't changed that much in subsequent viewings—is the fact that . . . the subject matter, a lot of it is so alien that it makes the surface of the film come alive. Much more so than a romantic film or a film with conventionally attractive people and beautiful sets.*

DL: Exactly, that's what I'm really interested in doing, like what you're saying. Yeah. I like to hit it from another angle.

GI: *In the family dinner sequence—now, there's an element that seems, when you stand away from it and think about it a little bit you think, "Well, it's not so unusual, the woman gets pregnant, the man is confronted by the mother and has to marry her, and they have this horrible . . . I mean I've seen that before" . . . but you've done it in a totally different way.*

DL: I didn't work that way because, some people, they say, okay, we're going to write a film on some social issue, you know? So they start with that as their goal, and then they create a film to back it up. *I did not work that way at all.* I started getting ideas. And that, most of the dinner sequence I wrote in one night, and I just, it just plopped out, like that. I mean I was hot, you know? I was really writing away. And that's the way ideas came. In fragments. And then I'd get a thread that would connect a whole bunch of fragments. And I'd be on to something. And once I got the thread, other things would fall in and I had it, in my head, then. And I love absurdity, you know, and I also had a lot of this, there's this humor that . . . it had to follow these rules. You know, how like the humor had to be able to be a certain kind of humor that could keep the film able to be able to go into fear, you know what I mean? Some humor would take you too far into safety, and you would never be able to turn around and go into fear again. It would never be real enough. So, that's part of these rules. That, once the world was established, you had to always make sure that you didn't leave it. It was like, you don't have that much freedom in a film, even if it's a strange film, because the moment you lock yourself into that, that Eraserhead world, then you were there. All these other options were closed off to you then. Only in the very beginning do you have the freedom, and then you lose out 90 percent of all your things.

GI: *Right. When he's walking along and he steps in the mud puddle, people think they're going to be seeing a Keaton film, or a Chaplin movie.*
DL: Uh-huh.

GI: *And then when he gets inside the whole thing changes.*
   You wanted to go into animation, because you were a painter.
DL: Yeah, for sure. Like, there were films that I liked, but no film that said I've got to get into film. At all. In fact, I thought I'd basically be into animation. But I don't like animation anymore.

GI: *I don't blame you.*
DL: There's way more. I love, there's things you can do with animation that you can't do with film, but I like trying to do them with the real thing. I like working with actors more and more.

GI: *Are the people who are in the film, do they work a lot in films, or do they work mainly...*

DL: No, Jeanne Bates used to be... she did a lot of pictures for Columbia Studios. And I saw her in one old picture, they were all B pictures, and now she's in a daytime soap opera, I think... she was, up until a year or so ago. And Allen Joseph, Bill, he does a lot of theater and does some television... and so was Jeanne... Jeanne was, I think Jeanne was the straightest of them all. And after one night, she came around. She was really with it. Then, Charlotte Stewart, I don't think she liked the film.

GI: *She's...*

DL: She's Mary. And she started doing *Little House on the Prairie*, after... *(Laughter)*

GI: *In reaction, probably...*
Was there any improvisation?

DL: No, not one bit.

GI: *Well, there are places in the film where you seem to be juggling ten things at once and they all come together and collide... and you don't know whether to laugh or scream or what, but there are different points in the sequence when the chicken starts...*

DL: Going, yeah.

GI: *That's been led up to by all these different things and it just seems there's an apotheosis at that point, where the mother starts having her fit, or whatever, and all through the film you seem to have those things... is that when everybody was really cooking and...*

DL: No, those were all rehearsed.

GI: *But it seemed like the right take to you?*

DL: Yeah, in fact most of the time, we would rehearse it so much that the most takes we really ever did was about four, I think, or six. And usually only one or two. And a lot of times the next take wasn't for actors, it was for maybe a camera bump or something like that.

GI: *How do you think of the ending? Now we're getting into what actually happens in the film...*

DL: A very happy ending.

GI: *It is.*

DL: Yeah, Henry goes to heaven.

GI: *When he kills the baby, there is a very loud background noise immediately after that that continues through the whole thing. How was that done?*

DL: An organ.

GI: *Just amplified, or . . .*

DL: Well, there's a lot of sounds that are going, but there's some chord of an organ that, actually they change, there's some changes that it goes through, but, yeah, it's up loud and it's with all these other sounds, too. That's a pretty thick soundtrack there at the end.

GI: *Oh. The worm that he gets in the mail. Is someone sending that to him, or is it in his mailbox, or . . .*

DL: Yeah . . . that was sent to him.

GI: *By whom?*

DL: Nnn . . . there might be, you might name someone, but if you don't that's fine too. But it was in my mind sent to him. In a way it's like, sometimes you get a message, and it sits, you know, for quite a while, and then suddenly it starts coming into your conscious mind. And in a way that's what's happening there.

GI: *Is this his death coming to him, or . . .*

DL: No.

GI: *No symbol, okay . . . What were the longest scenes to shoot?*

DL: In time? What took longest? Well, each thing took an awful long time to do, there wasn't one particular shot . . . well, a particular shot that was really hard to do, for us, was the, you know, the planet floating out in space, because we had, we did that also down at the stables (at the AFI), and we had to it in one weekend. And it doesn't sound like that much to do in one weekend, but there was a long dolly shot up to it, or away from it, and we shot it in reverse, but that thing we had, we hung about a 30 x 50 star germ-of-wheat bulb background, and we had this planet, and we had to mount it on a whirl head. We had these Beverly Hills Park garden boxes stacked up for a long dolly run, and then boards we got for this dolly track. And we had a rented Almack spider dolly with this jib arm, and we had to set all that up, and we started setting up Friday night and Monday morning, as the sun came up, we were getting our shot . . . as the sun was coming up. It was light. And the whole thing was no good. We had to shoot it exactly, we had to tear everything down and shoot the exact same thing the next weekend. That was real hell, that was really murder.

GI: *It sounds awful.*

DL: It was awful. We were carrying lead weights to hold the backdrop in the wind, and we had to; we couldn't, it was a nightmare really. And there were very, very few people working on it at any one time. I think we had a fairly good sized crew, maybe six people, or seven people working that night. And people working, we worked all day, all night, through the whole weekend just to light that and set it up and get it all worked out so that it would run right . . . and there were shots that went like that, there were things that just took a tremendous amount of time for one reason or another. And that was a particularly hard one.

GI: *One shot that was really incredible was, in the beginning, I'm not sure exactly where, but where you pan through blackness to that opening, that sort of hole . . . I mean the blackness becomes very real and you can sense the camera movement, even though the scene is totally black.*
DL: Well, you leave one movement . . . well, maybe you don't . . . you don't leave any movement, it's just the particles get thinner and thinner and then you're in black, and then you, you know you're moving when the hole comes in.

GI: *Yeah, but somehow—*
DL: You sense . . .

GI: *Yeah, the way that the shot is in the film, you feel the movement before the hole gets there, or maybe, as soon as you see the hole—*
DL: Yeah, you feel—

GI: *Feel it retroactively, or—it's really a wonderful thing . . . Where did you grow up? Where were you born?*
DL: Well, I was born in Missoula, Montana, but I lived in Spokane, Washington, Sand Point, Idaho, Boise, Idaho, Alexandria, Virginia, Durham, North Carolina, Boston, Philadelphia and California. L.A.

GI: *Which place did you like the best?*
DL: Well, for different reasons I liked them all, but I think Philadelphia, it took me about a year to get over the fear I was living under in Philadelphia. We lived in a real bad area of Philadelphia. All of Philadelphia is a bad area, really. There's a couple of very nice areas. But for instance a kid was shot to death just a half a block down the street from our house. And our house was broken into twice, and while we were in it. And, our house, a window was shot out of our house, our next door neighbor had some windows kicked in, and there was racial tension, and just . . . violence and fear. . . . I said to someone, all that separated me from the outside world was this brick wall, and they started laughing, like "What more do you want," you know? But that brick wall was like paper.

GI: *It's unfortunate the way that various people choose to describe this film. As Susan Sontag said about Jack Smith's film* Flaming Creatures, *the unfortunate thing about writing about this is that you have to defend it before you can say anything about it, and, I think the problem that anyone who is going to write about it is going to have is that, of course, you're writing for the public, you're always aware that there's a large public audience that has to see these things, has to see films like* Eraserhead *in terms of a gross-out, because they're not visually sophisticated, it's not a visually sophisticated audience that can handle a great deal of unusual material.*

DL: Yeah. Henry lives in this dark world, and it's just these strange things that happen there.

GI: *And I think we've kind of avoided talking about what actually happens in the film because the language to describe what happens in the film— I think there should be a new language to describe what happens in the film. Everything that people have written about it so far has been by way of taking sides without even really stating the fact that that's what they're doing. I don't think it's a grotesque movie, I think it's beautiful. And I wasn't grossed out by it . . . there were a lot of people that, you know, who were, or claimed to be, but these were the same people who were talking to the screen the whole time and not really letting themselves into what was happening. But . . .*

DL: There is a lot of talking in there.

GI: *Well, yeah, and that's the trouble with midnight movies. I mean, I think it's probably a good thing it's being shown every week, but on the other hand midnight movies have a kind of, uh, since they started, you know there have been articles written about midnight movies in magazines about how different the audiences are, and they are. They're noisy, they're loud, they talk back to the screen, they talk to each other through the whole film, and someone who just wants to sit back and really take it in is really inhibited by all the things he hears people saying around him.*

But then again, there was someone last night who laughed all the way through the film. I mean, cackled like a banshee at just about every new image that was hysterically funny . . . even though he may have been missing the point in places, at least he was getting his own particular input from it, and not . . . There was a couple sitting in front of me who necked through the whole movie. And this may interest you, they were necking and the man sort of had his head turned back to the audience, but every couple of minutes he turned away to look at what was going on on the screen and then go back to necking with his girlfriend. Interesting . . .

(laughter)

At the point where Henry cuts the baby apart he looked for a minute to see what was going on . . . quite a crowd, you know.
DL: Isn't it funny.

GI: *Yeah. I wondered what was going through his head.*
DL: Yeah. Crazy.

GI: *Do you want to say anything about, well, the story of the film?*
DL: Well, it's not . . . you could say, you know, I think, you know the story of the film, and I think, to me there's one level of the story; then it's, we get into our own personal interpretation on other levels, and so I don't want to say anything. Except, you know, on one level, like you say, it's a girl gets pregnant and there's a baby and they go off and live in his apartment, which is really what you see, but then there's other questions, that . . .
(laughter)

GI: *Well, there is this problem, it's very hard to describe the film in those terms and really give an idea of what it's like by saying that, and unfortunately the vocabulary to describe what's extra about the film tends to put a certain complexion on it . . . but . . . maybe my description will be different from anybody else's.*
DL: I think it will. I think you're going to do real well.

Director David Lynch—
From Cult Film to *Elephant Man*

JIMMY SUMMERS/1980

DAVID LYNCH'S FIRST feature film was *Eraserhead*, a black-and-white, low-budget horror film he made with help from the American Film Institute. His second film, *The Elephant Man*, is being released by Paramount, was financed by Mel Brooks's Brooksfilms, and stars Anthony Hopkins, John Hurt, John Gielgud, and Anne Bancroft.

It's a dramatic leap up for the thirty-three-year-old writer-director, and with such a gathering of experienced actors to direct for the first time one might think it would also be just a little intimidating.

"It's very intimidating," says Lynch, "and if you think about it, it could drive you nuts. But you can tell these people what to do because they're all such super professionals.

"They were all really nice to me and it's important on your first big film to have people who are supportive. It's very frightening, but they've been there themselves and they seem to understand."

Lynch had originally wanted to follow *Eraserhead* with *Ronny Rocket*, another specialty film over which he would once again have total creative control. But though *Eraserhead* was gaining a cult following on the midnight movie circuit, Lynch says it was not gaining enough for a studio to call him "one little bit bankable." He finally decided that if he was going to work at all, it would have to be with somebody else's material.

Stuart Cornfeld, a fan of *Eraserhead* who works for Mel Brooks, brought Lynch together with Jonathan Sanger, who had optioned a script called *The Elephant Man* from writers Christopher De Vore and Eric Bergren.

From *Box Office* (October 1980). Reprinted by permission.

Mel Brooks then entered the project and took on the film as a production for his Brooksfilms Ltd.

Although there was some question in the beginning as to whom Brooks would retain as members of the project, everyone remained with Sanger receiving producing credit and Lynch sharing writing credit with De Vore and Bergren. Lynch's position as director was apparently solidified when Brooks saw his earlier effort. "Mel saw *Eraserhead*," says Lynch, "and came running out of the theatre yelling 'You're a mad man! I love it!'

"So Mel," says Lynch, "set up Chris, Eric, and me in a little office across from his and told us to rewrite the script. We wrote two pretty much complete rewrites together before it was finally finished. We got along very, very well, which I would say is unusual. Ordinarily they wouldn't have wanted someone coming in and mucking with their script, but they tolerated it.

"It's important to say that their original script was really good. It was what inspired us all to get involved with the movie. But there were problems because it was so true to the material. Dramatically it had a build-up and then flattened out for a good part of the story. So there were two major rewrites based on ideas that Mel had, that I had, and that Chris and Eric consequently had.

"It became different, but the thing that stayed the same and that we were so keen on was the essence of John Merrick (the incurably and horrendously deformed man on whose life *The Elephant Man* is based). Staying true to him and his character was something we didn't fiddle with.

"Mel was on the set for about the first three days for about a half hour a day, being very happy and loving and supportive. But he wanted to keep a low profile. He said he was given breaks in life and he wanted to help out some people who were young and getting going. And it wouldn't have done any good if he had come in and done a power trip on us and taken over. He purposely protected the space and left us alone."

Lynch also has good things to say about Sanger, who made his debut as a producer of a feature film with *The Elephant Man*.

"Jonathan stayed with us in England (where the film was produced) and he did an excellent job. There are always things that go awry, but he really held everything together. For me it was important to just keep working, and around that Jonathan made sure things kept rolling."

Of John Hurt, who had to sit through seven hours of make-up a day for his role as John Merrick, Lynch says, "I don't know anybody any better than John Hurt. We wanted him because he's a real actor and not a personality. He gets so totally into a role that it's kind of magical.

"In the beginning I was afraid that if he didn't get the exact feeling that I knew was the Elephant Man, then directing him would be impossible and would take too much time. The truth of that guy's character had to come out of John Hurt.

"But he was so right on the money right from the beginning that we literally filmed his scenes with just one take."

Lynch has talked to De Vore and Bergren about working together again, but for now he feels it's more important for him to write something by himself. "Of the things that I really want to do," says Lynch, "I just feel I have to do them on my own. If you believe in a project and one or two other people involved don't, then it means making compromises. And to me it's really important to have as much control as possible."

You Can Have Any Colour So Long as It's Black

STUART DOLLIN / 1985

NOWADAYS—AND WE can assume that refers to at least the last ten years—it has always been assumed that a feature film would be in colour. To use black and white has been a conscious decision that goes against convention, but in the right hands can express more than the same scenes shot in colour.

Perhaps the most remarkable film of the last ten years to use black and white photography is *Elephant Man*. Directed by David Lynch (who since went on to make *Dune*) and photographed by Freddie Francis, it has often been held up as the example of what black and white photography is all about.

Style

The decision to shoot in black and white came from David Lynch but at the time this wasn't necessarily an important consideration for the cameraman, Freddie Francis.

"So far as I was concerned," he says, "this decision had already been taken. What is important to me is style. Black and white film is just another film stock. I might say that given the material I would choose the most appropriate style to cover the period and the feel we were trying to achieve. I think I could have made *Elephant Man* look just as good in colour, because I would have chosen a particular style that suited the film. If you look at my latest film, *The Doctor and the Devils*, this is set in much the same period, but it's in colour.

From *MovieMaker* (October 1985).

"Having said that, I was delighted we were working in black and white—I do have one crack-pot theory concerning subjects set in the Victorian era which is: this era was really the dawning of the photographic age and I firmly believe that an audience seeing a Victorian movie photographed in black and white will subconsciously accept the atmosphere as original."

For a modern cameraman who may have hardly used black and white material, adapting to its possibilities and peculiarities is not so straightforward as the other way round. Freddie Francis has been in the business since the mid-thirties and so quite naturally trained in the use of black of white film. As colour film was introduced he was again there at the start and could learn from scratch.

"Yes, it could be difficult if you've never touched black and white film suddenly going into this new medium, because frankly it's more difficult to do black and white. You have to create everything—with colour you have colours to help you.

Create Colour

"To photograph a film and make it look good in black and white you have to create your own colours, and when I say that I'm really talking about light and shade. In colour you can just put light on it and the colours take care of themselves—obviously it's not quite as simple as that, but you don't have to create as many things in colour as you do in black and white.

"If you are wearing a particular colour dress and you walk up against another particular colour, those two colours, in colour, will take care of themselves. In black and white you have to light them to register as the same colours, or different colours, or whatever. If you flat light in black and white the scene will *look* very flat—it's all on one plane. In other words you have to control lights much more finely in black and white than you do in colour."

This means that when shooting in black and white the cameraman has to be aware of what shade of grey each individual colour will make. To a cameraman as experienced as Freddie Francis it all boils down to an experienced eye. As he says, "There's only one thing a cameraman can rely on in the final analysis, and that's his eyes. If they're no good he might as well pack up and go home."

For the less experienced person it may well be a good idea to construct a grey scale chart by simply painting stripes of all the primary and secondary colours onto a piece of card—something like a video colour bar chart—and then photographing the result under bright light with black and white film. The resulting negative can be enlarged to 10 × 8 size, the individual bars labelled with their respective colours, and then cut out. If you're unsure of how colours will look when photographed together on black and white film then just place the two colour strips on top of each other.

Composition

Thinking of composition for a moment, yes you can use colour to aid composition—in colour. A brightly coloured feature in a room such as a notice board could be used as a compositional aid in the overall frame. In black and white you can't use colour but must turn to light and shade—dark and light. In other words colours in colour, and light and dark in black and white, mean the same thing when you're composing.

Having said all this, it still doesn't completely answer the question, well where do you put your light and shade, or indeed colours?

"Both for *Elephant Man* and *Doctor and the Devils* we were trying to create the same atmosphere. This was London of the 1840s and was very downbeat. There is one slight problem with colour. Normally if you just shoot straight it is very difficult to make anything look as downbeat and dowdy as required, although when you see *Doctor and the Devils* I think you'll see we've succeeded just as well as we did with *Elephant Man* which was shot in black and white."

Atmosphere

"Basically there is no magic trick, I just light the set until it looks right. Thinking about *Elephant Man* in particular, I try to picture the scene. If I were in London in 1840 at that time of the year, where would the light be coming from? There probably wouldn't be much light. Secondly if there *was* light it would be mixed with a lot of smoke coming from fires with burning filth on them and all these things you combine until that atmosphere which you can create on the set gives you Victorian London of 1840."

In a sense it's the same type of preparation that an actor might go through to find a character within a part, to create that particular character by finding those elements which make up something credible.

"This is something they didn't do in the early days of film. Whatever it was, it had to be lit 'properly'—bright shafts of light everywhere. Wherever the leading lady stood she had to have back lights so that her hair stood out, all of which made it terribly false.

"Don't be afraid of photographing things badly to create the right atmosphere. In the early days they were afraid to do that."

Availability

On a practical point of view—and it applies equally to 35, 16mm, or Super 8—is the availability of film stock and processing. *Elephant Man* was shot on Kodak Plus X film. All went well until several weeks into production Freddie discovered that the film stock had a defect and the whole batch had to be returned. Could they find any more Plus X? No chance. There was not one reel to be had on the whole planet. The film was nearly stopped but luckily a new batch arrived in time to avert total shutdown. The trouble was that it turned out to be one stop faster and seemed to need less than half the filler light that the previous batch had required. This took several days to get used to.

Like all professional filmmakers original tests had been done on the original stock, a practice that is well worth emulating by amateur filmmakers. It's far better to use one cartridge of Super 8 making sure that you get the results you expect at different camera settings than to plough on regardless only to find that all the material you have shot is not what you expected and probably useless.

Processing

Processing labs were another problem for Freddie Francis. As a regular user of Rank Film Laboratories, he was tempted to simply just go back there again, but because this was the first major black and white film for several years, he sent tests out to several labs.

Rank, however, seem to love a challenge—perhaps that's why they've taken a Queen's Award to Industry this year—and stripped down and refurbished all their old black and white processing machinery. The results were exemplary but only at the expense of stripping down the machines every day for cleaning and servicing.

Super 8 black and white users have similar problems and there is only one source for their processing—Ann Whitfield, 4 Drill St, Keigthley, West Yorks. Film stock can only be purchased in this country through The Widescreen Centre, but they do carry Kodak Plus-X, Tri-X, and 4X.

Concept

Freddie Francis, as cameraman, gave *Elephant Man* its style, but the original concept and direction came from director David Lynch. David is a native of Philadelphia and has been a filmmaker for a few years less than Freddie Francis. Why become a filmmaker at all?

"I was studying to become a painter and I started making short animated films which were a bridge between painting and movies. I didn't think I wanted to be a filmmaker but once I started I just fell in love with it. Also I had a lot of good luck in film, and not so good luck in painting—although I still love painting.

"My first big project was a thirty-four-minute film called *The Grandmother* which was a mixture of colour and black and white, animation and live action, and with this I was able to get a place at the Center for Advanced Film Studies in Beverly Hills. It was while I was there in 1970 that I started *Eraserhead*, although the picture was actually finished outside the school after I left."

Intuition

Even at this stage David was making conscious decisions to use either black and white, or colour. *Eraserhead* was not a commercial movie so the choice of medium was made for purely aesthetic reasons.

"I think that for me everything is feelings or intuition. There's not too much intellectualising, and if something feels like it should be colour, or something feels that it should be black and white then that's what I make it in. To me *Eraserhead* was absolutely black and white, as was *Elephant Man*.

"On the other hand the film I'm doing right now—even the title *Blue Velvet*—is colour. I've done tests in black and white, but it just doesn't feel right."

Of course this still doesn't answer the question, "What can black and white film do that colour can't?"

"This is a very difficult question to answer in words and it's something I've been asked many times. I chose one or the other mostly by feel, by intuition."

Power

"However, black and white does have the ability to take you into a world that's different, be it in the past as in *The Elephant Man* or in a parallel world as in *Eraserhead*. Sometimes with colour it's just too real and can't take you there so easily and it makes things more pure. You can see eyes and ears in a totally different way, so you really see them. You see shadows and contrasts and shapes because those are the things you end up working with. You don't see such a real picture which you glance over without a second thought. In black and white you really start to see things.

"It seems to make things in a way more powerful—it's removing you from reality. Now this may be a good feeling for the picture or it may not be. This is where you have to use your intuition."

Actually shooting in black and white does cause problems not found with colour. Freddie Francis has already outlined some of the difficulties but there are others which affect the creative direction of the film.

Problems

"You have to separate different objects with light. You have to think in terms of textures—shiny and dull, busy and slow—and I love thinking that way. In fact, getting down to the pure things, designing in black and white is so fantastic. Designing in colour is not nearly so much fun. You can get away with less in black and white. One or two things in a room look really beautiful. In colour it's empty."

On a more practical note, David would also echo the problems voiced by Freddie on black and white film stock.

"My main concern was the quality of the stock. We had great difficulty finding stock that was consistently good both for *Eraserhead* and *Elephant Man*. There's not so much of it made now and I guess that the film companies tend to regard it as film school stuff so they don't take so much care. You just couldn't get a guaranteed perfect black and white film."

Eraserhead is a very odd film—usual yet unusual. Where on earth could all the ideas come from?

"It came from my experience in Philadelphia—the experience of living there."

And why *Elephant Man*?

"Loving textures to start off with, and this idea of going beneath the surface was intriguing to me. There is the surface of this elephant man and beneath the surface is this beautiful soul. So much that everyone can identify with but so difficult to get to because of this surface. That is a neat idea to me. Then there's this texture in the middle of this industry, this kind of architecture and stuff, that is so fantastic-looking for me that I liked it from a visual point of view too."

Blue Velvet

David's latest movie, *Blue Velvet* is again a mood piece but a murder mystery set in an anonymous midwest USA city. This will be made in colour.

"We aren't going to do anything special with the colour," he says. "Having done tests in black and white and then combining shots to give a desaturated look, in the end it just looks dull. It has no magic. We're just going to put the colours in front of the camera and shoot them—we'll create the mood with light rather than use the film to add anything. It will do no more than simply record what's in front of it."

Creation

In the end David's influences come from other painters and places he has lived in and spent time with, rather than other directors. Light and shade, feeling and texture predominate rather than thinking in colours. Even his colour films use these concepts to build up the image. You create the mood first and then work upwards from that.

"Although I have written the screenplay for most of my films, it tends to be a blueprint, a feeling, an idea. Yes I do write with the final film in mind. That is the feeling and you have to stay true to that feeling. The more you veer away from it the weaker the idea and so the film becomes. What's there will dictate the sequence and pacing but in the end you have to sit down and remember the feeling that came with it."

Black and white does have a power all of its own. Filmmakers must never see it as an inferior substitute for colour, but recognise its potentials and capabilities to convey ideas that would be impossible in the full glare of colour photography.

Is There Life after *Dune*?

TIM HEWITT/1986

THE FIRST THING PEOPLE want to know when they find out you've met David Lynch is, "Is he weird?"

During a career that has spanned only three feature films, Lynch has established himself as something of a master of the absurd, the surreal, the grotesque, as often as not in the same movie. Although Lynch's first three features—*Eraserhead* (1977), *The Elephant Man* (1980), and *Dune* (1984)—were all born from different sources, the director has established a unity of style and vision that bind them to one another as surely as if they had all been created full-blown by the same imagination.

The newest entry in the Lynch canon is *Blue Velvet*, the first film since *Eraserhead* that Lynch has scripted from his own ideas as opposed to reworking the ideas of others. "Some parts of it, in mood, remind me of *Eraserhead*," Lynch said, "but it's not like *Eraserhead*."

Blue Velvet is a mystery, of sorts, involving murder, drugs, and a very bizarre sexual angle. The De Laurentiis Entertainment Group plans to release the film in September if Lynch can edit the film sufficiently to get an "R" rating. In plot the film is a complete departure from anything Lynch has attempted before, a film set in modern-day America and peopled with characters viewers will find, in some cases, as real as the people next door. In fact, Lynch characterizes *Blue Velvet* as a "neighborhood picture."

"It's a small mood film," he said. "I don't know if you'd call it *film noir*. There are a lot of dark sequences in it, but some light ones too. Mood is super important to me because that's the feel and the smell and the place of the picture and it has to be right. Then the picture becomes real."

From *Cinefantastique* (vol. 16, 1986).

Coming after *Dune*, *Blue Velvet* is almost a vacation for Lynch. It is his smallest film since *Eraserhead* and he welcomes its intimacy. He prefers working on the smaller scale and frowns at the suggestion of a *Dune II*. "They're not going to do that now. Or at least, *I'm* not going to do it." For all his work on the project, *Dune* still seems to hold a great deal of mystery for Lynch.

"There's something wrong with that movie," he said. "I don't really know what it is, and I'm not certain you could 'fix' it. It's just so big, you know, and there's so much there. A lot of it I like, but a lot of it I don't like. It's just got problems . . ." His voice fades as he stares at his most recent painting, an expressionistic industrial landscape.

"Is there a longer version of *Dune*?" I ask, having heard rumors of a director's cut running in excess of four hours. "Well, the rough cut was very long. It's a big movie. But it wouldn't have worked and that was never the final cut. I think what we ended up with is the best that could be done with it."

Despite his work in the genre, Lynch readily admits that he isn't a fan of science fiction or fantasy, or mysteries for that matter. What he likes is movies. "I love the idea of movies. I also love popcorn, so I love going to movies and eating popcorn. I like almost anything that moves. Sometimes if a film is close to something I love I'll become critical, but most of the time I'm open to what's happening and I don't judge things so much. I like a lot of different things when I'm watching them, but my own personal tastes are pretty narrow."

Although trained as an artist, Lynch doesn't acknowledge any artists as being particularly influential to his vision, nor does he cite any cinematic or literary influences.

"My interior thinking," he said, "comes more from the influences of places I've been and people I've met than from anything else. But sometimes I get ideas and don't know where they come from. I'm sitting in a chair and I get ideas. And they're not particularly related to anything. It's exactly like going fishing and catching a fish. It doesn't matter if you like that particular kind of fish, that's the fish you caught. My ideas are like that."

Even though Lynch doesn't like mysteries as a genre, traditional whodunit type stories, he is captivated by mysteries in a broader sense. "Everything is a mystery, really, isn't it? Darkness to me is a mystery. I don't know what's there and that's what draws me there. It's not necessarily evil, although that would exist there."

Often what the darkness reveals for Lynch are absurd, disquieting images such as those of *Eraserhead*, commonplace things made frightening. For Lynch the surface of things is only the beginning of the vision. "Everything goes in degrees. Just a human face, if you look at it really close, becomes rather strange. And if you look at it *real* close, it becomes grotesque, even the most beautiful woman's face. It's all in such a tender state, all this flesh, and it's an imperfect world."

What the grotesque seems to represent for Lynch is a closeup vision of aspects of ourselves that are otherwise masked by the everyday normalcy of appearance.

"I like things that are within other things," Lynch added. "Like *The Elephant Man*. The outside was one way and the inside was another. *Blue Velvet*'s like that too. It's about a surface that's beautiful, but underneath becomes stranger and stranger."

Lynch's script involves a college student named Jeffrey (Kyle MacLachlan of *Dune*) who returns home because of his father's illness. The mystery begins with the discovery of an ear—a human ear—in a vacant lot beside the home of a nightclub singer (played by Isabella Rossellini). The police are reluctant to become involved; a single ear is not sufficient evidence that a murder has occurred, if indeed one has. As Jeffrey takes it upon himself to investigate he becomes aware of a dangerously mysterious character who seems to have control over the singer. Dennis Hopper plays the villain.

Elements of the script do recall *Eraserhead* in that the same aspect of sexual tension is present throughout. There is an uneasiness in *Blue Velvet* that belies its commonplace setting.

Filmed in Wilmington, North Carolina, *Blue Velvet* reunites Lynch with director of photography Fred Elmes, who shot *Eraserhead*. An early scene in the film, set miles away from the principal action, was shot in the basement of the Cape Fear Hotel along Wilmington's waterfront. A better set couldn't have been built. The basement is dingy with plenty of exposed pipes, many wrapped in crumbling insulation. Hotel junk is scattered about and there are pools of water on the floor. Nothing was ever new here. It looks like it belongs in a David Lynch film.

The scene involves a college student who has sneaked away from a party upstairs and brought his girlfriend to this secluded location in order to do some serious petting. Before long the boy is trying to force himself on the girl who is desperately protesting. Only a sudden shout to stop from Jeffrey, who has followed them down, allows the girl the time to get out of the situation.

"I like all of this stuff," Lynch said, indicating the decay of the basement. "I love textures." The pipes and machinery in the basement also recall another of Lynch's preoccupations: factories. Lynch loves them, views them as places of creation, yet they usually appear dark and threatening in his films.

"Well," he said slowly, "accidents can happen in factories. Factory workers are like heroes in a way, like coal miners. They go down and they risk their lives and they get into this thing because each of them knows about their factory life and when they go home their families don't know about it. There's certain things that surround a factory and a certain way of life and a certain rhythm. It's a generalization, but I like that as the basis for a story. I've never done a *real* factory picture, I guess, because I've never thought of one or been offered one. But I'd like to do a film about certain kinds of steel workers. Maybe use that as a background for a film."

Back in his office at Dino De Laurentiis's North Carolina Film Corporation, Lynch looks like a baby-faced schoolmaster. He wears exactly what I expect: black leather jacket, a white shirt buttoned to the top, khaki pants, and tennis shoes. It's the same as in almost every picture printed of Lynch.

There are photographs of Lynch's "kits" lying on the couch. Usually for each film he makes a "kit," dismembered animal parts mounted on a board with instructions for assembling the creature. The chicken kit, he explained, is separate from the feathers kit. Has he made a kit for *Blue Velvet*? "I've got six mice in deep freeze right now and I'm going to make a mouse kit, but I haven't had the time yet."

One wall of the office is dominated by Lynch's new painting. The canvas holds much of the same mood you would expect to find in a David Lynch film, although the painting is less representational. With a smile Lynch explained that the large red square in the painting dominated by brown hues "had to be there. It just had to. It didn't necessarily have to be a square. It could have been any one of ten things. But it couldn't have been eleven things."

Lynch doesn't associate his paintings with his films, preferring to keep the two activities separate. "*Blue Velvet* and *Eraserhead* are the closest of my films to my paintings, but they're not *like* the paintings. Different parts of the brain produce different works. When I'm painting it doesn't have a lot to do with what I'm doing when I'm making a film."

Blue Velvet and *Eraserhead* are personal films for Lynch, and when I commented on his physical resemblance to Jack Nance (Henry from *Eraserhead*) and Kyle MacLachlan, he nodded his head. "I'd never really noticed that. But I suppose there's something to that. I am Henry in a way, and I'm Jeffrey in a way. I'm not the Elephant Man, and I'm not really in *Dune*. But *Eraserhead* and *Blue Velvet*, I'm in them."

Another film that might have had more of Lynch in it is *Ronnie Rocket*, the long-discussed project that now seems to be on permanent hold. "I'd love to do a comedy," Lynch said with his gentle, whimsical smile. "*Ronnie Rocket* would have been a comedy. I don't know if I'll ever do it now. I rewrote it and I love it. It's a huge, long script, and it's really absurd, an absurd, abstract comedy. The thrill is gone, I'm sorry to say. It would take me along time to do it. I personally love it, but I don't know if anybody would ever care to see it."

But even without *Ronnie Rocket* there will no doubt be other scripts, other films, each uniquely Lynchian in their vision. *Blue Velvet* will bring Lynch's feature production to four films, films as rich as an artist's canvas, films unlike any others.

"Is he weird?" they ask about David Lynch. Well, yes, but not the way you might think.

Out to Lynch

DAVID CHUTE/1986

(PARAGRAPHS IN ITALICS are excerpts from an interview with David Lynch by David Chute, conducted at the Bob's Big Boy, corner of Wilshire and Highland in Los Angeles on Saturday, June 21, 1986.)

Blue Velvet is not a movie for everybody. Some people are going to really dig it, but we've experienced some extremely negative reactions, too. We had a sneak preview in the Valley that was a disaster. People thought it was disgusting and sick. And of course it is, but it has two sides. If you don't have the contrasts, then maybe. But you can push the limits out much wider than Blue Velvet. I believe that films should have power, the power of good and the power of darkness, so you can get some thrills and shake things up. And if you back off from that stuff you're shooting right down into lukewarm junk."

"I don't know if you're a detective or a pervert," remarks Sandy (Laura Dern) to Jeffrey (Kyle MacLachlan) at a crucial juncture in the harrowing new David Lynch picture, *Blue Velvet*. We never are told which term really applies, although writer-director Lynch (who created Jeffrey as a lookalike alter ego) would surely insist that he is both at once. The puppyish curiosity of the eager-beaver boy investigator, who gets into a sicker brand of trouble than an American small town is supposed to be able to encompass, may not be entirely blameless in his wide-eyed naivete. He is so amorally awestruck by crime and horror that he could be accused of fraternizing with the forces of human soul-rot.

The movie is a nightmarish coming-of-age story, a Hardy Boys thriller with running sores and pustules. It was made by, and about, a compul-

---

From *Film Comment* (no. 22.5, September/October 1986). Reprinted by permission of David Chute.

sive lifter of rocks who secretly adores the slimy creepy-crawlies he uncovers. But the picture also toys with the notion that happiness is a matter of confining yourself stubbornly to the sunny surface of things, of not probing too deeply into their wormy innards. And who can deny that he has a point?

"This is all the way America is to me. There's a very innocent, naive quality to my life, and there's a horror and a sickness as well. It's everything.

"Blue Velvet *is a very American movie. The look of it was inspired by my childhood in Spokane, Washington. Lumberton is a real name; there are many Lumbertons in America. I picked it because we could get police insignias and stuff, because it was an actual town. But then it took off in my mind and we started getting lumber trucks going through the frame and that jingle on the radio—'At the sound of the falling tree. . . .'—that all came about because of the name.*

"*There is an autobiographical level to the movie. Kyle is dressed like me. My father was a research scientist for the Department of Agriculture in Washington. We were in the woods all the time. I'd sorta had enough of the woods by the time I left, but still, lumber and lumberjacks, all this kinda thing, that's America to me—like the picket fences and the roses in the opening shot. It's so burned in, that image, and it makes me feel so happy. That was in a lot of our childhoods.*"

A brainy, small-town kid, MacLachlan's Jeffrey finds a grisly clue in a field one day and dutifully hands it over to the straight-arrow local constable. Later on, partly to impress the cop's daughter, Dern's Sandy, a raw-boned teen angel, with his own boldness, Jeffrey follows his few skimpy clues straight into the dark heart of a violent sexual mystery. It's as if the living room wall in a Frank Capra movie opened up to reveal an assaultive ritual choreographed by de Sade unfolding on the other side—a ritual in which purity is sacrificed (for love) to monstrosity and is irrevocably tainted by it.

Isabella Rossellini's porcelain-skinned Dorothy, bruised and defiled by the seething, wheezing, vile Frank (Dennis Hopper in full froth), standing naked in Jeffrey's living room, in front of Sandy and Jeffrey's mother, screaming, "He put his disease in me!" is not a spectacle anybody will enjoy. (The nudity is meticulously de-eroticized.) And poor Jeffrey doesn't know how to react; he isn't sure which of the implications of this outburst he has to accept like a man and which he can still righteously fend off.

Because he is implicated. He imagines that he's falling in love with Dorothy (even though the center of the story is Sandy's radiant sanity), and when they're in bed and she reflexively says, "Hit me," he recoils, but complies.

"Blue Velvet *is a trip beneath the surface of a small American town, but it's also a probe into the subconscious or a place where you face things that you don't normally face. One of the sound mixers said it's like Norman Rockwell meets Heironymous Bosch. It's a trip into that as close as you can get, and then a trip out. There's an innermost point, and from then on it pulls back.*

"Jeffery has seen enough and gotten in there enough so that the opportunity is there and the desire is there. But it's something he doesn't like about himself at all. It comes back at him pretty quick. And that's something about life, you know. At times, you push the limits out as far as where you think you can live with yourself. Even though Jeffrey could understand it and get there, it's not his scene. That's his, I dunno, his conscience. You can't keep doing things you can't live with. You're going to get sick, or you're going to go crazy, or you're going to get arrested, or something's going to happen."

For David Lynch, gazing in rapt fascination at diseased bodies (or souls), in *Eraserhead, The Elephant Man, Dune,* and *Blue Velvet,* the spectacle may be no more gross or disgusting than wriggling bacteria glimpsed through a microscope. His curiosity is not tainted by irony, malice, perversity, or condescension. His studious outlook has an almost scientific purity. He doesn't smirk, he doesn't wink, he doesn't judge. The wisps of classical religious music on the *Blue Velvet* soundtrack are no ironic jape. David Lynch could be putting his most profound religious feelings into this picture, quasi though they be. This is probably the most nakedly exposed he's been in a movie, and no artist as sophisticated as Lynch would take such flagrant risks unless he felt driven to it, unless he felt he'd hate himself if he turned tail.

It will be observed that *Blue Velvet* has story problems. It probably could have benefited from the services of a freelance "thriller doctor" like, say, Ross Thomas. The generic mystery story elements are skimpy. On the level of bare craftsmanship, *Blue Velvet* sometimes feels downright klutzy. It stumbles over the basics of setting up characters, of leading us along step by step so that we'll always know just how to interpret everything. It "bungles" all those neat, businesslike devices for eliminating ambiguity. But it revels in the kind of demented, go-for-broke amateurishness that cuts through to perceptions that ordinary professionalism, valuing correctness beyond everything, can't touch.

"I've met John Waters, liked him, and feel a definite kinship with his stuff. But there are a lot of differences. His way is making so much fun of those banal, absurd, polyester things. I want to come at them sideways in a drier way,

for that certain kind of humor. And also so that you can slip into fear: See, Ronnie Rocket, the film I've been trying to make for five years, is very absurd but also can turn slightly and become very frightening. You can't just be so camp or so blatant. Waters is very up front, sorta like a loud saxophone, and I want to back off into something a little different."

The billowing blue velvet draperies under the opening credits have an Italianate lushness, a rotting romanticism that recalls Luchino Visconti. But they also look like something that's alive and throbbing: an engorged membrane. In this movie, Lynch's trademark thumping noises make us feel trapped inside an organism, wedged into an intestine or a pulsating ventricle.

All the organic elements in *Blue Velvet* exhibit a similar hectic vigor. The flowers look swollen with color, the greenery mysteriously overnourished, like the thick blades of grass over a cemetery. In the calender-art first image of a glowing-white picket fence and top-heavy blood-red roses, the colors are psychedelically heightened, like the blossoms on the plants in H. P. Lovecraft's *The Color Out of Space* that were raised on unearthly fertilizer.

The underlying horror of *Blue Velvet*, of course, is that there's nothing unearthly or inhuman about any of this stuff. It's the rampaging, devouring vitality of the most noisome critters that so unsettles. The rot in a human monster like Dennis Hopper's Frank is, in this scheme of things, a moral abscess, and Hopper's performance (as wacked-out as it is) has a lot of pain behind it: the anguish of a spiritual gangrene case wracked by uncanny jolts of energy. You feel he could crush brains with his bare hands in the throes of some feverish spasm.

"Laura Dern's Sandy has to balance out a lot of darkness. Laura looks like Sandy should look, and she understood what she had to do, and she had everything that it took to do it. Sandy is the counterweight but she is also the person who got Jeffrey into this. He would probably have walked home that first night, after talking to her father, and forgotten all about it."

The implications of *Blue Velvet* could slightingly be reduced to a fistful of platitudes—it's a yin and yang, ego-id, can't-have-the-light-without-the-dark view of life. But Lynch clings to such a tough-minded version of this basic attitude, without a trace of romantic nature worship, that it doesn't feel like a reduction. He's willing to construct a working model of the scheme of things that incorporates the vile, the revolting, and the monstrous—and he calls them by their right names.

Death and decay also feed a teeming undermass of scavenging beetles and bacteria, and Lynch always seems subliminally aware of the odorous organic processes that are gnawing at the very roots they fertilize. His camera keeps trying to burrow into that wriggling, black, bug-infested subsoil—literally, at first, when Jeffrey's father suffers a stroke while watering the front lawn and a chasm opens up and we can hear the clattering hum of thousands of leathery black mandibles. And, like a painter schooled in anatomy, his sense of what's beneath the surface affects the way he photographs it.

"The one artist that I feel could be my brother—and I almost don't like saying it because the reaction is always, 'Yes, you and everybody else'—is Franz Kafka. I really dig him a lot. Some of his things are the most thrilling combos of words I have ever, ever, ever read. If Kafka wrote a crime picture, I'd be there. I'd like to direct that, for sure. I'd like to direct a movie of The Trial. Henry, the hero of Eraserhead, gets into Kafka's world a bit.

"Henry is very sure that something is happening, but he doesn't understand it at all. He watches things very, very carefully, because he's trying to figure them out. He might study the corner of that pie container right there by your head, just because it's in his line of sight, and he might wonder why he sat where he did to have that be there like that? Everything is new. It might not be frightening to him, but it could be a key to something. Everything should be looked at. There could be clues in it."

Some moviegoers will react to the brutalization of Isabella Rossellini in Blue Velvet with unalloyed disgust. Those sequences could invalidate the film for them. It is a peculiarity of the visceral way we respond to movies that we don't necessarily assume that the disgust has been evoked intentionally or that the director shares this feeling. The person who staged the action, who dreamed it up, often becomes the object of the negative reactions it provokes.

And, in a sense, this is perfectly proper. A novelist, for instance, doesn't have to draw anybody else into a depiction of depravity. He doesn't have to force anyone to walk through it. The act of moviemaking draws close to the acts it depicts or explores, because the acts have to be staged before they can be photographed. You can even assume that if a director found any human activity too disturbing even to simulate, he wouldn't be able to make a film about it.

"Some people may have this stuff in them, but they live through television or movies or someone else to satisfy the urge. So it's one step removed and it's cleaner. They don't get their hands dirty, but they're still there. The people watching the soap operas are digging this sick stuff so much, and they understand it—and if they had the chance, they would do the same sick stuff.

"Sex is such a fascinating thing. It's sorta like you can listen to one pop song *just so many times, whereas jazz has so many variations. Sex should be like jazz. It can be the same tune, but there are many variations on it. And then when you start getting out there, it can be shocking to learn that something like that could be sexual. It would be kind of, you know, strange. But it's a real fact of life just the same. There's no real explaining in* Blue Velvet *because it's such an abstract thing inside a person."*

A character in John Updike's novel *The Witches of Eastwick* (an enjoyable book that presents magic as a vestigial nature-religion) delivers a guest sermon at a local church. It's a pretty weird sermon, too, all about the emotions of the roundworm nestled in your small intestine, "when a big gobbety mess of half-digested steak or moo goo gai pan comes sloshing down to him. He's as real a creature as you and me. He's as noble a creature, designwise—really *lovingly* designed."

David Lynch shares the fascination of this amateur biologist (and amateur minister) with the complex shapes and ingenius functions that even the groddiest natural processes can assume. And it's somehow even more diverting when the phenomena are poisonous or stomach-churningly ugly.

"The 'disease' Dorothy talks about is an abstract sort of thing. It doesn't mean AIDS, or anything like that. There was, in the script, even more on that theme. Dorothy's had that done to her before, and she understands that thing, that sickness. People mention William Burroughs to me a lot, but I've never read any Burroughs. I know I should, but. . . ."

As it happens, Lynch's dreamily evocative visual gifts are a perfectly adequate substitute for intellectualism and analysis. He is such a wizard at infecting us with his creepoid perceptions that he really doesn't need to work through the intermediate steps of figuring out what it all means. As if entranced, he translates his intimations of toxic mortality directly into imagery.

"In a way, this is *still a fantasy film. It's like a dream of strange desires wrapped inside a mystery story. It's what could happen if you ran out of fantasy."*

The in-and-out structure of *Blue Velvet* mirrors the "journey into hell" format of such recent American political epics as *Missing, Under Fire,* and especially *Salvador.* The new myth of discovery in these stories is a journey into a dark place where very few of the (legal or natural) laws we take for granted seem to apply any longer. Everything is leveled by the feral, surreal savagery that bubbles up from within people when they're liberated from the social tether. The last fillip of horror comes with the recognition that this chaos is somehow a direct consequence of those beliefs and of our attempts to enforce them on other people. We peer into the abyss of political decay and see our own faces staring back at us, slack jaws dappled with innocent blood.

In the face of the lobotomized, yuppie-careerist, expedient optimism that ate Hollywood, the most acidulous pessimism can be a sign of life—an act of independent judgment.

"*I really believe it's like the Beach Boys said: 'Be true to your school.' You gotta be true to the ideas that you have, because they're even bigger than you first think they are. And if you're not true to them, they'll only work part way. They're almost like gifts, and even if you don't understand them 100 percent, if you're true to them, they'll ring true at different levels and have a truth at different levels. But if you alter them too much then they won't even ring. They'll just sort* clank.

"*No matter how weird a story is, as soon as you step one foot forward into that story you realize that this world has rules, and you have to follow them or the audience will sense that you're doing something dishonest. That's part of being true to your ideas. Some films operate so much on the surface it doesn't feel like there are any kind of real rules. Maybe in those cases you can actually go further, here and there.*

"*Anytime there's a little bit of power, somebody might think it was sick or disgusting. A lot of the time when you go out to an extreme, you can make a fool of yourself or a fool of the film. You have to believe things so much that you make them honest. I'm really just trying to be true to those ideas, not to manipulate an audience; to get in there and let the material talk to me, to work inside a dream. If you just experience it, ideas will pop and you'll be in that world, and then you're OK. If it's real, and if you believe it, you can say almost anything.*

Blue Movie

JEFFREY FERRY/1987

NO FILM IN RECENT memory has so divided public opinion. Subjecting Isabella Rossellini to harrowing scenes of sexual degradation, *Blue Velvet* arrives here in March as the most controversial movie in years . . . and some say the sickest. Director David Lynch remains defiant.

At last October's New York Film Festival, amidst the cosmopolitan cacophony of the luxurious mock-Renaissance hotel horror which served as unofficial film biz HQ for the week, I stopped abruptly by one of the city's leading agents.

"You absolutely must see *Blue Velvet*," she hissed, red talons sinking into my forearm for emphasis. "Everybody's talking about it. It's the most controversial movie in years." She darted off backwards, no doubt to take another meeting and sign another million-dollar deal.

No film in modern memory has so divided American opinion as David Lynch's low-budget surprise-hit thriller. At every screening of this lurid tale of murder, violence, and sadomasochism set in bucolic small-town America, at least a handful of the audience walks out in the middle of the film.

Others love it. According to *Newsweek*, a heart-attack victim in Chicago fainted while watching *Blue Velvet*, was rushed to hospital to have his pacemaker adjusted, and then rushed back to the cinema to catch the end of the film. Critics Roger Ebert and Gene Siskel, who do a sort of Mutt-and-Jeff movie reviewing act on American TV's *Tonight Show*, had their bitterest-ever disagreement. Ebert labelled *Blue Velvet* "one of the sickest movies ever made," while Siskel called it one of the year's ten best.

From *The Face* (no. 82, February 1987).

Blue Velvet is a coming-of-age movie. It is the story of a young man's discovery of the forces and emotions lying just below the surface among his family, his friends, and his neighbours. In writer-director David Lynch's view, those forces include love, hatred, murder, perversion, corruption, and degradation. *Blue Velvet* is a kind of journey inwards to the land of Original Sin.

It is a film of extremes. In the timber-felling town of Lumberton (a real town in North Carolina), the birds always chirp, the white picket fences glow like summer clouds, and the neighbours are so genial and friendly they might have walked in off *Petticoat Junction*. Yet the criminals are so evil and vicious, the degradation so intense, that the movie evokes a kind of primordial fear in the viewer. The fear would be almost unbearable at times, if not for the chunks of wacky college-boy humour interspersed throughout. Like *The Exorcist*—to my mind the most genuinely frightening horror film of the 1970s—the fear *Blue Velvet* inspires is not an external fear—of a monster or a murderer—but internal fear—of the evil within our own minds and souls.

"It kind of strips you to the bone," said a friend of mine, who loved it. He added that two of the four people he went to see it with walked out halfway through.

For many Americans, the most controversial aspect of *Blue Velvet* is the character of Dorothy (Isabella Rossellini), a down-on-her-luck nightclub singer forced to submit to violent, sadistic sex by the terrifying pervert Frank (Dennis Hopper).

That's the good news. The bad news is that Dorothy enjoys it. She gets turned on by being beaten and degraded. When she seduces Jeffrey (Kyle MacLachlan), she implores him to beat her. He complies. The Dorothy character has been denounced as an embodiment of the worst of male fantasies, a denial of the last twenty years of feminist progress, an incitement to rape, and so on.

"The only thing worse than being talked about is not being talked about," said dear old Oscar. David Lynch apparently does not agree. The forty-year-old director has been so unnerved by the torrent of criticism his film has provoked that he has become exceedingly cautious in discussing it. Which is a shame, because *Blue Velvet* is very much a personal creation. Part of its strength is that it is not a product of the usual Hollywood committee with the usual checklist (Hero, Villain, Love Interest, Plot Line, Resolution, etc.), but of an individual with a vision so powerfully all-embracing that it convinces by its very intensity. The fact that certain plot details are sketchy or unclear hardly matters in the context of the eviscerating story Lynch wants to tell.

"The only thing to say about all the controversy," says Lynch, opening up at last to my prodding, "is did I make all that up, or are there examples like that in real life? And there are countless examples like that in real life. So why do they get so upset when you put something like this in a film?"

With a shock of lustrous brown hair falling over his forehead, round inquisitive eyes, a white shirt buttoned primly up to his neck, and a twangy golly-gee-whillikers style of speaking, Lynch is very much the all-American boy. You have only to watch him for thirty seconds to see that the film's young protagonist—earnest, curious, intelligent college student Jeffrey—is very much an autobiographical creation.

He stands by his most controversial character, the sado-masochistic Dorothy. "People get into all sorts of strange situations, and you can't believe they're enjoying it, but they are. And they could get out of it, but they don't. And there are lots of reasons for it. It gets you into psychiatry."

Dennis Hopper's portrayal of Frank gives us one of the most chilling, terrifying, homicidal maniacs the screen has seen. After years of internal exile in Hollywood as a "drinker-drugger" (his own phrase), Hopper is back, with a performance destined to go down in cinematic history alongside Tony Perkins's Norman Bates.

"Dennis Hopper called me up one day," says Lynch, "after reading the script. He said, 'David, you have to let me play Frank, because I *am* Frank.'

"That scared the hell out of me."

On the subject of Frank, we get a hint of what probably lies behind Lynch's motivations in making *Blue Velvet*.

"Frank, to me, is a guy Americans know very well," he says. "I'm sure most everybody growing up has met someone like Frank. They might not have shook his hand and gone out for a drink with him, but all you've got to do is exchange eye contact with someone like that and you know that you've met him."

According to Lynch, Frank is not so much evil as twisted. "Frank is totally in love. He just doesn't know how to show it. He may have gotten into some strange things (like sadistic sex with incestuous role-playing, murder, dismemberment, helium inhalation, drug-dealing, and latent homosexuality, to name a few), but he's still motivated by positive things. *Blue Velvet* is a love story."

David Lynch loves to tell the story of his first meeting with Isabella Rossellini. He was introduced to her at a restaurant by a mutual friend when he was in the process of casting *Blue Velvet*. Struck by her serene

European beauty, he told her, "You could be Ingrid Bergman's daughter." "'You idiot,' my friend said to me," Lynch recalls, "'she *is* Ingrid Bergman's daughter!'"

Lynch claims he was not aiming to provoke a furore with *Blue Velvet*. Rossellini was chosen for the part of Dorothy because she projected the sense of sophistication and mystery, along with vulnerability and helplessness, that Lynch was looking for. But if Lynch was after controversy, he could not have done better than Isabella Rossellini.

As the daughter of Ingrid Bergman and "the face" of Lancome cosmetics, she is in the highest constellation of American stars those who, like the Royal Family in Britain, are "nationalised" by press and TV to become the property of the public. Before the fearless invigilators of *People* magazine and their imitators, every visit to the supermarket by these celebrities becomes public property. With Isabella Rossellini playing the sexually perverted Dorothy, *Blue Velvet* was instantly transformed from a minor art movie from an avowedly weird director into a major attack on American morality.

In person, in an almost frumpy black cardigan and minimal make-up, Rossellini wears her superstardom with quiet dignity. As we sat down to lunch at Sam's Cafe, a moderately pretentious (by New York standards) media hangout, Isabella wondered if the film company had chosen Sam's Cafe because of its resemblance to Rick's Cafe "in my mother's movie *Casablanca*," and David Lynch began enthusing over the coffee cups, "the biggest I've ever seen—don't they make you kinda feel like you're shrinking?" I began to despair in the thought that the two of them had been rehearsing their roles, superstar's daughter and art school product, in front of the mirror prior to the interview.

But when I offered the opinion that Isabella's mother was, according to a very great authority on 1940s Hollywood (namely my mother), the most beautiful woman in all of Hollywood in that decade, Isabella reacted ("Oh, thank you very much") with a sweet and genuine gratitude, even a hint of surprise, so spontaneous I was touched.

Moving adroitly from the sublime to the slime, I said, "Isabella, critic Rex Reed said that your mother would turn in her grave if she saw the part you played in *Blue Velvet*."

"I don't want to comment on that," she replied quietly. "My parents are dead. It's hard enough for me to live without them, so I leave it to others. I think it must be morbid people who say these things because they make good copy. It's not up to me to stir up the tombs.

"I don't know whether they would have liked the film or not," she continued determinedly. "They aren't here to see it. All I do know is that mother loved *Elephant Man* (directed by Lynch) and father liked David very much when he met him."

For those readers just returned from a forty-year vacation on another planet, Ingrid Bergman created an international scandal in 1949 when she left her first husband in Hollywood for Italian film director Roberto Rossellini, by whom she was pregnant. Hollywood, reacting as if Ingrid Bergman had invented adultery, banned her from the American picture industry for more than a decade. Rossellini, a genius of a film director but no saint where women were concerned, left Ingrid when Isabella was a small child.

I ask Isabella if she was aware as a child that her father was a genius. "As a little child," she says, "I thought he was God. Then as I got older I had to come down a little bit, and say he was a genius. My mother, too, was a goddess, but I was always closer to my father. I was a daddy's girl."

For most of her childhood, Isabella lived in Rome with her father, often visiting her mother in Paris. In 1972 she moved to New York, where she worked first as a television journalist for Italian state TV and then as a fashion model. She signed a five-year contract, renewed last year, with Lancome cosmetics, for two million dollars, making her one of the highest paid models in the world. Thirty-four is rather old for any fashion model, let alone one so successful.

"Once you become the image of a company, it's very hard for the company to change its image, so they keep you for a long time," Isabella explains with unmodel-like modesty.

In taking the part of Dorothy, Isabella knew exactly what she was letting herself in for. Like Lynch, she feels the character is realistic and interestingly complex. She has little time for the one-dimensional career-woman characters currently fashionable in Hollywood. "I see Dorothy very much as a victim and as someone who is suffering," she says. "Yes, she does get herself into this situation, and yes, she does enjoy being beaten, but she was probably totally twisted and totally crazy and sad. And she does begin to come out of it as the film ends.

"The film is basically a search into the unknown. In a search, you find something. You begin to understand something, whether it's good or bad, about yourself, and the world and that you have choices. It's a process of knowledge, and experience.

"I tried to portray not just a character, but a character development." In her independence and her commitment to acting, she is very much her mother's daughter. Not to mention that when she smiles that familiar warm radiant smile, you want to pull your trilby low over one eye and drawl out of the corner of your mouth something about the cares of two people not amounting to a hill of beans in this crazy world.

Since *Blue Velvet*, Rossellini has had several small acting parts ("I hate waiting around doing nothing") and one major role, opposite Ryan O'Neal in Norman Mailer's film of his book, *Tough Guys Don't Dance*. Impressed by her performance in *Blue Velvet*, Mailer rewrote the part specifically for her. She was less than overwhelmed by Mailer, and does not expect great things from the just-completed film.

"I am still a beginning actor, and Mailer is a beginning director. I think we were all kind of lost together. It had its problems."

She says she would act full-time "if every film would be like *Blue Velvet*." Unless and until more opportunities like that arise, she is keeping an open mind on making a full-time commitment to acting. "My father always encouraged curiosity, and he always found an incredible pleasure in finding out, in knowledge. And for me the best thing in life is to extend yourself, to fulfill your deepest curiosity, not just the gossipy part, but the knowledge. That, to me, is happiness."

If, in the century of its imperial ascendancy, the United States has made any original contribution to world culture, it is probably the development of an art form devoted to the examination of surfaces and external images, both in themselves and as clues to underlying meaning. This approach, or sensibility— it might be called the Warholian sensibility—is especially appropriate to modern consumer society, where the products we have to deal with each day become ever more complex, while the packaging and advertising which sell them strive ingeniously to make them appear ever simpler.

David Lynch has brought this sensibility to filmmaking. Here he is describing Henry, the hero of his 1977 cult classic, *Eraserhead*: "Henry is very sure that something is happening, but he doesn't understand it at all. He watches things very, very carefully, because he's trying to figure them out. He might study the corner of that pie container, there by your head, just because it's in his line of sight, and he might wonder why he sat where he did to have that be there like that. Everything is new. It might not be frightening to him, but it could be a key to something. Everything should be looked at. There could be clues in it."

On *Blue Velvet*: "There's always the surface of something and something altogether different going on beneath the surface, just like electrons busily moving about, but we can't see them. That's one of the things films do, is show you that conflict."

The key image in *Blue Velvet* is the severed ear Jeffrey finds lying in a field. When Jeffrey turns it over, it is infested with hundreds of crawling ants. All that follows in the film flows from Jeffrey's decision to investigate how the ear came to be there. According to Lynch, the ear is "a ticket to another world."

Lynch spent his childhood years in small towns in America's rugged, wooded Pacific Northwest. His father was a scientist with the U.S. Forest Service.

"I spent a lot of time out in the woods, building fires."

"Did you like the woods?"

"No."

"What were you trying to do, burn them down?"

"No, I was trying to cook something."

When a teenager, his family moved to suburban Washington, D.C. "I got the woods out of my system. Now I like cities. I still like the woods though." After high school, he attended three art schools: the Corcoran School of Art, the Boston Museum School, and the Pennsylvania Academy of Fine Arts. "I love art and I love painting, and I still do it."

Ask Lynch about art, and the mood suddenly lightens. He becomes cheerful and enthusiastic. It is as if, interviewing Rod Stewart, one suddenly switched the subject from music to football. *That* was work, *this* is fun. One of Lynch's favourite encapsulations of *Blue Velvet* is "Norman Rockwell meets Hieronymous Bosch." I asked him why he liked art so much. "The art life is . . . (pause) . . . it's just another way of saying the great life."

"David," interjected Rossellini, with an almost maternal solicitousness (she is mother of a three-year-old daughter, Elektra, by former husband Jon Weidemann), "now you're being too enigmatic."

Rossellini seemed worried that Lynch's secretiveness would prevent me from appreciating his talents.

His key influences include filmmakers Stanley Kubrick, Hitchcock, and Jacques Tati; the films *Sunset Boulevard*, *La Strada*, and *Lolita*; and the writer Franz Kafka. When I asked what his single greatest influence was, he did not hesitate for a second.

"Philadelphia."

"You mean because it's horrible?"

"Yes, horrible, but in a very interesting way. There were places there that had been allowed to decay, where there was so much fear and crime that just for a moment there was an opening to another world. It was fear, but it was so strong, and so magical, like a magnet, that your imagination was always sparking in Philadelphia.

"I just have to think of Philadelphia now, and I get ideas, I hear the wind, and I'm off into the darkness somewhere."

Urban renewal, says Lynch, has since cleaned up Philadelphia and destroyed the magic.

He is very happy that *Blue Velvet* is now into profit on its six-million-dollar cost. "Nobody ever thought it was going to be commercial. Now that it's made money, it goes down as an exception. It's fantastic when that happens."

The film's success will also help him get his next project, *Ronnie Rocket*, off the ground.

"I've been writing it for ten years, since I finished *Eraserhead*. It's an absurd mystery of the strange forces of existence. It's about electricity."

Of course. Electricity. What else?

For some months now, the rumour has been circulating that Isabella Rossellini and David Lynch (both divorced) are romantically involved.

"Isabella, I understand you two are involved?"

"That's none of your business."

"David, if the story of *Blue Velvet* had continued past the ending, which of the two girls would Jeffrey have ended up with, the blonde all-American, or the dark, mysterious foreign nightclub singer?"

"I've got my ideas, but I think the movie should end there, where it ended. Anyway, it's pretty apparent."

"I'm sorry, we have to go now."

The actress and director smile gently and rise. Both dressed demurely in black, both silent, they file out of the restaurant.

A Dark Lens on America

RICHARD B. WOODWARD/1990

AT THE EDGE OF the French Quarter in New Orleans, where the city's charm falls off into skid row, David Lynch is directing a scene from his new film *Wild at Heart*. On a scouting mission during the morning he had liked several of the people who gather here in the bars before noon and has now decided to incorporate them into the shots. The action of the film, which stars Nicolas Cage and Laura Dern as young lovers, has the couple always on the run from sinister, adult forces. New Orleans is only one of their many hideouts.

The script calls for Sailor to pick up Lula in his car at a seedy hotel; there's a bit of dialogue, then a drive-away. Lynch positions an older woman from the area by the hotel door, patiently coaching her about what he wants. "Ruthie, have a smoke, drink your beer and when they drive up, look over casually," he says through his speaker-horn from across the street. "Don't look at the camera, no matter what." On cue, Ruthie performs flawlessly, adding a sour note of realism to a throwaway scene.

A crowd of tourists and locals has gathered on the median strip to watch the film-making, giving Lynch another idea. He whispers to the assistant director, who whispers to his assistant: "Round up the ten weirdest people you can find and get them ready. We're going to do it again." By the time the camera starts rolling, a group of forty or fifty is standing on either side of the hotel door. This time, as Cage arrives for Dern, Lynch signals the crowd to shout, "Goodbye, Sailor! Goodbye, Lula!" after which Cage floors the '65 Thunderbird convertible, leaving a patch of rubber on the street and the director beaming. "That was fun," he says. Whichever take eventually passes the final cut—gritty and low-key or

From the *New York Times Magazine* (14 January 1990). Reprinted by permission of the New York Times Syndication Sales Corp.

off-the-charts euphoric—it will bear the mark of David Lynch, a homegrown surrealist whose love for dark and light extremes yields a warped revision of common American places and experience. His eye for the absurd detail that thrusts a scene into shocking relief and his taste in risky, often grotesque material has made him, perhaps, Hollywood's most revered eccentric, sort of a psychopathic Norman Rockwell.

From his astonishing feature debut, *Eraserhead*, in 1977, through his first mainstream success with *The Elephant Man* in 1980, which earned him two Academy Award nominations (best director and best adapted screenplay), through *Blue Velvet*, his erotic detective story that won the National Society of Film Critics Award for Best Film of 1986, Lynch has developed a peculiar signature. Within established moods of dread and mystery, disturbing things happen in the frame or on the soundtrack. A low wind blows throughout *Eraserhead*, which features an evening meal in which chickens suddenly move their wings and spout blood. The criminal Frank Booth in *Blue Velvet*, played by a maniacal Dennis Hopper, needs an oxygen mask to reach orgasm, and he terrorizes people while quoting Roy Orbison. There is an ominous and exciting sense in a Lynch film that anything could befall his characters. And that they take in stride any number of bizarre circumstances gives them comic dimension, which often only serves to make the scary parts even scarier.

From the beginning, his films have raised issues of exploitation. *Blue Velvet*, a critical and commercial triumph, nonetheless brought charges that Lynch relished its kinky sex and violence. Some critics deplored the treatment of the character Dorothy Vallens, who enjoys being beaten up. Many people feel uncomfortable sitting through his films, acknowledging at the same time that they can't stop watching them. Pauline Kael of the *New Yorker*, a critic who admired *Blue Velvet*, reported overhearing someone say upon exiting the movie: "Maybe I'm sick, but I want to see that again." Lynch doesn't censor his most unsavory fantasies; they go right up there on the screen.

"David is plugged into the American psyche," says Harry Dean Stanton, who plays a private detective in the new film. "He takes things to the edge, which we're badly in need of now." Whether to the edge or beyond it, Lynch makes movies that resemble no one else's. And however much he may be wired into the country's nightmares, he is even more in tune with himself—with the tensions between the security and wonder of childhood and something adult, unknown, and dangerous. Despite two marriages, two divorces, and two children, Lynch has managed to stay very much a curious boy for whom the world is alive with discoveries, both good and evil.

Everyone who meets David Lynch for the first time is struck by how normal and clean-cut he seems. His work often brings to mind the European surrealists Buñuel and Cocteau, but in person he is wholesomely American. His body is average, unathletic; the hair thick and conservatively styled. He usually wears white socks and keeps the top button of his shirt fastened—a retro 1950s look, as though he were still in grade school instead of forty-three years old. Mel Brooks, who produced *The Elephant Man* and hired Lynch to direct it, calls him "Jimmy Stewart from Mars"; and Lynch certainly shares the actor's sweet face and folksy voice—haltingly sincere, twangy.

But to talk to him means first to catch him. For the last year and a half Lynch has been on a creative tear that allows little time for anyone not involved in his many projects. Dino De Laurentiis's film company, which produced Lynch's *Dune* (an adaptation of Frank Herbert's science-fiction classic) as well as *Blue Velvet*, went bankrupt in 1988, tying up the director in several scripts that were never filmed. As if to make up for this frustration and lost time, Lynch has exploded with an array of new work.

His status as a cult figure—on the order of Laurie Anderson or David Byrne—allows him access to other media. In addition to *Wild at Heart*, which is now in postproduction and scheduled for fall release, he continues to make and exhibit his soft, moody paintings that float between abstraction and figuration. He has produced and written lyrics for an album by the singer Julee Cruise, whose "Mysteries of Love" was the closing number in *Blue Velvet*. And last November he came to New York for a performance at the Brooklyn Academy of Music of his *Industrial Symphony No. 1*. A theatrical work he wrote and directed with the composer Angelo Badalamenti, it included a midget who sawed wood on stage, a half-nude woman acrobat, and a finale in which dozens of baby dolls were lowered on strings from the catwalk.

Perhaps most remarkably, Lynch is about to infiltrate prime-time television. *Twin Peaks*, a series that he cowrote and codirected, will be seen on ABC in the spring. Rather than the bowdlerized, shrunken show one might expect, *Twin Peaks* is unmistakably Lynch. It's an intense fantasy about high-school life in a Northwest mill town following the murder of a prom queen, who turns out not to be as pure as everyone thought. The series explores the town's involvement in her death and the F.B.I.

investigation of it. It's kind of a languorous, finely textured soap opera, injecting the form with hallucinatory power. Like the director himself, it is conventional but crazily bent.

A hint that Lynch is not as prosaic as he looks is dropped after we sit down for lunch at one of his favorite Manhattan restaurants, Jerry's in SoHo. Lynch has many rituals. On the New Orleans set of *Wild at Heart* he would retreat every day at lunchtime for meditation, a practice he has followed for seventeen years. Another ritual, it turns out, is restaurants. He likes to eat at the same place and order the same thing every day. He was at Jerry's the day before, and knows what he wants.

"I'm in something of a crisis because I heard something about combining certain foods and their chemical reactions," he says, between bites of his BLT. "Now I really don't know what to eat anymore because everything I eat is wrong and I don't know what to eat that's right. It's not just a problem for me but for millions of people."

He isn't kidding. He looks genuinely worried as he pops another french fry into his mouth. This is a man who has kept his house in the Hollywood Hills largely unfurnished for years so that he "wouldn't have to think about it." He also didn't want people to visit him there. "I was doing things I didn't want them to see," he says. Pressed about what those might be, he will say only: "Things." "I like things to be orderly," he says, still on the specifics of food. "For seven years I ate at Bob's Big Boy. I would go at 2:30, after the lunch rush. I ate a chocolate shake and four, five, six, seven cups of coffee—with lots of sugar. And there's lots of sugar in that chocolate shake. It's a thick shake. In a silver goblet. I would get a rush from all this sugar, and I would get so many ideas! I would write them on these napkins. It was like I had a desk with paper. All I had to do was remember to bring my pen, but a waitress would give me one if I remembered to return it at the end of my stay. I got a lot of ideas at Bob's."

Talking to Lynch can be like interviewing a teenager. He uses words such as "neat," "thrilling," and "coolest," as in describing two of his favorite directors: "Kubrick is the coolest, and Marty"—Scorsese—"is right next door." Lynch shies away from critical analysis, either for fear that he will jam the flow of images or because he honestly doesn't know where his ideas come from. "They're based in abstraction or nature," he says vaguely, although a high sugar intake is another explanation. Isabella Rossellini, who played the tortured Dorothy Vallens in *Blue Velvet* and is now Lynch's romantic companion, calls him "seraphic, blissed. Most people have strange thoughts, but they rationalize them. David doesn't translate his images logically, so they remain raw, emotional. Whenever

I ask him where his ideas come from, he says it's like fishing. He never knows what he's going to catch."

This angelic medium is at the same time firmly grounded. He gardens and builds things. On the set he is preternaturally calm and sure of what he wants. Responsible, aware of budgets and schedules, he almost never storyboards a scene, leaving himself open to chance or suggestion. He is not a flake. Like a true subversive, he can pass for ordinary.

"I didn't know what to expect when I met David," says Gary S. Levine, vice president for dramatic series development at ABC, "but what you get is a gentle, almost timid person with a very clear vision that he adheres to. He's incredibly responsible and focused. *Twin Peaks* came in under budget and on time. I think it was all in his head even before he walked in the office."

Born in Missoula, Montana, in 1946, Lynch is the son of a research scientist for the Department of Agriculture. The job moved the family around the Northwest, from Sandpointe, Idaho, to Spokane, Washington, and finally east to Alexandria, Virginia, where he went to high school. *Blue Velvet* and *Twin Peaks* clearly reflect this early all-American adolescence: growing up in lumber country with its small, mostly white communities, attending public schools, cruising downtown at night for kicks.

"As a teenager, I was really trying to have fun twenty-four hours a day," says Lynch. "I didn't start thinking until I was twenty or twenty-one. I was doing regular goofball stuff." According to the director Jack Fisk, who went to high school with him, Lynch and his girlfriend were voted "cutest couple" and are pictured in the yearbook aboard a bicycle-built-for-two. "I think David has fought his upbringing in middle-class suburbia," says Fisk. "But a part of him is really attracted by that kind of stability. He knows it's an illusion, but he draws on it for his films."

Unlike many of his Hollywood contemporaries, Lynch did not grow up besotted with movies. Instead, he wanted to be an artist. He and Fisk had their own studio, which they painted black. Upon graduation, after Lynch had tried and hated the Boston Museum School, the pair set off for Europe to study with the expressionist painter Oskar Kokoschka. Planning to spend four years there, they lasted ten days. Lynch moved back to Alexandria, to the chagrin of his parents, and proceeded to get dismissed from a succession of low-paying jobs. It wasn't until he moved to Philadelphia, where he and Fisk enrolled at the Pennsylvania Academy of Fine Arts, that Lynch found himself. "I had my first thrilling thoughts in Philadelphia," he says. He often credits the city as the source of the visions in *Eraserhead*, a slow, bleak film about a miserable couple and their mutant baby, set in a poor, industrial landscape where it is always dark. "I started to appreciate the absurdity of life," he says. He would wake up at five o'clock in the afternoon, and work all night. Lynch and Fisk rented a house in a crime-ridden poverty zone, next door to Pop's Diner and kitty-corner from the morgue. "David would dress up to visit the morgue," says Fisk. "He was fascinated, and he would always wear at least two ties, one for luck." In the neighborhood, at the time, murders were not uncommon. "I saw so many things in Philadelphia I couldn't believe," says Lynch. "I saw a grown woman grab her breasts and speak like a baby, complaining her nipples hurt. This kind of thing will set you back."

For an art contest at school Lynch made his first film: an animated ten-second loop that features six heads, which throw up and then catch on fire. He shared first prize. A fellow student, who loved the piece, gave Lynch $1,000 to build a sculpture with a working film loop in it for his living room. After working on it for months and exhausting the money, he discovered that a defect in the camera had produced "one long blur. There weren't even any frame lines." For some reason, he wasn't upset. "It was a very weird thing. I remember thinking I should be depressed." He looks back on this as "fate," the path that led him to filmmaking. Fate and luck are vital concepts for Lynch, who describes himself as "a Hindu, I guess."

With money from his father, Lynch made *The Alphabet*, a four-minute film with animation and live action, but without a story. He sent it to the American Film Institute in Los Angeles, which gave him funds to make *The Grandmother*, about a disturbed boy who plants a seed that grows into his grandmother.

Accepted into the institute's Center for Advanced Film Studies in 1970, Lynch studied with the Czechoslovak filmmaker Frank Daniel, whose course on film analysis shaped his writing and directing habits. "It's a simple thing he taught me," says Lynch. "If you want to make a feature film, you get ideas for seventy scenes. Put them on three-by-five cards. As soon as you have seventy, you have a feature film." Except that he now dictates to an assistant, Lynch still works this way.

But dissatisfied again with school and divided between film and painting, he was prepared to quit. When the film institute asked him not to leave and to say what he really wanted to do, he said: *Eraserhead*.

From 1971 through 1976, this obscure, terrifying, original film consumed Lynch and a small group of friends, with whom he has remained close. "David was developing a film grammar all his own," says the cinematographer Frederick Elmes, who also shot *Blue Velvet* and *Wild at Heart*. Most of *Eraserhead* was shot at the Greystone Mansion, an estate in Beverly Hills then the headquarters of the American Film Institute, where Lynch was illicitly living after separating from his wife. With blankets over the windows, his room became his world. He would ask Elmes to padlock him in at night so the watchman wouldn't suspect.

In 1967, Lynch had married a fellow art student; a year later, their daughter Jennifer was born. It isn't hard to see in the film the terrors of someone who finds that he can't really handle the responsibility of fatherhood. One of the agonizing motifs of the film is that the helpless, monstrous baby never stops crying. "David went through a spiritual crisis when he was making *Eraserhead*," says Jack Nance, who played the befuddled husband. "That's when he developed his program of meditation."

In other interviews Lynch has talked about the importance of the "art life," in which the discipline and time required for making art takes precedence over everything else. "An artist's life is very selfish," he says today. "But it's thrilling to create something, and you need a certain set-up for the process to take place. You can't have a lot of obligations.

"It's not a hardship for me. It's a hardship only if I see I'm hurting other people. But maybe they were holding me back." (He has remained on good terms with his former wives and his children. Next month, Jennifer Lynch, his twenty-one-year-old daughter, will make her debut as a director with *Boxing Helena*, a film she wrote herself. The story of a girl whose boyfriend cuts off her arms and legs and keeps her in a box, it is, in her words, "an obsessive modern-day love story." Asked about how much this plot may owe to the influence of her father, she says: "Actually, he was quite offended by the subject matter. But he thinks I've written a hell of a script.") *Eraserhead* took five years to complete because Lynch kept running out of money; it was finished with help from many people, including his parents. In 1977, it opened at the Cinema Village in New York for a midnight show and, after a slow start, became a hit on on the horror circuit in Los Angeles, San Francisco, and London. That same year, Lynch married Jack Fisk's sister Mary (in 1982 they had a son, Austin) and, living in Los Angeles, began what could be called his "shed building" or "early Bob's Big Boy" period. As his only job he had taken a paper route delivering the *Wall Street Journal* and, with wood he collected on the streets, he built L-shaped, gable-roofed, and Egyptian-style additions to the garage in which they lived. He was perfectly content; he had discovered sugar, which he calls "granulated happiness." But two years later, restlessness took him back to film as one of the writers of *The Elephant Man*. After every studio turned down the script, Mel Brooks decided that his company, Brooksfilms, would produce it. When Lynch's name came up as a possible director, Brooks went to see *Eraserhead*. After the screening, with Lynch waiting nervously outside, Brooks came out yelling, "You're a madman, I love you, you're in."

The mood of *The Elephant Man*, its palpable vision of blanketing darkness and pockets of light in industrial-age England, owes much to Lynch. And for the only time in his career, his gift for atmosphere was joined to a clear dramatic story: the relationship between the pathetically deformed John Merrick and his doctor. A box-office success, the film elevated Lynch above cult status. He was given money by Dino De Laurentiis to develop original scripts, one of which became *Blue Velvet*.

But between these two hits, Lynch made *Dune*, a $40-million disaster for De Laurentiis and an emotional failure for the director, who still finds it "extremely painful to talk about." A futuristic epic about dynastic families and a boy's coming to power on a waterless planet, *Dune* had chunks of narrative lopped off, without Lynch's consent, in order to run at normal theatrical length. A messy, sluggish film, it is nonetheless visually enthralling. "The experience taught me a lesson," says Lynch. "I would rather not make a film than make one where I don't have final cut." On *Blue Velvet*, Lynch had artistic control. With scenes that originated on the napkins at Bob's, it seems to have jumped out of the director's subconscious, the Freudian storyline innocent of textbook programming. Jeffrey Beaumont, a young man who has returned home to see his ailing father, finds a human ear while walking in the woods. This discovery, and the detective work that follows as he tries to determine its owner, lead him to uncover corruption in the heart of the town and to witness, from a closet, a horrifying re-enactment of the primal scene between Dorothy Vallens and Frank Booth, whose oxygen mask resembles the gear his father wears in the hospital. Jeffrey enlists the aid of a high school girl, the daughter of a detective, and together they root out the villains. Love reconquers the world, darkness lifts, robins sing, and the boy's father is healed.

Both an X-rated Hardy Boys adventure and a riveting study of the pleasures and dangers of voyeurism, *Blue Velvet* dramatizes a young man's fear of adults and his need to know more about grown-up sex and death. Many of Lynch's friends see Jeffrey Beaumont, played by Kyle MacLachlan, as a stand-in for the writer. "I saw so much of David in the Kyle character—his walk, his mannerisms," says Jack Fisk. This lack of distance can be unsettling; it feels as though we're peeping in on the director's own overheated fantasies. As Pauline Kael wrote in her review: "If you feel that there's very little art between you and the director's psyche, it may be because there's less than the usual amount of inhibition." And if the happy ending seems ironic, too pat, given what Jeffrey has seen, both Lynch and Laura Dern, who played the coed Sandy Williams, disagree. "David is as much of a believer in the robins as in Frank Booth," she says.

As he has paid attention to his childhood anxieties, Lynch has charged this material with his own, consistent film style: slow dissolves, spotlighting, extreme close-ups, figures who emerge out of darkness, shots held an extra beat to catch the sound and texture of a place or thing. He has an interest in facial deformities, exaggerated noise, sick puns, and comically banal dialogue. Characters can be ridiculously specific. "Details give the film a certain quality," says Frederick Elmes. "It has to be that brand of beer to please David. He's thought a lot about the kind of car a character would drive." These details are often chronologically confused—brand names from different eras—so that everything takes place in dream time.

Twin Peaks, the new television series, named for the small town in which it is set, includes all of these elements. It bears a direct relationship to *Blue Velvet*; the first image in the pilot—a bird in a tree—picks up from the robins. "I see my character as Jeffrey Beaumont grown up," says Kyle MacLachlan, who plays the Federal agent. "Instead of being acted upon, he has command of the world." However, the agent has his typical Lynchian quirks: he can't get used to the tall trees in the area, and he recites his every thought into a micro-cassette recorder.

The town itself is full of eccentrics: a woman who carries a log everywhere; a policeman who cries at the scene of any disaster; and a couple of budding, teenage sociopaths. The cast includes Jack Nance, Michael Ontkean, Piper Laurie, Joan Chen, and, from the old television series *Mod Squad*, Peggy Lipton. Indeed, the series is laced with references to other television shows (J. R. Ewing's initials figure in the plot), to *Sunset Boulevard*, and to *West Side Story* (Richard Beymer and Russ Tamblyn, who played in the movie, are in the show).

As with *Blue Velvet*, the town existed before the characters. "We drew a map," says Mark Frost, Lynch's cowriter and coproducer. "We started with the image of a body washing up on a lake. We knew the town had a lumber mill, but the specifics we weren't sure of." After three months of concentrated discussion, they wrote the script in ten days.

There are two versions: a two-hour video cassette that resolves the murder mystery; and the series, with the killer still unnamed after the first group of episodes. The sex and violence are underplayed in *Twin Peaks*, although the murder involves drugs, flesh magazines, and bondage; and the title of the show is a male joke about women's breasts. The Western landscape does, after all, prominently feature the Grand Tetons.

If there is one image that, for Frost, epitomizes Lynch's mind at work, it is the scene in the pilot in which the F.B.I. agent checks the body of the dead girl lying in the morgue. He is probing with tweezers for a bit of evidence he thinks may be lodged under her fingernail, an image many viewers may find unsettling. "David likes to get right under there, beneath the surface of things, and make people uncomfortable."

Lynch likes the scene too, but for other reasons: "The thing I love about it is that Kyle's obsessed. Not in a bad way. He's goofy."

"Everyone is a detective," he continues. "All of us want to know what's going on." Without trying to exploit an audience's fears, he concedes that he wants people "to sit in their seats differently."

"There is a magical line that you have to feel or you get into trouble," he says. "And sometimes you think that you feel it but you don't. It's interesting to go up to the line—you should go up to the line. But you shouldn't cross over. The fingernail is near that line."

Executives at ABC have only a vague idea how America will react to this eerie, experimental soap opera. "We did a cable test that was pretty positive," says Gary Levine. "Not overwhelming, but positive." The constraints of television, with its censors and blocks of time, don't seem to have bothered Lynch. "We lucked out on the pilot, and everything fit just right," he says. "But any time limit is arbitrary and absurd. There's no law that says you have to end a show at a certain time. Other countries don't end shows on the hour. I don't know which countries. But I heard they did."

The persistent violence of television, however, genuinely concerns him. "The worst thing about this modern world is that people think you get killed on television with zero pain and zero blood," he says. "It must enter into kids' heads that it's not very messy to kill somebody, and it doesn't hurt that much. That's a real sickness to me. That's a real sick thing."

At Jerry's, as the meal winds down, the only comestible left a half cup of coffee, Lynch deflects another question about the intricate process of his film-making. "I don't think about technique," he says. "The ideas dictate everything. You have to be true to that or you're dead."

Whether or not a television audience can accept Lynch's weirder ideas, he has movies for his more unbridled fits of imagination. *Wild at Heart* is even more violent and sexually twisted than *Blue Velvet*, and includes a torture scene so creepy—featuring a ritual resembling a carnival game, except that it involves masturbation, a gun, and a pair of soda bottles—that Lynch was afraid to show it to anyone. "I thought they would lock me up," he says. The scene is nowhere to be found in Barry Gifford's book, the basis for the film. Where the idea came from, Lynch can't say.

The waiter walks over with a coffee refill, but Lynch puts his hand over his cup. "No thanks," he says with a smile. "I've finally got it mixed just the way I like it."

David Lynch

DAVID BRESKIN/1990

DAVID LYNCH WAS born in Missoula, Montana, in 1946. His father worked in the woods for the government; his mother worked at home, raising David and his brother and sister. The family made stops in Spokane, Washington, and Sandpoint and Boise, Idaho, before settling in Alexandria, Virginia, where Lynch unhappily went to high school. (He ran for class treasurer; his slogan, "Save with Dave." He lost.)

After attending both the Corcoran School of Art in Washington, D.C., and the School of the Museum of Fine Arts in Boston, and after an aborted trip to Europe to study with a painter whose work he greatly liked, Lynch wandered through a series of sad jobs, marked only by his talent for being fired. Mired in extended adolescence, he retreated to art school, this time to the Pennsylvania Academy of Fine Arts in Philadelphia. There he began by studying painting, but ended four years later by making his first live-action movie, *The Grandmother*, in which a distraught, bedwetting boy, abused by his parents, secretly grows a benevolent grandma from a seed.

In 1970, Lynch enrolled at the American Film Institute in Los Angeles as a fellow in the Center for Advanced Film Studies. His first advanced film, *Eraserhead*, wasn't released until 1977, because he'd spent a lot of time painting, delivering the *Wall Street Journal*, collecting garbage, building sheds, dissecting animals, getting divorced, smoking cigarettes, slurping shakes, and sitting in a chair, silently, thinking. *Eraserhead*, a blackly comic, pleasurably disgusting meditation on bringing up baby—a virtual feast of anxiety!—became a midnight movie hit. His next film, *The Elephant* Man, was refined and subtle, if not sentimental, by comparison. A tone poem on Victorian England, a place, to Lynch,

---

From David Breskin, *Inner Views: Filmmakers in Conversation* [Expanded Edition] (Da Capo Press, 1997). Reprinted by permission of David Breskin.

where the beast *was* the beauty, it won eight Oscar nominations and commercial legitimacy for its director. This he quickly bastardized on *Dune*, his only commercial and critical bomb. Lynch tried to thread its gigantic narrative through the eye of his trancelike moods and methods, and failed, quite spectacularly.

Blue Velvet was a return to form, scale, and intuition. A wickedly funny, overripe orchestration of all of Lynch's obsessions, set in small-town USA, *Blue Velvet* was arguably the most original and powerful American movie of the 1980s. Remembered and discussed mostly for having put the vile back in violence, it moved Lynch to the forefront of American directors.

His next film, *Wild at Heart*, went even further with the kind of surreal psychosexual slapstick that's become his "name brand." Despite the Palme d'Or prize it won at Cannes, it wasn't the masterpiece *Blue Velvet* was—its weirdness felt applied and artificial, and it came perilously close to self-parody. Still, *Wild at Heart* was still a curious and engaging film—a hokey, jokey joy ride through the bottomlands of Lynch's own imagination.

Between those two films, Lynch and a partner, Mark Frost, unleashed *Twin Peaks*. A whimsical subversion—but not destruction—of all TV's codes, it served up that strange slice of American pie where distortion meets recognition, producing a kitschy sugar high, Lynch à la mode. Accompanied by a feeding frenzy of media attention, the first season of *Twin Peaks* in the spring of 1990 was brilliant: nine hours of dancing dwarves and echoing owls and an aura unlike anything in the history of American television. But the second season proved flaccid and banal, and the show was soon canceled. Lynch, frustrated, sought the last word, which in this case would be the first word. A cinematic prequel, *Twin Peaks: Fire Walk with Me* would be his continued attempt to explore the improbabilities of this mythic town, free from the restrictions of commercial television.

In addition to screenwriting and directing, David Lynch has also written naive song lyrics, produced pop albums and the nonsymphonic *Industrial Symphony No. 1*, and for years drawn the cartoon "The Angriest Dog in the World" for the *L.A. Reader*. He takes pictures, paints, makes perfume commercials, and is preparing a coffee-table book of his collected visual work, which will reflect, in part, his interest in dental hygiene.

Our two conversations occurred in late June and early July of 1990, between the first and second seasons of *Twin Peaks*. The initial session took place at the midtown Manhattan apartment/studio of his music maven, Angelo Badalamenti, who was at work in the adjoining room; the subsequent, in a booth at the Studio Coffee Shop in Hollywood, an antitrendy diner much favored by Lynch.

Lynch was prompt, courteous, and completely uncomfortable with the process of analysis and verbalization demanded by an in-depth interview. His aw-shucks Americanisms and anti-intellectual bias—the Jimmy-Stewart-from-Mars persona—is delectably odd: funny, comfy, yet coolly distanced and distancing. I felt he'd thought about everything I asked him: he just didn't want to lug all his bags up out of the basement.

Session One

DB: *When you've talked about your childhood, you've said it's filled with beatific memories but also with traumatic horror. Could you elaborate on this a bit?*
DL: Well, it's hard to elaborate, but I kept coming to Brooklyn to visit my grandparents, and that was part of the horror. *Part* of the horror. In a large city I realized there was a large amount of fear, because so many people were living close together. You could feel it in the air. I think people in the city obviously get used to it, but to come into it from the Northwest it kind of hits you like a train. Like a subway.

In fact, going into the subway, I felt I was really going down into hell. As I went down the steps, going deeper into it, I realized it was almost as difficult to back up and get out of it as to go forward and go through with this ride. It was the total fear of the unknown—the wind from the those trains, the sounds, the smells, and the different light and mood—that was really special in a traumatic way.

Then there were traumas in Boise, Idaho, too, but they were much more *natural*, I would say. There was more light around the place, and not so much fear in the air.

DB: *You oppose the blue skies, picket fences, and cherry trees of your youth with the red ants crawling out of the cherry tree—*
DL: That was in Spokane, Washington, where we had a cherry tree in the backyard, and it was a real old one. There was this pitch oozing out of it—but really, *really* oozing out of it—and then ants just, like, *alive* on the tree. That was something I would stare at for hours. Like watching TV.

DB: *It was a pretty normal scene at home. You say your parents didn't smoke or drink and never argued; but that you were ashamed of them for that. You wanted them to carry on. You wanted a strangeness that wasn't there.*
DL: Yeah, it was like in the fifties: there were a lot of advertisements in

magazines where you see a well-dressed woman bringing a pie out of an oven, and a certain smile on her face, or a couple smiling, walking together up to their house, with a picket fence. Those smiles were pretty much all I saw.

DB: *But you didn't believe them.*
DL: Well, they're strange smiles. They're the smiles of the way the world should be or could be. They really made me dream like crazy. And I like that whole side of it a lot. But I longed for some sort of . . . not a catastrophe, but something out of the ordinary to happen. Something so that everyone will feel sorry for you, and you'll be like a victim. You know, if there was a tremendous accident and you were left alone. It's kind of like a nice dream. But things kept on going, normally, forward.

DB: *Did you secretly wish to be orphaned?*
DL: Well, I wished to be, not orphaned, but I wanted to be special and set aside. Maybe it's an excuse for not having to do anything else. You're instantly important. You've kind of got it made in a certain way. I was thinking about things like that. I was sort of embarrassed that my parents were so normal.

DB: *More abnormal things were going on in your friends' households?*
DL: Oh yeah! Yeah.

DB: *So you pursued a kind of danger on your own to bring this into your own life?*
DL: I didn't get into too many dangerous things. And I don't talk about a lot of dangerous things. People are going to do what they do anyway, but it's not so good to sell the idea—because you don't need to do a lot of dangerous things to be creating. Just to introduce a thought of certain things is not so good.

DB: *You wanted your parents to argue, but you've said elsewhere that you didn't like tension or conflict, that you were always trying to smooth things over.*
DL: Yeah, I did that. It goes back to feeling this bad thing in the air. I'd see my friends who just moments earlier were getting along, and then it would all fall apart. And I'd try to make it go back and be smooth. Just so we could all have fun.

DB: *The "smile" that you talked about, in the ads, were you feeling something akin to this smile inside, or were you feeling very different?*

DL: No, I had a tremendous smile. I have pictures of me underneath the Christmas tree with a smile that is like total and pure happiness. I sort of had a happiness.

DB: *But at the same time there was something about it you didn't trust.*

DL: You know, that's another thing: there are too many possibilities for something to go wrong—so you could always worry about that. And there are many things that are hidden and seeming like many, many secrets; and you don't know for sure whether you are just being paranoid or if there really are some secrets. You know little by little, by studying science, that certain things are hidden—there are things you can't see. They've run experiments; they know there are things like atoms, and a lot of things that you can't see. And your mind can begin to create many things to worry about. And then, once you're exposed to fearful things, and you see that really and truly many, many, many things are wrong, and so many people are participating in strange and horrible things, you begin to worry that the peaceful, happy life could vanish or be threatened.

DB: *What were the things you thought were hurtful or worrisome?*

DL: Just every sort of negative thing you feel in the air was bringing the situation down.

DB: *Let's try to be concrete. You're the master of the specific, come on—*

DL: [Laughs.] Yeah, right! Like in Philadelphia a family is going to this christening. I happened to be upstairs at home painting the third floor black. And my wife at the time, Peggy, was taking my daughter, Jennifer, who was one, out in this perambulator. It was like the Cadillac of perambulators, that we got at Goodwill for about a buck, but it was unbelievable. It had springs—it had a ride like a giant Cadillac. Anyway, Peggy was taking this down the steps. And a large family was going to a christening of this small baby. And a gang came swooping down on the other side of the street and attacked the family. And in the family there was a teenage son who tried to defend the whole bunch, and they beat him down, and they shot him in the back of the head. Those kind of things will spoil the atmosphere—permanently—and bring it way down.

DB: *Is art your only defense against things like that?*

DL: There is no defense. Your horror of horrors is that all of us are so much out of control, and if you start thinking about it you can worry about that for a long time.

DB: *But you've managed to survive things like that.*
DL: Well, you go along. But you realize that basically you're pretty lucky to be able to just go along.

DB: *You've said that as a kid you felt "a force, a sort of wild pain and decay, accompanying everything." What did that pain feel like?*
DL: I don't know what I was talking about there, but whenever you finish something, it starts decaying. Instantly. Just like New York City. The idea of New York City is a great one: you can have business and residential things all together, and people all together, and really fine restaurants and theatre, movies, and great architecture! Buildings that look so great and were built so well. They're functional, but also sculpture. But then time goes by and the bridges—they're rotting so bad! The roads, the buildings are falling apart. New ones are going up but they're not built the same way. This thing about decay and nothing remaining constant is another thing to worry about.

DB: *Our bodies are like that, too.*
DL: They sure are. They grow, and then they start reversing themselves. And strange things happen. You say, "That won't ever happen to me. No way!" But then one day you look in the mirror and it's happening.

DB: *What have you seen happening in the mirror that was traumatic for you?*
DL: Well, right above my ears there's these kind of silver, fish-scale silver hairs.

DB: *And when you first saw them?*
DL: I couldn't really believe it.

DB: *That wasn't the first time you had a sense of your mortality?*
DL: Uh, no.

DB: *That "wild pain" you talked about—what makes it wild?*
DL: Because it's not able to be controlled. See, a small world like a painting or a film gives you the illusion that you're more or less under control. Or that you're in control, rather. So I guess the smaller the world, the more safe you feel, and in control.

DB: *So you build a world.*
DL: You build it, yeah. I love going into another world, and film provides that opportunity—*Eraserhead* way more than any other film, because I really did live in that world.

DB: *You lived on the set.*

DL: I lived on the set, and in my mind I lived in that world. And the set helped a lot; the lighting, the mood of it helped. And since it took so much time I really sank into it. But now films go so fast: you move into a set, you check and make sure the mood is correct, and the next moment you're shooting it. And moments later it's being bulldozed. So it's captured on film, but it's real fun to live in it for a while, too.

DB: *You don't feel you're getting to inhabit your own films the same way you used to?*

DL: No. It's not as long and as satisfying.

DB: *This kind of worry you talk about—what's the nature of it? Why not accept the decay?*

DL: Well, you have to sort of learn to accept things. But I don't like it. Nobody likes to accept things. You fight decay by painting those bridges. The Golden Gate Bridge in San Francisco, they don't ever stop painting it. You've got to do something to maintain things. And the more you let it slip, the harder it is to bring it back to the original condition. And a lot of things, when they get older, if they have been maintained, get another degree of quality. Nature goes to work on them a little bit, but they have been maintained, and so they are called antiques and you can get a lot of money for them.

DB: *A patina of rust can be beautiful.*

DL: A patina. Exactly. Absolutely.

DB: *Would anyone who looked at you on your fifteenth birthday, this little worried Eagle Scout, in uniform, down by the White House seating VIPs for JFK's inauguration parade—would anyone have thought you were unusual or had some different ideas?*

DL: No. I was like a regular person. There wasn't much happening upstairs. I didn't really *think*, at all, not that I can remember, until I was about nineteen.

DB: *What triggered that?*

DL: I don't know. I think Philadelphia.

DB: *When things started happening upstairs, was it always in terms of images?*

DL: And sounds, but I didn't really know about that part, until later on. Always since I was little, I was drawing. And then I got into painting. But there wasn't any thought behind the drawings.

DB: *Your parents were supportive of your early work?*

DL: Oh, very supportive. My mother probably saved me: she refused to give me coloring books. Which is pretty interesting, because there was lots of pressure to color—and once you have that coloring book the whole idea is stay between the lines. Not having that restriction . . . and paper! My father worked for the government, and he'd bring home lots and lots of graph paper, and one side was old news and the other was blank. So I had lots of paper, and I was able to draw whatever I wanted all the time. My father also helped pay rent on a painting studio when I was in high school, and helped pay for my first film.

DB: *Yet you were rebelling like crazy at the time.*

DL: Yes, I was.

DB: *From about age fourteen to about age thirty?*

DL: Yes, and my theory is that most people rebel that long these days, because not counting accidents or strange diseases, we're built to live longer. And so all the stages consequently last longer. And so you're going to find people living at home, going through these strange rebellions. And maybe they'll be sixty before they realize they're an adult, and get serious about things.

DB: *What were you rebelling against?*

DL: I never really thought about it. They call it rebellion. I just didn't want anything to do with anything except painting, and living the Art Life. Nothing else was fun.

DB: *You didn't want them to know about what you were doing, did you?*

DL: I was doing many things that I figured they would not enjoy knowing about. So I was forced to live a secret life.

DB: *Now, there's a kind of power in having a secret.*

DL: There's a horror in secrets, too.

DB: *What's the horror?*

DL: You know, trying to keep it secret.

DB: *What's a secret? A secret is something you absolutely have to tell someone!*

DL: Well, yeah. There's that problem too.

DB: *Did the fact that they didn't know what you were up to—living this very nocturnal Art Life—help you start to feel like your own person?*

DL: Yeah. I felt like my own person before that, but I didn't think about things in the same way. I mean, I was smoking cigarettes; that was before any kind of drug things. I don't know if I would have gotten into drugs, but I was absolutely born to smoke. I loved to watch my Grandfather Lynch smoke cigarettes. I could hardly wait. I loved the taste of tobacco. Being addicted to it was one thing, but I really and truly loved every part of smoking: the texture of the smoke, all the business, the lighters and matches. The taste of it, particularly.

DB: *What was sex like as a teenager? Scary?*

DL: Umm, what kind of an interview are we doing, David? [Laughs.] I tell you what: sex was like a dream. It was like a world that was so mysterious to me that I really couldn't believe that there was this fantastic texture to life that I was getting to *do*. It was so fantastic, and I could see a world opening—this sexual dream. It was another great indication that life was really great and worth living. And it kept on going, because I see that the vast realm of sex has all these different levels, from lust and fearful, violent sex to the real spiritual thing at the other end. It's the key to some fantastic mystery of life.

DB: *But there's a sense in your films that the flesh is not to be trusted.*

DL: Well, I think until a person has reached a certain degree of evolution there's no such thing as trust.

DB: *What stage of evolution would that be?*

DL: [Pause.] If you were to believe in evolution, you would see that there are different levels of human growth. Degrees of awareness or consciousness. You could see a person being totally aware and totally conscious at the end of this evolutionary trail. And dealing with a full deck. And if you are able to deal with a full deck, I think then you'd be pretty trustworthy.

DB: *How many cards are in yours?*

DL: I don't have any idea, but it's not fifty-two.

DB: *The Europe experience, very briefly—*

DL: And it was a brief experience—

DB: *Austria was too clean—*

DL: Austria was way too clean. I didn't know why I was waking up there so early, but looking back I know why. It was early enough in the trip for me to be getting jet-lagged. But I was so young it didn't slow me down, I just woke up early, which is completely unusual for me. I attributed it to the clean air in Austria. At that time, part of the Art Life for me—since

I grew up in a place so clean, with forests and all—was about American city life, so I didn't really take to Salzburg. I was glad I went, but once that fell apart the whole trip unraveled. But the Orient Express was an incredible journey.

DB: *The Art Life means: stay up late, smoke cigarettes, don't get married, don't have children, stay dedicated to seeing beneath the surface, drink coffee. And yet you got married, not once but twice, and had two children.*
DL: [Pause.] These things happen.

DB: *Happen to you, or you make them happen?*
DL: Well, it's a two-way street. Nothing happens to you. It takes two to tango, and this is what happened to me.

DB: *How was it, living inside those contradictions?*
DL: It was kind of tough. But again, absolutely good and meant to be. Sometimes a jolt of electricity at a certain point of your life is helpful. It forces you a little bit more awake. It makes something happen inside you. I didn't really understand what was happening, but because I had these new responsibilities, I think it really helped—it overlapped into the work. I was just starting to make films, and it made me focus in and take things more seriously. I might have been drifting around for a lot longer had these things not happened.

DB: Eraserhead *seems to be, on one level the work of a man completely unprepared for, and terrified by, fatherhood.*
DL: *Eraserhead* is an abstract film. It's hopefully not just about one thing. But that's definitely in there. [Smiles slyly.]

DB: *Going to the morgue in Philadelphia was another turning point.*
DL: Well, Philadelphia itself was the turning point. Seeing a lot of different things. The morgue was kind of a clinical thing. It was very powerful, but it wasn't a twisted thing to me. It was more like seeing my neighbor's dog. That was another image I'll never forget. Their dog, they fed so much, it looked literally like a water balloon with little legs. The legs kind of stuck out. Almost couldn't walk, this dog. Had a little bitty head. It was like a Mexican Chihuahua with a watermelon in the middle. And there were lots of little bowls of candies in the room, and these things stuck with me a lot.

DB: *Was the dog your first link to surrealism or were Dali and Buñuel?*
DL: I never saw, I still haven't seen a lot of Buñuel and I saw *An Andalusian Dog* a lot later. I don't even know that much about surrealism—I

guess it's just my take on what's floating by. I wasn't exposed to too many sophisticated things.

DB: *What was the spiritual crisis you underwent during the filming of* Eraserhead?

DL: The spiritual crisis was that I thought I had every reason to be completely happy. I was making a film I wanted to make. I had the greatest crew and friends working. The list of things that I thought were going to do it for me were all checked off. I was sitting right where I thought I should be completely happy. And I wasn't happy. So I really wondered about that. It made me think about the idea of happiness, and what it might be.

DB: *Did you want it, badly?*

DL: Oh yeah, you betcha!

DB: *Is it still paramount?*

DL: Well, it's another word for lots of things. It's another word for: fifty-two cards.

DB: *That unhappiness led to Transcendental Meditation?*

DL: That's right. That's what it did.

DB: *And did that at least start shuffling the deck?*

DL: Yeah, it did. I don't really talk about meditation. A lot of people are against it. It's just something I like and I've been doing it since 1973.

DB: *It seems like your background as a painter led to a film style focused on texture and the single image—it demands real examination of the frame. Was that something conscious for you when you moved from the canvas to film?*

DL: No. I forget the word . . . oh, composition. This thing of composition is so abstract. It's so powerful, where you place things and the relationships. But you don't work with any kind of intellectual thing. You just act and react. It's all intuition. It must obey rules, but these rules are not in any book. The basic rules of composition are a joke.

Really sophisticated composition works like really sophisticated pieces of music: you can't believe what you're seeing. You could spend years looking at one great work and still find new things in it that are so perfect. Like great symphonies. You can't believe that that chord flows into that, and then *that* swoops in. It's too great. Too thrilling. And how they come to be is a mystery.

DB: *So you don't find particularly compelling parallels between your painting and filmmaking?*

DL: No. They obey some of the same rules, that's all. And these rules are found in nature. Like the duck. You could pick any animal, but let's take the duck. The duck is real good for many things—like textures, proportions, shapes. How a duck is made and where the different things are on a duck can give you a clue to a more or less perfect composition for a painting. If you could interpret a duck, if you could work with the rules of a duck, you could get something close to a well-composed painting that had neat things happening.

DB: *Your famous first Botched Commission, where in art school you worked for two months shooting and came out with one long blur because the camera was broken—you point to this as something that led you on into film, but isn't that twenty-twenty hindsight?*
DL: It felt funny. It was a very weird thing. It took two months to shoot two minutes and twenty-five seconds. I remember holding the film up to the light to see frames, and I saw no frames. I was not depressed, I was curious to know what was happening. There was no depression. I remember someone asking, "Aren't you upset?" I said, "No." The hindsight part came in later. If that had come out and I had sent that to the American Film Institute, it wouldn't have been good enough to get me the grant I got later. And of course that grant I *had* to have, if I was going to get into film. So fate was smiling on me.

DB: *The feeling you had after a subsequent film didn't turn out right wasn't quite as uplifting.* Dune.
DL: But I learned a lot of stuff on *Dune*. I started selling out on *Dune*. Looking back, it's no one's fault but my own. I probably shouldn't have done that picture, but I saw tons and tons of possibilities for things I loved, and this was the structure to do them in. There was so much room to create a world. But I got strong indications from Raffaella and Dino De Laurentiis of what kind of film they expected, and I knew I didn't have final cut. And little by little by little—and this is the danger, because it doesn't happen in chunks, it happens in the tiniest little shavings, little sandings—little by little every decision was always made with them in mind and their sort of film. Things I felt I could get away with within their framework. So it was destined to be a failure, to me.

DB: *Well, the failure of* Dune *saved you from having to do* Dune II *and* Dune III.
DL: Yes, that's a plus. Though I was really getting into *Dune II*. I wrote about half the script, maybe more, and I was really getting excited about it. It was much tighter, a better story.

DB: *Did you feel like a failure?*

DL: Yeah. I was made to feel like one, and I felt like one too. There were times before, like on *The Elephant Man*, I went through some things that I thought would be the end of me, but *Dune* was pretty bad. Even in post-production, I started feeling the writing on the wall.

DB: *What did you think would be the end of you on* The Elephant Man?

DL: I was supposed to build the Elephant Man's makeup. And again, I worked for two months, maybe more, two months in England, and what I built was a complete and total disaster. It was a disaster because I wasn't prepared to build things for a human. And I didn't know how certain things worked. Though parts of what I did were interesting, it was a disaster. For four days I had nightmares at night, but when I woke up, being awake was worse than the nightmares. Mel Brooks [the film's producer] came over to England and found a guy to do it in the time we had. Mel's good attitude pulled me out of the torment of being a complete failure.

DB: *Had you ever felt like that before, during those years doing all those lame jobs, before and after school?*

DL: No. There I felt like, not like a failure, but very frustrated. There are an awful lot of people who feel this way, and I felt this way for a long time. In order to do a painting, you've got to have canvas, stretchers, paint, brushes, turpentine. You have to have a place to paint. You have to have time to paint. And you have to have a certain mental freedom, to think about the painting. And if you have a job or any kind of other responsibilities or an apartment where you're going to be sued for getting paint here or there? There are so many obstacles to getting set up to paint. That initial outlay of cash to just get set up. It's almost too much to overcome. It's staggering to get set up to do anything. If you are going to do photography, just to get a darkroom—there are so many things that can stop you. It's pretty frustrating. I felt frustrated during all those times, because I never could get set up to work.

DB: *Let's shift gears. I'd like to talk about some elements that seem to be present in all your films, despite the differences between them. First, you have an obsession, with obsession.*

DL: Yeah, I got that.

DB: *Now, during* Blue Velvet, *when you were filming the scenes of Frank [Dennis Hopper] abusing and raping Dorothy [Isabella Rossellini], apparently you were beside yourself with laughter. You thought this was sort of funny on some level?*

DL: I'm sure pretty near every psychiatrist could tell me right now why I was laughing, but I don't know. It was hysterically funny to me. Frank was completely obsessed. He was like a dog in a chocolate store. He could not help himself. He was completely *into* it. But I was laughing and I am a human being; there must be some logical reason why. It has something to do with the fact that it was so horrible and so frightening and so intense and violent that there was also this layer of humor.

I don't know what it is, but it's there, and it has to do with this degree of obsession, where people cannot help themselves. In New York, especially, you see it on the street all the time. And because you see it on the street, you know it's happening in their apartments too. But the poor people on the street don't have any place to go do it privately. These kind of things strike me as humorous sometimes.

DB: *Are you obsessive?*
DL: Yeah, I'm sure I am. Habits are obsessive things. Having things a certain way. This is sometimes humorous.

DB: *That can come from feeling out of control, using habits as centering devices—*
DL: Oh, absolutely. I must be completely out of control.

DB: *Because you are such a creature of habit?*
DL: Yeah. I like to try to control my local environment as much as I can. And it's impossible to do it.

DB: *Do you really feel out of control?*
DL: Yeah. There are certain times when it's an illusion that you have some sort of control. It's a gift just to get just a little bit of that feeling. There are so many things that can come in and pull the rug out from under you so fast.

DB: *Is there a freedom in understanding you don't have any control? Then you don't worry about it so much.*
DL: Well, yeah. But you still strive for it as much as possible. It's not control for control's sake; it's to get something a certain way. Making something a certain way is really, really hard because there are so many forces at work to undermine what you're doing. And to stay one jump ahead of it, or even two or three jumps behind it instead of ten or twenty jumps behind it, is sort of fun. It's sort of what it's about.

DB: *Is it scary to feel out of control?*
DL: Yes. Very scary. And there's nothing you can do about it.

DB: *What's the worst that can happen?*
DL: I'm sure that's the kind of thing a psychiatrist might ask you: "What's the worst thing that could happen, David?" [Laughs.] And then if you could face that, you could face anything. The worst thing that could happen is that . . . [Long pause.] I don't know. There's also the fear of the unknown—who knows what could happen? In the case of a film, the worse thing that could happen is something like *Dune*. Where the film is halfway there and halfway not.

DB: *Let's look at something else that seems central to your work: the presence of cruelty and physical and mental abuse.*
[Angelo Badalamenti comes in, asking if anyone wants coffee.]
DL: Angelo, you've said the magic word! Light! With sugar! . . . Cruelty, uh-huh.

DB: *Where does it come from?*
DL: Beats me.

DB: *I'm not denying it's out there on Thirty-fourth Street, but it's very much there, specifically, in your vision of the world.*
DL: It could be a lot of different things. It could be partly what I feel is out there. Partly the stories that attract me. That tension. See, I see films more and more as separate from whatever kind of reality there is anywhere else. And that they are more like fairy tales or dreams. They are not, to me, political or, like, any kind of commentary or any kind of teaching device. They're just *things*. It's another world to go into, if you choose to. But they should obey certain rules. The same as a painting. And these rules are abstract and found in nature.

And one of them is Contrast. It can't just be a flat, straight line of pure happiness. People fall asleep. So there are conflicts and life-and-death struggles. I like murder mysteries. They get me completely, because they are mysteries and deal with life and death. So I'm hooked right away. The letdown is if the story is too simplistic or it's not structured properly so it doesn't have a lot of satisfaction. But initially, if you say "mystery" and "murder," that always gets me, and if you throw in the word "hotel" or "factory" I get even more involved.

DB: *So you don't know where this predilection for cruelty comes from?*
DL: No. I was not tortured as a child. And I didn't ever see anybody get tortured. So either it's a coincidence that this is all through there or the reason lies beyond, somewhere else.

DB: *Okay, let's look at one aspect of "Contrast." In your work, there's a constant dichotomy between Good and Evil, between Light and Darkness, and Innocence and Knowledge, where Knowledge is aligned with guilt, danger, horror—Knowledge as a kind of sickness.*

DL: Uh-huh. Knowing the wrong thing, like the man who knew too much, is sometimes a real drag.

DB: *I guess what I'm wondering is whether, outside the constructed world of the films, you see the world as having these very strong dichotomies between Good and Evil, as opposed to a kind of complex, integrated—*

DL: No, I know it's complex. Everybody's got many threads of both running through them. But I think in a film white gets a little whiter, and black gets a little bit blacker, for the sake of the story. That's part of the beauty of it, that contrast, the power of it. Maybe it would be very beautiful to have a character that had an equal mixture of both, where the forces were fighting equally. But maybe they would just stand still.

DB: *You mentioned life and death. It's compelling that all your movies have a birth scene—or some kind of abstracted birth scene—and also death scenes, scenes of murder or murderous intent. Finally, in* Wild at Heart *the birth scene is a death scene—an abortion. How we start and how we finish seems the biggest subject on the table for you?*

DL: Absolutely. [Pause.]

DB: *Is it on your hard disk?*

DL: I guess so. [Laughs.] It must be. You know, it's in interviews that you can sometimes see some sense to it. Most of the time the thinking exists on a more abstract area. You don't even worry about what things you've done before, or if these things are out there or are they just in here, is it out of proportion, or whatever. You're just going along and catching this fantastic train that leads to a new world and another story.

DB: *What I'm saying is that the trains run to all kinds of destinations and through all sorts of scenery—*

DL: But might be going all to one place. [Laughs.]

DB: *No, not at all: but wherever they're going, they're still in Lynchville! Even in* The Alphabet, *your first four-minute animated film, the capital letter* A *gives bloody birth to little a's.* The Grandmother *has an excruciating birth,* Eraserhead *has any number of disturbing births,* The Elephant Man *and so on—what gets you about it?*

DL: For a long time, and I suppose, still, the idea of birth was a mysterious and fantastic thing, involving, again, like sex, just pure meat and blood and hair. And then at the same time, this feeling of life and the spiritual thing. There are too many things going on there not to be fascinated by it. [The coffee arrives.] Angelo, bless your heart, I sure am gonna dig this!

DB: *Did you attend the birth of either of your children?*
DL: Both. For Jennifer, in those days, at the hospital in Philadelphia, they wouldn't let fathers in there. And so I was real proud of myself, because I could convince the doctor that I could handle it. I did, because he kept taking blood from my wife Peggy, and I figured more of it than he needed to take, just to see if I would pass out or something. And when he saw that I was able to handle that, he said okay, I could come in. So I scrubbed up and put on the green shoes and the outfit. I went in and, like twenty-five billion people, witnessed this thing. And it's not so much what you see as an abstraction you feel. It's the weirdest thing. It's real weird.

DB: *All of a sudden there's someone else in the room.*
DL: There's a *lot* in the room, it feels like! Things you can't see. It's pretty powerful.

DB: *Could you make a film without birthing or dying?*
DL: Sure, you could do it. But it's putting the cart before the horse. Some people get on a kick. They say, let's make a film about *this*. And then they create a whole story to support this idea. It's backwards. Later on, you maybe find out what the film is about. I'm not saying it's good, it's just more natural for me. And they don't all happen at once: they happen in fragments. Even a book, you're reading in fragments, one chapter after another. You're carried forward by these things and a world is starting to go in your mind. But for me, the world of the mind, it's fuzzy. It's not complete. It has holes in it. It can't be shared so well. When you make it specific and concrete and have so many elements swimming together, it becomes so powerful and shareable.

DB: *Now let me bring up a touchy subject. The position of women in your films. For* Blue Velvet *you took some abuse about—*
DL: Because people have an idea that Dorothy was Everywoman, instead of just being Dorothy. That's where the problem starts. If it's just Dorothy, and it's her story—which it is to me—then everything else is

fine. If Dorothy is Everywoman, it doesn't make any sense. It doesn't add up. It's completely false, and they'd be right to be upset.

Ideas are the weirdest things. They're out floating, and you catch them, and you can build them into something. Like a table. It's right there floating. And then it appears in your mind: suddenly you've caught it, it bubbles up, shows itself to you, and you can go in your shop and put it together. And that's how these things go.

DB: *Let's try to talk more concretely about women in your films—the "disease" that Dorothy has. There's a kind of physical threat that hangs over women in* Twin Peaks *and* Wild at Heart *and* Blue Velvet. *And there's a certain amount of female complicity in it. Even in* Twin Peaks, *Ronette Pulaski, who's beaten to within an inch of her life, rates four red hearts in the department store manager's secret book of call girls, and we know Laura Palmer, who's brutally murdered, is not Snow White. Are you ever afraid that you sidle up close to a sort of "blaming the victim"?*

DL: I know what you're talking about. Again, it goes to Ronette Pulaski not being Ronette Pulaski as Everywoman, but just Ronette Pulaski. Everyone can picture in their mind a situation where the girl—for one reason or another—went along with the situation. And everyone can picture in their mind where the girl said, "I'm not into this one little bit!" and got *out.* And then there's a borderline, where it's right on the edge for a person: where it's interesting, but it's sickening, or it's frightening or it's too much, or almost, or not quite. There's every different combo in this world. When you start talking about "women" versus "a woman," then you're getting into this area of generalizations, and you can't win. There is no generalization. There's a billion different stories and possibilities . . .

DB: *In the naked city—*
DL: You betcha!

DB: *Now let's talk about these women. Both Dorothy in* Blue Velvet *and Laura in* Twin Peaks *have the "disease." Laura gets off on a man almost killing her, because it makes sex great. What's the "disease" to you? Can you be more up front about it?*
DL: Um, no.

DB: *Come on, David.*
DL: No, because just the word "disease" used in that way . . . it's so beautiful just to leave it abstract. Once it becomes specific, it's no longer true

to a lot of people, where if it's abstract there could be some truth to it for everybody.

DB: *But come on, we know there's a kind of masochism at work here—*
DL: But even *that* can be so complicated that even to start talking about it wouldn't do it justice. It would always make it be less than it really is, because it's so *unbelievably* complicated. And if it wasn't complicated, people could be fixed and made perfect so easily. It just is so complicated.

DB: *One critic pointed out that in* Blue Velvet *women were either abused of useful to men, and that the only choices women had were those put before them by men.*
DL: That's this person's take on it. How would what he said have anything to do with Sandy [Laura Dern]? She wasn't totally manipulated by anybody, you know, any man. She did tons of stuff on her own. She liked certain things. She didn't like certain things. She made decisions on her own. She acted and reacted with her own apparatus. She gets Jeffrey into the situation on her own. On her own. But instead of *her* going over to that woman's house, she is able to catch the interest in Jeffrey and fire it up, so that he does the dirty work. Meanwhile, Aunt Barbara and they are at home, all they can do is watch it on TV, they don't even want to go out of their house. They'll see it in the safety of their living room. But they're interested in it. It's all about an interest in things that are hidden and mysterious. Sandy is very smart and very together. What he said was kind of a general thing, and when you put it against what's really there it doesn't make a whole lot of sense. [Lynch assumes, wrongly, that the critic is a man.]

DB: *How about Lula, though, in* Wild at Heart? *Lula [again, Laura Dern] in the movie is certainly a step back as compared to Lula in the book in terms of her assertiveness, her aggressiveness, her control over the world around her. In the book, Lula tells Sailor where to get off, orders him when to drive. She finds him dancing with another woman at a club and throws a bottle at him, which hits him, and lets him know how pissed she is at him; whereas in the movie there's a club scene where Sailor [Nicolas Cage] sort of "rescues" her, and defends his territory when another man tries to dance with her. Couldn't one say that Lula is made a less modern woman through the way you've channeled the book?*
DL: [Long pause. Irritated] Well, I don't know about modem women. Except that Lula is . . . it just so happens that both those other scenes were

shot, and because of time and one thing after another, they didn't get in. It may not be that she throws a bottle at him, but there are still lots of indications that she would be very pissed off at Sailor if he ever did something like that. You can tell that from the way she just is. The thing that got me about Sailor and Lula is their relationship: they're so really good to each other and in love and they treat each other with respect, in my opinion. I don't know about a modern man or a modern woman, but that's a modern romance. Because Sailor can be cool and masculine, but still have tenderness toward Lula and treat her as an equal. Never talk down to her. He just talks to her. And the same with Lula to him. One of the reasons I love this relationship and this book is them being equals.

DB: *But in the book she's sensitive to the fact that he might be talking down to her. She doesn't like being called "Peanut" all the time. She says, "I don't know that I completely enjoy you callin' me Peanut so much . . . puts me so far down on the food chain."*
DL: Oh, I don't even remember that. No, she *loves* to be called Peanut.

DB: *It's in the book. Now, there's an Oedipal thing happening in your films. You either have a kind of mystical reunion with the lost mother or you have—*
DL: Well, that's The Elephant Man. That's specific to that story. For the Elephant Man, his fondest memory was of his mother. His whole life was built trying to live up to something he imagined her wanting for him. So that when he died it needed to be that way: with the mother. It felt right. What other films?

DB: *You have, in* Blue Velvet, *and elsewhere, a kind of "sex with mom" thing going on.*
DL: How's that?

DB: *Frank is like an infant, calls Dorothy "Mommy" and says at one point, "Baby wants to fuck!"*
DL: He's either daddy or he's baby.

DB: *And in* Wild at Heart, *Lula's mom [Diane Ladd] comes on to her boyfriend, Sailor—*
DL: And that happens in *Eraserhead*, too!

DB: *Right, Mary's mom comes on to Henry [Jack Nance]. And now, on* Twin Peaks, *we get to see Benjamin Horne confronting his daughter Audrey in a whorehouse bedroom. There is a pattern here.*
DL: Well, yeah, the trouble is if you do more than one of anything, then people start comparing. A lot of times it leads you into strange conclusions

that have no bearing on reality or the way it came about. It could just be a coincidence that each story . . . some of them I didn't write, I didn't think up, even though I was involved in the script. Ideas come along. How much is something inside me? I think the inside-you part dictates a lot, but then the idea part coming in from outside is a big part of it, too. I don't know. There's a lot of things that human beings do that are completely fascinating, and at the same time you think they are somewhat strange.

DB: *That seems to be the way we're built.*
DL: That's exactly right. And those are the things that are so interesting to work with in films. If things are real normal, you might as well just stay home—they're strange enough there. In film, things get heightened. You see things a little bit more and feel things a little bit more.

DB: *You seem kind of defensive about this.*
DL: Because I don't know if it's true that there are these similarities.

DB: *Well, let me bring up one more for observation. There's a sense, at the ends of your films, in the redemptive power of fantasy, of the imagination itself. There's a, not childish, but maybe childlike sense that you want to see or imagine something brand new, that the possibilities of your imagination are what save you.*
DL: Yeah. It's tough, again, to talk about some general thing, but I guess—for myself—I believe in this force of evolution. Being in darkness and confusion is really interesting to me, but behind it you can rise out of that and see things the way they really are. That there is some sort of truth to the whole thing, if you could just get to that point where you could see it, and live it, and feel it and all that. I think it's a long, long way off. In the meantime, there's suffering and darkness and confusion and absurdities, and it's people kind of going in circles. It's *fantastic*. It's like a strange carnival: it's a lot of fun, but it's a lot of pain.

DB: *Is it all darkness and confusion?*
DL: Everything is relative. I'd say this world is maybe not the brightest place one could hope to be.

DB: *One of the confusions seems to be over whether art has to mean anything. Let me quote you: "Why do people want art to make sense when they accept the fact that life doesn't make sense?" First off, I don't think people accept the fact that life doesn't make sense. I think it makes people terribly uncom-*

fortable. Religion and myth were invented against that, to try to make some sense out of life. Don't you think that's where art comes from too?

DL: Maybe some of it does. But for me, I'm of the Western Union school. If you want to send a message, go to Western Union. It's even a problem with responsibility. You have to be free to think up things. They come along, these ideas, and they hook themselves together, and the unifying thing is the euphoria they give you, or the repulsion they give you (and you throw those ideas away). If they're all stringing themselves happily together and they're forming a story that's carrying you forward, the first way you can kill that is to start worrying about what other people are going to think. Then you start worrying about, what your immediate friends or family are going to think—that can kill it right there. The next thing to worry about is the general public. It's so abstract, you kill it instantly. Then you have to worry about the future people, and you can't even imagine what they're going to be like, so you'd have to figure they're not going to like it. You have to just trust yourself. If you have any sort of moral thing or boundaries you won't cross over, that's going to shape your story. Then, if you're given permission and the money to make this into a film, you say, this is just the way it is. Please walk out of the theatre if it's upsetting you. If you don't like it, fine. I'm real sorry you had to see even a frame of it. People have to be able to create these things.

DB: *But that's not to say they don't mean anything?*

DL: No, but if you start worrying right away about the meaning of everything, chances are your poor intellect is only going to glean a little portion of it. If it stays abstract, if it's in an area where it feels truthful, and it hooks in the right way, and it thrills you as it moves to the next idea, and it seems to move and make some sort of intuitive sense, that is a real good guideline. There's a certain kind of logic and truth and right workings that you have to trust. That's the only thing you have to go by. Fifteen trillion decisions go through this same process: it's either kicked out or taken, or turned this way or that way. That's how it goes along.

DB: *So you don't resist the idea that your films mean something?*

DL: Not a bit. But they mean different things to different people.

DB: *Let's hope so.*

DL: Yeah. But even so, some mean more or less the same things to a large number of people. It's okay. Just as long as there's not *one* message, spoon-fed. That's what films by committee end up being and it's a real bummer to me. *No message* is hard to do, because people will read into anything. You can't do a no-message film, it's impossible.

DB: *So to say that art doesn't need to make sense because life doesn't make sense—*

DL: Life is very, very complicated and so films should be allowed to be too. That's more like the way it is.

DB: *Is there an element in this filtering process—the fifteen trillion decisions—where there's a line, or boundary, that you'd like to cross, your intuition tells you to cross, but which you pull back from because it would be too much for people to take?*

DL: Yes. And that happened on *Wild at Heart*. When you make a film, it's like a soup. And so much is evaporated out before you get it in the bowl, and probably some is lost off the spoon, and some is stuck in your tooth that you spit out later on: it's only important finally what gets in your stomach, what gets on the screen. And so this process of making the film doesn't stop until someone sits down in the theatre. Like they say, the projectionist has final cut. They can chop off certain things, rearrange the reels. So you keep on checking what you're doing with the intuition thing, or, like in *Wild at Heart*, if vast numbers of people get up out of the audience and leave the theatre, you've got a decision to make.

DB: *They're straining the soup.*

DL: They just don't like the soup.

DB: *You had two test screenings of* Wild at Heart *where you had an elephant-stampede out of the theatre—during a scene that involved masturbation, gunplay, and bottles—*

DL: It didn't even involve that. Yes, that's the scene, but it didn't really involve those things that way. The scene is almost there in its entirety now. But it really taught me something: an audience can really be with you, but if you rub it in their face too much—which I didn't think I was doing—they say, "That's enough!" and out they go. And you can't blame them. I thought it was more powerful that way, but it reached a point where it was too much.

We lopped off the end of the scene, and that brought it back into the good zone. The scene is necessary. At one point I took it out entirely, and without that scene, there was no life-or-death threat, and it was very important to underlie the rest of the film.

DB: *What do you think causes such discomfort for people watching certain images?*
DL: I don't know. There again, an experienced doctor could tell us. All I know is, it went one step too far, and it snapped their involvement in the story. They rose up out of the story, then they rose up out of their seats, and they eventually got out of the theatre. And the ones that stayed never got back into the film after that. I can't really blame them.

DB: *Is there anything you can't watch yourself, other than for reasons of boredom?*
DL: Oh, sure. Sure. I don't know what they are, but there are a lot of things all of us don't want to see.

DB: *What won't you look at? What have you turned away from or turned off because you couldn't handle it?*
DL: [Long pause.] Umm, let's see. [Long pause.] I can't remember. I can't remember.

DB: *Have you seen the footage from the concentration camps?*
DL: Well, that would be hard to watch and hard to not watch. A lot of people could not watch it. The stuff that human beings do to one another is sometimes impossible to understand or believe, but they still do. So you want to watch to get a hint of how far we'll go as human beings. It's just unbelievable. So you could question your motives for watching and question your motives for not watching. It's a complicated thing.

DB: *Were you surprised that it took an external stimulus, a test audience, to tell you to take that scene out of* Wild at Heart?
DL: Yeah, I was. That's when I started changing my ideas about these test screenings. There's something about several hundred people sitting in a room. It's not what they write on their cards at the end of the screening, it's the feeling you have sitting in the room with them. It doesn't matter who they are. There's a certain thing we'll all do if three hundred people are together. It's important to see your film with that *presence*. You can learn so much. If there was a machine that could give you that feeling of them being around you . . . but there isn't. It needs to be those souls sitting right next to you. You feel things completely differently. It's unbelievable. It's so frightening but it's so important. The reason people don't like it is because it's so hard to endure. So they say, "I don't dig test screenings. I don't believe in them." Well, I believe in them, but I don't dig them. I really believe in them now.

DB: *So even though on an important level you don't care what the audience thinks, you want to communicate, don't you? You're not just making these things for yourself.*

DL: No, you don't make them for yourself; but you don't make them for... uh, it's, well, I don't understand how it works. You can *think* that you're making them for yourself, but when you sit with the three hundred people you realize that if you were really making it for yourself you would have done this a little differently. I don't understand exactly how it works, but they tell you certain things by being there. Certain things you tricked yourself into thinking were working you see honestly and truly are not working when you have three hundred people there. So it's really a way of checking yourself, by having them there.

Session Two

DB: *Let's talk about some of your work that hasn't been produced, starting with the oldest project,* Gardenback.

DL: *Gardenback* is a good example. It should have been a short film. Very abstract. It's the script I submitted along with *The Grandmother* to the Center for Advanced Film Studies. No one really understood what I was trying to do with it. I don't blame them.

DB: *You described it as "an abstract film about adultery."*

DL: And it was, but they made me say that. Finally, Frank Daniel asked me, "Is this film about adultery?" I guess it is, but it's about other things, too. A guy who was making low-budget horror films told me he'd give me $50,000 to do it if I'd turn it into a feature. He didn't understand it either. But it had a monster in it—which is all that he cared about. He *thought* it was a monster. Fifty thousand dollars was like someone now giving me five million. But it had to be expanded to be a feature...

DB: *And that killed it?*

DL: That killed it for sure. Because it became less and less abstract and more and more "normal" in a boring way.

DB: *Have you been able to steal from the corpse?*

DL: Maybe a little bit. It crept into paintings and lots of things. I was fascinated with gardens: people standing in gardens in paintings, form in a garden, at night. I really loved that. Then I became really frustrated, but all that was good because it led to *Eraserhead*.

DB: *Your most celebrated unmade work is* Ronnie Rocket. *Is it dead in the water, completely?*
DL: No, no, no, no, never, not in a million years. It's hard to say I'm going to make *Ronnie Rocket* next. I don't know if it'll ever be made. It's definitely not dead. I've talked about it so much and scripts of it are around—I'm waiting for the next step to happen to do it, if there is a next step. I'm waiting for a time where I don't really care what happens, except that the film is finished. I do care, now, enough so that a film like *Ronnie Rocket* is frightening, because it's not a commercial picture. It's an American smokestack industrial thing—it has to do with coal and oil and electricity. It might be a picture that I would love, but I don't know if too many other people are going to dig it. It's very abstract.

DB: *There's not an arrow of narrative?*
DL: Well, I think it's pretty straight ahead. I think it's kind of plain. But it is kind of absurd. It's not like a regular picture. And I want to have time to go into that world and live in it for a while, and that costs money. I don't really want to have a normal eleven-week shooting schedule on *Ronnie Rocket*. I'd rather go with a smaller crew, and build the sets and live in them for a while and let it build up that patina that we were talking about.

DB: *Is there anybody out there who would afford you that opportunity?*
DL: There are some people, kind of coming around, that have *so* much money that they don't really care, necessarily, about making a profit. They wouldn't mind getting their money back.

DB: *Would you junk narrative if you could? Would that be the first thing to go if you could work outside commercial Hollywood cinema?*
DL: No way. What are you calling narrative? The story?

DB: *Yes, the linear "A leads to B leads to . . . ."*
DL: Well, not necessarily. Sometimes it really works and you need it. Sometimes the linear thing isn't really so hot. It doesn't take you underneath the surface and allow for surprise or thrill. But I really believe in a story. How it's told is the key to the whole thing.

DB: *After* Blue Velvet, *there were a couple of other projects you were interested in. What about* Red Dragon, *the novel Thomas Harris wrote before* Silence of the Lambs?
DL: I was involved in that a little bit, until I got sick of it. I was going

into a world that was going to be, for me, real, real violent. And completely degenerate. One of those things: No Redeeming Qualities.

DB: *So that movie couldn't even get into your country club?*
DL: The way I was thinking of it, I didn't want to let it into my country club. It was made. It was called *Manhunter*.

DB: *Your first project with Mark Frost, which never got onto its feet, was* Goddess. *What can you tell me about that?*
DL: That's when Mark and I first met. I always, like ten trillion other people, liked Marilyn Monroe, and was fascinated by her life. So when this came along I was interested, but, you know, what's the drill? I got into it carefully. They were going to put a writer on it. CAA [Creative Artists Agency] loves to package people together. So they packaged me with Mark. I met with him and liked him, and we had a plan. We met with Anthony Summers, who wrote the book. The more we went along the more it was sort of like UFOs. You're fascinated by them, but you can't really prove if they exist. Even if you see pictures, or stories, or people are hypnotized, you never really know. Same thing with Marilyn Monroe and the Kennedys and all this. I can't figure out even now what's real and what's a story. It got into the realm of a bio pic and the Kennedys thing and away from this movie actress that was *falling*. I got cold on it. And when we put in the script who we thought did her in, the studio bailed out real quick.

DB: *For political reasons?*
DL: Yeah.

DB: *Who did you finger?*
DL: Never mind. Never mind. [Laughs.]

DB: *Was your attraction to Monroe another example of what Wendy Robie said was your attraction to "broken beauty"?*
DL: I don't know what it is. It's a sadness in the beauty. It's like mystery and beauty and sadness.

DB: One Saliva Bubble. *Steve Martin, Martin Short. Kansas. A ray from a military satellite. And then what happens?*
DL: And then all kind of wacko hell breaks loose. And out-and-out wacko dumb comedy. Clichés one end to the other.

DB: *Your version of* It's a Mad, Mad, Mad, Mad World?
DL: Well, sort of. It makes me laugh. Mark and I were laughing like crazy

when we wrote it. I thought of this idea on an airplane. Steve Martin and I had met and we were interested in this one particular project way back when. We had both read a book, I've forgotten what it was. He loved it, and he still loves it. The only problem is, every time I get ready to commit to it, I think the problem for me is that there's not enough meat to it. I feel like a lot of people could do it.

DB: *Where did the title come from?*
DL: It came from a funny accident that caused the satellite to go off.

DB: *What about* The Lemurians?
DL: *The Lemurians* was a thing Mark and I were going to do as a TV show. Based on the continent of Lemuria, which was fictitiously thought of as a very evil continent. It was sunk way before Atlantis even rose— sunk because they were so evil. Jacques Cousteau inadvertently moved a rock, very early in his travels—part of it was "Jacques, Jacques, had to move that rock." A lot of poems in it. Part of the lore surrounds the leaking of Lemurian essence from the bottom of the Pacific Ocean. Anyway, the essence is leaking, and becomes a threat to all goodness in the world. It's a comedy!

DB: *NBC said "Thank you very much—"*
DL: "—It's real nice seeing you fellas." The problem with *The Lemurians* is it's a complicated show.

DB: *There are detectives tracking extraterrestrials, right?*
DL: Yes, and all sorts of things. It's so complicated that we don't have time to introduce another TV show right now. It would mean cutting your concentration down to where it's impossible . . .

DB: *Too thin a pancake gets—*
DL: I'm a real thin pancake! I'm right on the edge.

DB: *What about* The Cowboy and the Frenchman?
DL: I really want to release that. I was in Paris with Isabella. And we were taken to a restaurant by this Frenchman. The restaurant was really, really good!

DB: *Almost as good as this one!*
DL: Yeah, when are we gonna get some food? I'm getting so hungry. It's 4 p.m. for you. You must be just going insane! So this guy said he was interested in doing this thing—the French newspaper *Figaro* was going to have six directors do short films commenting on the French, for their

two-hundred-year anniversary. And I was going to be the American director. So I said, "I'm flattered that you asked me, but I don't have an idea about it right now. And I'm busy. But if I get an idea in the next two weeks, I'll call." It was a real small thing.

That night I got an idea. I called him. He said, "That's great, two clichés in one!" I said, "You got it!" So I made it. It was supposed to be four minutes long. Mine turned out to be twenty-one minutes long. I didn't really go over budget, just over time—because I was having so much fun. It was Harry Dean Stanton, Jack Nance, Tracy Walter, Michael Horse, and the Frenchman, Pierre. We had strange music and horses. We were on a little farm outside of town.

It's an absurd comedy. A Frenchman was in New York City and some very kind people gave him some pills in Central Park. Then he took them, and the next thing he knows is he ends up at a ranch in the West and Harry Dean Stanton is the foreman and Jack and Tracy are the sidekicks. And they don't know what he is, until they start going through his valise. Finally, they figure out that he's a Frenchman. And it goes from there.

DB: *That piece is very dreamlike. Do you use your own dreams in your work?*
DL: No. One time. Well, twice. There was a scene in *Eraserhead* that was cut out. And in *Blue Velvet* I'd been having a lot of trouble solving the ending—not the "ending" ending but near the end. One day I went over to Universal Studios, I forget why I was over there, and I had my script with me, and I was trying to finish it, and I was sitting in a chair, there was a receptionist, and I started writing, and as I was writing I remembered I'd had a dream the night before, and it suddenly became clear. The dream was the scene in Dorothy's living room. And in the dream I saw Jeffrey reach into the man in the yellow suit's pocket. Two things came from the dream: the police radio and the pistol in the yellow man's jacket. Then I went back in and wrote the scene where they're driving to Ben's and he says, "Hide the police radio," so Frank would know that Jeffrey knew he had it. So anyway, those things came from the dreams. That's the only time it's happened like that.

DB: *What about your acting debut in* Zelly and Me *in 1988? It seemed like such an odd choice for you—because the movie itself was so precious and sticky-sweet, and everything your work is not. I couldn't understand the choice, except that Isabella was the star.*
DL: It was all Isabella. I consequently met Tina [Rathborne, writer and director] and liked her a lot. I don't think Tina set out to make the movie as sweet as it was. It was her first feature film, one thing happened af-

ter another. Mainly I did it because I had a fascination to see if I could do it. Mainly to overcome this fear of acting, which is phenomenally fearful.

DB: *You mean you didn't do it so you could expose your manly chest?*
DL: I was afraid I would cause a lot of guys to feel very bad about themselves. I'm sorry.

DB: *Are you still making any kits? [Lynch used to dismember small animals to make "kits," like organic hobby-shop models.]*
DL: I have a strong, strong desire to make kits. I did a duck kit and chicken kit during *Dune*. I did a fish kit. I didn't do anything during *Blue Velvet*. I haven't done anything lately. My duck kit didn't turn out well. The photograph was very blurred, you couldn't read the writing. I wanted to do a mouse kit. I have a photo which may go into a book of a children's fish kit—which is much more simple than the adult fish kit.

DB: *The period after* Blue Velvet, *when you were all tied up in the bankruptcy of your producer, Dino De Laurentiis, was that a—*
DL: Trying time?

DB: *Yes, sir.*
DL: Yeah, it was. I almost was going to make *One Saliva Bubble* then. We had all our scouts, had it cast, was right there ready to go. Dino kept delaying it, delaying it, delaying it. It became obvious it wasn't going to happen: there wasn't any money. Shortly thereafter his company went bankrupt. We saw the writing on the wall.

DB: *Was there a period when you were kept from working?*
DL: No, but if I had wanted to make *Ronnie Rocket* then, I wouldn't have been able to do it, because I found out that Dino owned it. And *Up at the Lake* and *One Saliva Bubble*. Not only did he own it, but he had made money on it. And so when I finally got it back, I found out that if anybody makes any of those projects they will have to pay, out of first profits, a bunch of money to DDL that Dino has already taken.

DB: *How has Dino made money on them?*
DL: He paid himself a salary.

DB: *That's nice. How was your parting with him?*
DL: Very amiable. Dino does his thing. You can't fault the guy. He's just one or two steps ahead of everybody in a certain way, and by the time you learn the game, you've already been hurt bad. [Laughs.]

DB: *Let's go to* Twin Peaks. *You've been to the Philadelphia Museum of Art, haven't you?*
DL: I used to live right next door.

DB: *That's what I figured! But in an interrogation, David, sometimes one has to ask even the obvious questions. Do you know a piece by Marcel Duchamp, dated 1946–66, so it would have been finished just before you got to Philly?*
DL: No.

DB: *Well, the piece is called* Given 1) The Waterfall 2) The Illuminating Gas. *It's a dark, empty room. Along one wall are dark wood boards, nailed up. In the boards, at eye level, are two peepholes, and through them you can see a constructed scene. And in the scene is a naked sort of dead woman, lying on her back, and off to the right pulses this amazing waterfall. Except for the fact that it's not a lake, it feels like the beginning spark—*
DL: —Of *Twin Peaks*. I'll be darned!

DB: *With TV being the modern peephole, exposing the darkness, in a paradoxical way. I just thought you might have seen it?*
DL: Maybe so. Maybe so. But the waterfall was not in the script. We didn't know there was a waterfall up there. And the girl would have been naked, but it was on television—you can't do that.

DB: *She seemed naked but we couldn't see—*
DL: Underneath the plastic. But everyone is naked underneath their clothes. [Laughs.]

DB: *How did you feel watching the pilot, at your New York City hotel room?*
DL: Actually, it was pretty depressing. I was amazed by the poor quality of the image and the sound. There's a gigantic, huge loss of quality. If we could know the way it should be, and experience that, it's a whole different thing.

DB: *So you were depressed?*
DL: Yeah, but the commercials didn't depress me. I liked them. The commercials, I thought, were sort of thrilling. It was live. It was all around the country. It was kind of nice.

DB: *But before* Twin Peaks *ever aired you called commercials "big, violent interruptions" that you thought were pretty absurd, that the system didn't work—*
DL: Well, I still think they're absurd.

DB: *But by the end of the first year of the series you were watching to see who were the advertisers, and you were glad they were big companies; you'd changed and become more of a participant in the world of commercials.*
DL: Yeah, I . . . I . . . that's true. I'm joining in the absurdity. [Laughs.]

DB: *Did that change your attitude about making them, or was it a check someone decided to write you?*
DL: No. I've only done one legitimate commercial.

DB: *For heroin, right?*
DL: For Opium. [Laughs.] Now I'm doing one for another company, but we're not going to mention it [Calvin Klein's Obsession].

DB: *It's going to be tough to keep under the rug. Are you doing it for essentially financial reasons, or you like the challenge, or you've always secretly in your heart wanted to sell products?*
DL: Let's see. It's sort of, it's—obviously, it's got to be partly the money. But, these commercials. I liked the idea of them. And I like to—I've got kind of a thing now about keeping busy. It's sort of getting a little bit absurd.

DB: *Ultra-frantic creativity?*
DL: Yeah, something like that. I hope I'm not biting off too much. The Opium spot aired a long time ago. I like it, it's kind of pretty.

DB: *Back to* Twin Peaks. *There's a sense that there's a lack of respect for certain characters on the show. There's a thin line between laughing at a character and making fun of them—*
DL: Who are we making fun of?

DB: *Maybe Nadine with her eye patch, or Leland in his grief, or Johnny in the headdress banging his head up against the dollhouse. These are things I found spectacularly funny, but there's a part of me that isn't comfortable with my own laughter in some cases. Do you feel there's a danger here?*
DL: There's danger around every corner. I think . . . it's, uh . . . it depends. If Johnny had a disease or something that you were making fun of, that would be one thing. He could just have an emotional problem and could come out of it. He could be pretending this whole thing, too. It sort of depends on how you see it. It's not meant in my mind to be offensive or to make fun of anybody, really. But at the same time, because he's the way he is, there's a humor side you can't avoid. A lot of times, someone who's in bad shape can do something funny—you laugh. At the same time, there can be a lot of compassion underneath that laugh. And

yet it's the way the world is. It's so screwy—we're all kind of in this thing together, and there's got to be some room for a realistic attitude towards things. You can't just—TV and all these things would be reduced down to Tarzan movies, and we'd have nothing more.

DB: *Have you heard of the "Moment of Shit"?*
DL: [Very interested.] No, I haven't heard that.

DB: *The "Moment of Shit" is what TV writers call it when everything comes together, and you have that edifying moment, when you are supposed to get the Message, and the Morality comes across—*
DL: We have a lot of moments like that. [Laughs.]

DB: *The nice thing about* Twin Peaks *is that it turns the fan on all that. Now, is it true that, filming* Eraserhead *in 1972, you looked at Catherine Coulson putting on her glasses and said, "I see a log in your arms. One day I'll do a series and you'll be the Log Lady"? It seems wildly impossible.*
DL: It's sort of true. What happened was, Cath and I did another piece called *The Amputee*. It's about four or seven minutes long. I'd like to show it to you. She's a very interesting actress. Through *Eraserhead* she got into the other side of the camera and became a camera assistant, and she's been doing that ever since, until the Log Lady.

I had an idea for a show I wanted to call "I'll Test My Log with Every Branch of Knowledge." And that is true. And I wanted her to be a woman who lived with a son or a daughter, single, because her husband was killed in a fire. Her fireplace is completely boarded up, his pipes are there, his sock hat, stuff like this. And she takes the log to various experts in various fields of science or whatever. Like, if she goes to the dentist, the log would get put into the chair. With a little bib put on it. The dentist would X-ray the log, even to find out where its teeth were. Or he'd say to the little kid, "Let's say the log had a cavity. First I'd give it novocaine." And go through all the steps. So, through the log, through this kind of absurdity, you would learn, you'd be gaining so much knowledge through the show. A lot of times they wouldn't even go to the scientists. They'd stop off at a diner, and there'd be stories there. This was my big show.

So when it came time for shooting the *Twin Peaks* pilot, I called Catherine. And she got herself up to Seattle on her own, stayed at a friend's house, and came in and did this thing. Flicked the lights at the town meeting. "Who's that?" "We call her the Log Lady." And that was pretty much it. Except it was just one of those things that just stuck, so consequently, it became more than that.

DB: *Let's talk about the psycho-killer. In* Blue Velvet, Twin Peaks, *and* Wild at Heart, *you have characters who are very attractive, in an almost magnetic way, who are psychotic killers. What's the pull for you in using these characters?*
DL: I think it's the scariest thing to know someone, or suspect someone, that has a very intelligent mind—really nothing is wrong with them in any way—but who is possessed by evil, and who has dedicated themselves to doing evil. This is so unbelievable, so hard to figure.

DB: *You think it's just an act of volition for these people? That they just "decide" to do evil because they're in the mood for it?*
DL: No, I think it's a complicated thing. I think there is some disturbance, electrical or chemical, and some people might believe it is even beyond that. Some disturbance where they're smiling at you, but something you see in their eyes gives you the willies. And your smile back to them doesn't change their mind. The meals that you buy them, the schools they go to: none of that makes one bit of difference to these people. They do what they do, regardless.

DB: *The public obviously has a great appetite for characters like this, not only in film and TV, but on the news as well, as if they free us from the bounds of our own civility. There's a kind of wild freedom in what they do that's attractive.*
DL: I don't think it's that at all. We don't want to do these things. We're fascinated only because—I've never exactly figured out what the fascination is, but I think we want to understand it so we can conquer it. First of all, we want to really see it, so we can see if it's true. And then, we want to learn about it enough that we can do something about it. It's just too, too . . . there's something that captures our interest, but it's not a sickness, I don't think.

DB: *It was ten years for you between* Eraserhead *and* Blue Velvet, *and I'm interested in why, after such a long stretch between original pieces, you would turn after* Blue Velvet *to essentially someone else's story,* Wild at Heart.
DL: Well, it's hard to figure, you know. [Long pause.] A lot of my stories from that time were owned by Dino. And when you've been thinking about something in your mind, it was just forming up so nicely, certain things I was thinking about, and Dino, or anybody, takes that—and you can't do that. Your mind refuses to—you want *those* ideas, and in order to go to the next step in your own work you have to do the ones that are there. I couldn't finish *Eraserhead*, but I couldn't start anything else until

it was done. So I was really in a frustrating place. This last go around, after *Blue Velvet*, the ideas that were really my own were locked off from me, and when I read Barry Gifford's book it was just what the doctor ordered. So many different things in the air pointed toward this way to go. Sometimes you go and you get nothing but red lights, and you can fight it for a while, but pretty soon it's like you drive a block and stop, drive a block and stop. This one just got green lights like crazy.

DB: *Obviously, a film and a book are always going to be different animals—make different noises and eat different things—but you really radically changed this book. There are whole plot development and feeling differences in the movie. How did you come to these things?*

DL: When I read the book, they came to me. Barry said, "I don't care what you do with this—there will be Barry Gifford's *Wild at Heart* and David Lynch's *Wild at Heart*. Go with it. Go for it." So it became a point of departure for a lot of things. But Sailor and Lula, what I really loved about the book, stayed always through it.

DB: *Did you know at the beginning that the* Wizard of Oz *thing was going to be so blatant?*

DL: No, that kind of crept in at different times. The last piece that came in was the character Jack Nance plays, talking about, "My dog barks some. You may even picture Toto from *The Wizard of Oz*."

DB: *You make an interesting aesthetic choice to make it so front and center, as opposed to subtle or subliminal. Was that a difficult decision?*

DL: Sailor and Lula just have this fascination with *The Wizard of Oz*. It's just part of them, like it's part of so many people.

DB: *Do you share this fascination?*

DL: Oh yeah. Yeah.

DB: *Is that where Dorothy in* Blue Velvet *got her name?*

DL: I think so.

DB: *Also in* Blue Velvet: *Frank Booth and the Lincoln Apartments—Booth and Lincoln—I thought was not coincidental.*

DL: No, there are all sorts of things like that.

DB: *Another of the changes involves Lula. In the book, she's raped but in the movie it's much more violent, more traumatic. Why did you change this?*

DL: Because I didn't really believe the book. [Laughs.] I wanted Bobby Peru [Willem Dafoe] to go to work on both Sailor and Lula. And I wanted what he did to Lula to tie into what she'd been through before. It also pointed out that Lula plays tricks on herself; like we all do—she blocks out many parts of reality so that she can still continue to be Lula.

DB: *I thinks that's called denial. Denial is a river in Eygpt.*
DL: Yeah, denial. Thanks, doctor. [Laughs.]

DB: *How would you describe* Wild at Heart? *You can't say, as you have, "a road picture, a love story, a psychological drama, and a violent comedy."*
DL: Well, I wouldn't be able to describe it then. [Long pause.] I don't have a one-sentence thing that captures it.

DB: *You described* Blue Velvet *as a moral picture—*
DL: I did?

DB: *Yes. You said that Jeffrey learns about the world and that he helps Dorothy in the process. Would you make the same claim about* Wild at Heart?
DL: Well, like I always say, we're all coming at things from different angles. And I think that Sailor and Lula are trying to live *properly*. They're struggling in darkness and confusion, like everybody else. It's hard to say. I don't know for sure. The idea that there's room for love in a really cool world, that to me is really interesting.

DB: *At the end of the picture, the Good Witch in a bubble tells us, "Don't turn away from love, don't turn away from love, don't turn away from love." Might one accuse David Lynch of going to Western Union to send a message?*
DL: No. That's the Good Witch talking.

DB: *But you resolve the story and the movie in a way that seems to pull back from what's happened—*
DL: In a way. But not . . . see, I didn't buy the ending in the book. In the first script, the ending was true to the book [Sailor and Lula go their separate ways]. But emotionally, it wasn't ringing true at all! I couldn't think of a reason when Samuel Goldwyn asked me, "Why is he leaving?" He hated the ending. If it had been honest, I could have given him an answer. But I said, "I hate the ending, too." I think they've learned a lot more, and grown more, even through fantasy, this way. The other way was a real . . . defeat.

DB: *Does the happy ending make you happy?*
DL: Well, the thing is . . . yeah, of course it does. And it rings true, to me, also. I think that Sailor and Lula are so fantastic a couple—I really like them a lot.

DB: *So you don't feel that, when push came to shove, you ducked on the harsh realities of love with—*

DL: With the happy ending? No. It was even the reverse of that. Even Siskel and Ebert were talking about it—that commercially, a negative ending isn't so good. So, I almost wanted to do a miserable ending just to show that I wasn't trying to be commercial. And that's wrong—doubly wrong. And so, like I said, it's got to feel honest, and if it does, that's what you have to do.

DB: Blue Velvet *has a happy ending—with a twist.*

DL: There's the same . . . there's a resolution in both films. Both of them have happy endings.

DB: *They both rely in the end on the power of imagination and fantasy to conjure up something: the robin, although the robin may come with an insect in its mouth, or your own good witch, making fantasy real. What happens, though, when you run out of fantasy?*

DL: Things get kind of boring.

DB: *In your first student film, that ten-second animated loop, heads catch on fire and then they throw up. In* Wild at Heart *fire is the controlling image and vomit is a recurrent motif—*

DL: [Laughs.] I can't get away from it!

DB: *There are not many movies in which you get to see both a mother and her daughter throw up!*

DL: Yeah, it's a real thrill. That alone is worth the price of a ticket.

DB: *And the flies on the vomit—*

DL: That's my favorite shot! When the door opens—they take off, they lift up as Sailor comes in.

DB: *That's your favorite shot in the film?*

DL: It's one of several favorites. I do like it.

DB: *But it's interesting that these motifs are there even in your earliest work.*

DL: Yeah, a lot of things. There are a lot of things *in* The Alphabet that keep coming back. And *The Grandmother,* too. Maybe you do keep doing the same thing over and over.

DB: *In the past, you've argued for Life as the inspiration for your work, as opposed to Art, which puts you—almost strangely—in the modernist, not postmodernist, camp. But in our last session, you said you're increasingly feeling the separation of film from life. Is there a change here?*

DL: No. To me, stepping into a film was always going way far away from regular life. Way far away.

DB: *But does your inspiration remain life its own self?*
DL: Oh yeah. Because the closer to the source of an idea you can get, the more power there is.

DB: *You've said that you never want to be too busy, because if you're too busy then you can't dive down and catch the big fish. Well, now you are crazy busy!*
DL: Yeah, and I'm not getting any big fish. Right now, I'm in a speed boat, and I'm dragging everything I can to catch what won't slow me down—it's the fish near the surface. I'm going to have to cut the gas off and throw the line in, and let it roll out all the way.

DB: *Years ago, you said your films both reveal and hide your fears. Do you still think it's true?*
DL: Yeah. Oh yeah. When you go with intuition or subconscious or whatever, you can't really filter that stuff out. You kind of have to let it come out and happen, without interrupting it. Once you start intellectualizing too much or talking to the doctor about it, you might say, "Oh my god, man, that's very bad, I don't want people to think that!" so you'd start filtering, chopping off that little conduit. So it's better not to know so much, in a way, about what things mean or how they might be interpreted, or you'll be too afraid to let it keep happening.

DB: *But how do the films* hide *your fears?*
DL: Well, they hide them, because when they bob up, they may already be hidden. They don't come up and tell you so realistically. They're more like a dream thing. It might be one or two steps removed from a sentence describing your illness. So they're more like symbolic things that could be open for interpretation. Just like you talk about a piece of decaying meat. If you happened upon it in a certain setting, you could almost hear people oohing and aahing about its beauty. Until they realized what it was. Then they would not find it beautiful anymore. As soon as it had a name to it.

DB: *Sometimes there's no beauty in anything with a name attached. Isn't that feeling what kept you out of psychoanalysis?*
DL: Well, no, I went once. People have—at least I have—habit patterns, I wanted to look into one particular one.

DB: *It was disturbing?*
DL: It was disturbing to me and other people.

DB: *Self-destructive?*

DL: No. It was . . . yeah. In a way, yeah. So I decided I would go see this psychiatrist, who was recommended by a friend. I liked this person and we sat down in his office and talked for a little bit, and it was kind of interesting. I realized that so many times you want someone to talk to who isn't judging you. And that's kind of cool about it. I could see it would be very good for getting ideas. Just to pay someone to listen to you. But even more than listen, someone who is fascinated from a technical aspect—so they kind of egg you on. It was interesting, and then I asked him about whether it could affect creativity—and he said, "Maybe." And that was it.

DB: *Affect it doesn't necessarily mean ruin it. Maybe change it?*

DL: Anything that would improve it, fine. But I think I asked him if it could effect it negatively, or interrupt it, that wouldn't be too good. I could see how if you disturb the nest too much you're liable to . . . you don't know what could happen.

DB: *You might not want to know so much.*

DL: I want to go about it in a different way.

DB: *Your own method of exploration?*

DL: Yeah.

DB: *Were you afraid that psychology barks up the tree you've so happily climbed?*

DL: What it does is destroy the mystery, this kind of magical quality. It can be reduced down to certain neuroses or certain things, and since it's now named and defined, it's lost its mystery and the potential for a vast, infinite experience.

DB: *And do you still have the same disturbing habit pattern?*

DL: Yeah!

DB: *Would you like to share it with the class?*

DL: [Laughs.] It wouldn't make any difference.

DB: *You used to have this kind of fear that dominated you, the fear of being restricted.*

DL: Yeah, I guess I did.

DB: *How did you get over that?*

DL: I'm not over that. I think that's why I love money so much. I think that the freeing power of money is a very healing sort of thing. Because all we want to do is to be able to do what we want to do. And if we can do that, we get the sense of freedom.

One of my frustrations, one of the limiting things, was the lack of money. And I still don't have enough to do all the things I want to do yet. But at least I have more than I had then. In terms of painting, I don't have a studio, a place to paint, but I have enough money to get good canvases made, and enough paint. I really like to paint thick.

DB: *Camus, in one of his last books, proposes that to solve the existential problems of life you need money, because money is freedom.*
DL: Yeah, up to a certain point, it sure is. It won't help you if you've got a bad disease. And it won't help you if you desperately want to go to Mars.

DB: *There was a period in which you were actually afraid to go out of your house.*
DL: Luckily, school came about. But I had a touch of that disease where you are afraid to go out.

DB: *And what makes you the angriest dog in the world?*
DL: Well, I had tremendous anger. And I think when I began meditating, one of the first things that left was a great chunk of that. I don't know how it went away, it just evaporated.

DB: *What was the anger like? Where did it come from?*
DL: I don't know where it came from. It was directed at those near and dear. So I made life kind of miserable for people around me, at certain times. It was really a bummer. Even though I knew I was doing it, there wasn't much I could do about it when the thing came over me. So, anger—the memory of the anger—is what does "The Angriest Dog." Not the actual anger anymore. It's sort of a bitter attitude toward life. I don't know where my anger came from and I don't know where it went, either.

DB: *You've said both that you have to be happy to create and that you have to create to be happy. There's a serious chicken-and-egg problem here.*
DL: Yeah, it's like, creating things maybe makes you more happy, but if you're really, really miserable, you don't feel like creating stuff. But if you're kind of into it, it's a certain kind of happiness: happy gluing one piece of wood to another. You kind of like the wood, and the sun is just right, and the glue, you've got enough of it. Some little bit of wire. And you know what the wood does and you know what the glue does, and

the wire, and your imagination is seeing the whole thing. And a little bit of action and reaction. It's a fantastic thing, and it can make you more happy—the doing of it. In the beginning, you're in the mood to do it, which is a certain kind of happiness.

DB: *Are you more attached to process or to achievement?*
DL: To me, the process has got to be enjoyable. You can't just think about the end result. Otherwise, I think eventually you'd have to stop. I don't see how you could wake up—if you hated the process so much. You'd soon be out of the business. You sort of have to love the trip.

DB: *A number of years ago, you said your life was split between innocence and naiveté, and sickness and horror. Do you still feel that polarity?*
DL: Yeah, I think my father . . . he's in his seventies, but I see him as real innocent, and a little bit naive in the same way I am. I think it's good, up to a point, until you become a fool. Europeans are so much more sophisticated, generally speaking. There's an innocent, naive thing still swimming around here.

DB: *What are you innocent of?*
DL: Well . . . [Long pause.] Maybe it's not so much innocent as unsophisticated. More easily shocked, or at least not afraid of showing shock at something. Certain things I still can't believe are happening.

DB: *That in Africa a few years back Bokassa threw his rivals into pits of crocodiles? Or that he dined on the flesh of his victims? That still shocks you?*
DL: You bet!

DB: *What's horrific and sick, on the other hand, about your life?*
DL: No, you don't want to know all that. [Laughs.]

DB: *I do, David, I do.*
DL: There are many things that swim together.

DB: *Besides semen.*
DL: [Laughs.] There are all kind of things going on.

DB: *That are horrific and sick?*
DL: Yeah. You know, just ideas. Mainly it's all on the idea level. I think that's the last frontier.

DB: *Anything disturb you these days?*
DL: Oh yeah, a lot of things disturb me. I'll tell you what's disturb-

ing me now. It's something in the air again. The decay I feel is spreading faster than the building.

DB: *Well, the very air around us is decaying.*
DL: Well, yeah, everything is falling faster than we can clean it or build it or make it right. So that side of nature is winning. And it's our own nature. It's not really our fault in a lot of cases, 'cause we didn't understand what we were doing, like to the ozone. But when you visit New York City every now and again, you notice each time it's fallen further. It's not maintaining, it's falling. And that's an indicator of something happening in a lot of other places, but it's harder to see.

DB: *What about politically? You've indicated that you don't think of your films as political, but the two most famous men of the 1980s who called their women "Mommy" were Frank Booth and Ronald Reagan.*
DL: [Surprised.] Really?
DB: *You know he called Nancy "Mommy."*
DL: I didn't know that. I'll be darned.
DB: *You met him twice at the White House.*
DL: I sure did. I know there are a lot of very intelligent, wonderful people that would be upset at me, but I really like Ronald Reagan. There's something about Reagan I liked from the very beginning. I can see why people didn't like him, and when he was governor I wasn't feeling the same way. I think I saw him make one speech one time and I must have been moving into some right-wing frame of mind, or something. It was something in the air again. I mostly liked that he carried a wind of old Hollywood, of a cowboy and a brush-clearer. And I thought that, for a while, he was like a real unifying thing for the country. Maybe not for the intellectuals, but for a lot of the other people. Maybe for a lot of the intellectuals too.

Anyway, there's no winning in politics. It's something I don't even know a little bit about. Zip!

DB: *But you voted.*
DL: But all you have to do is pick up a pencil. Not even a pencil.

DB: *Well, most Americans stampede away from the polls. I think there's never been a democracy in the world where a lower percentage of eligible voters vote.*
DL: Yeah.

DB: *So you vote because you feel very patriotic, like a real American?*
DL: Yeah. But the way you say that is like— [Laughs.] Do you vote?

DB: *Yeah. I feel very patriotic. I can't imagine living anywhere else.*
DL: The thing is, America is suffering such a . . . everybody's got a . . . maybe it's changing a little bit now, it's coming back a hair. But for a while we were all so down on ourselves, it was not one bit cool—just the word "patriotic." Because we'd done a lot of things in the name of that that were so, so bad. Anyway, it's a losing game and it has nothing to do with the films I'm making.

DB: *You think not?*
DL: Not one bit.

DB: *But don't you think the things that led you to vote for Reagan—not necessarily intellectualized, but the feelings you have inside—involve the decisions you make aesthetically, and what you choose to show, and how you portray x, y, or z?*
DL: [Long pause.] You could say so, but not really. But so many things start from an idea. It seems very foreign to me. I know it's important, but it doesn't seem so important to me.

DB: *Knowing your work, I wouldn't have imagined that you voted. I could imagine you might be interested in the weird personalities of politics, or the power itself, but not that you would necessarily cast a ballot.*
DL: No, I did. There was quite a period when I didn't. Maybe I didn't realize it was voting day.

DB: *What were these White House events like?*
DL: The first time I went there was for a state dinner. I forget who all was up there, I think it was for the president of Argentina. You go to the White House, you meet the president, and then you have dinner. It's kind of incredible.

DB: *How did you get invited?*
DL: I don't know how I got invited. The first time, *Dune* was going to open at the Kennedy Center. The next time Isabella got invited, and she took me.

DB: *Do you think politics is serious business?*
DL: See, you *know* I don't like talking about this.

DB: *Well, David, if I was just trying to be your friend I wouldn't make you.*
DL: [Laughs, pauses.] I guess it's very serious, you know.

DB: *The implications are: If you're writing a story and you open one door, the characters walk through that door and there may be no getting back to open a different door, and each door leads to two more doors and you need to make decisions. Elections and politics are just like that, don't you think?*
DL: See, you should just take a certain number of pages and write out what you feel, and that would just be fine with me.
DB: *Well, I want to know what* you *feel.*
DL: I'll tell you what. I'll tell you what's really sick. See, I just—I'm involved with something over here, and I know nothing about this business of politics. It's totally absurd for me to comment on it. I don't know anything about it.
DB: *Well, you had your vote, Citizen Lynch, which you exercised.*
DL: And that's about it.

DB: *I feel your discomfort here, but I feel that people who know your work were very surprised—because your work seems to shred so many mythologies, and to penetrate under the surface—that you would make a political decision based on what seemed like very superficial things: that you liked the guy's haircut, that he's happy, you liked that sense of a brush-clearer, an old Hollywood actor. And I think that itself disturbed people, or confused people. You are in the public realm, for good or bad.*
DL: That's why I say it's a no-win situation. All those things that are aside from the film are not one bit important. There's nothing I can say about it.

DB: *But there are even times in talking about the films when you say there's nothing you can say.*
DL: Yeah. Uh, the words . . . unfortunately that's what this is all about.

DB: *I actually thought of giving you a sketch pad so that if you couldn't answer a question you could sketch me out an answer.*
DL: I could draw you one, yeah.

DB: *Let's go back to something we talked about last time: secrets. You put a line in* Wild at Heart *for Sailor that was not in the book: "We all got a secret side, baby." It's a repeated motif in your work. I said there's a certain power in a secret, and you said there's a horror in it, too. Can you address yourself to both sides of that equation?*
DL: Well, it's like common sense.

DB: *How's that, Doctor Lynch?*
DL: We talked about the man who knew too much. There are so many

different kind of secrets. Part of the thing about secrets is that they have a certain kind of mystery to me. A dark secret. Just the words "dark secret" are so beautiful. Again, for the same reason I don't want to go back to Spokane, Washington. I don't want to see something so clearly that it would destroy an imaginary picture. And I'm real thankful for secrets and mysteries, because they provide a pull to learn the secret and learn the mystery, and you can float out there. And I hope, in a way, I don't ever get the total answer, unless the answer accompanies a tremendous rush of bliss. I *love* the process of going into a mystery.

DB: *You're secretive yourself, wouldn't you say?*
DL: That's a possibility, yeah.

DB: *Jack Nance says you're the most secretive guy he's ever known.*
DL: Well, I'm probably speaking much too much with you. [Uneasy laugh.]

DB: *There were some pieces written in the mid-eighties that made mention of the fact that you didn't have any visitors. Your response wasn't that you didn't like the way your house was, or, "I have a small house, I can't have visitors," or, "I'm never in town"—any of which would have been perfectly fine excuses—*
DL: What was my response?

DB: *Your response was, "I'm doing things that I don't want people to see."*
DL: At the time, I probably was. I'm not always doing these things in my house. [Laughs.]

DB: *See, but you didn't tell anyone what you were doing.*
DL: No.

DB: *So you* created *a secret.*
DL: Well. I suppose I did. In an answer to a question, I created a secret.

DB: *I'm just wondering if part of your attraction to secrets is that there's a kind of power, a kind of control in secrets. I think one reason secrets are so important to teenagers is that for them the world is completely out of control.*
DL: I don't know. Secrets then were totally traumatic to me, because I was doing so many things that I thought could change my world in a negative way. I was living in a fearful state. Secrets and mysteries provide sort of a beautiful little corridor where you can float out and many, many wonderful things can happen in there.

DB: *Now it's come time to deny the rumor or admit to all America that you've a woman's uterus in a bottle somewhere.*
DL: What have you heard about this?

DB: *We know you're interested in body parts. We heard that a woman producer was having a hysterectomy and you asked her to save the tissue.*
DL: It wasn't that way at all! This woman was having this operation, and *asked* the doctor to save this for me, as something she felt that I would want to have. A gift.

DB: *Sort of like a valentine.*
DL: Yeah. It's like, there's many things I have in my house, right? But some things—like the Log Lady—have stuck with certain people as very interesting things. So I guess that could be one of them.

Interview with David Lynch

MICHEL CIMENT AND HUBERT NIOGRET/1990

MICHEL CIMENT & HUBERT NIOGRET: *What was the starting point for* Wild at Heart*?*
DAVID LYNCH: The novel itself. My friend Monty Montgomery is one of the producers of the film, and he was reading the novel by Barry Gifford, *Wild at Heart: The Story of Sailor and Lula,* though it hadn't been published yet. He was looking for unpublished stories, and this one stood out because he had met the author, Barry Gifford, who used to work with the California publisher Black Lizard. Since Monty wanted me to help him write the script so he could direct it himself, he had me read the book. I asked him jokingly: "OK, but what happens if I like it so much that I want to direct it myself?" He said that in that case, I could direct it. So what started as a joke was exactly what happened. The book impressed me a lot with that title: *Wild at Heart*, this wild and crazy world, and in the middle, this love story, these people you can't imagine being tender, loving, and at peace. And I also liked the flashbacks as a way to take a more indirect approach.

MC & HN: *How did you approach the adaptation, which you wrote yourself?*
DL: I changed quite a few things because the novel's essentially a character study. There's not really very much that happens. Certain characters and certain stories are mentioned only briefly, and these secondary elements appealed to me so much that I brought them into the main storyline. I also changed around the flashbacks. And then I found myself with a depressing ending: Sailor and Lula break up. I wanted my script to be wild [*sauvage*], but the ending of the first draft was still too violent.

From *Positif* (October 1990), translated from the French. Reprinted by permission.

That's the version that I submitted to most of the big production studios, and they all rejected it. They found it too violent and didn't see any commercial potential for it. Then I met Samuel Goldwyn, who was the only one to tell me that he hated the ending, and he asked me why I liked it. I tried hard to defend it, but didn't succeed, and finally I told him that whether or not he decided to produce the film, I was going to change the ending. He may have wanted a different ending for commercial reasons, but still I think that it really didn't work. Going through the ending again, I changed a lot of other things, and the whole tone changed, especially when I incorporated the bit from *The Wizard of Oz*. The script moved to another imaginative level, and I think that if I'd proposed the second version to the studios, things would have worked out a lot differently. And that's the script that I shot.

MC & HN: *Although generally in American cinema, flashbacks are psychological or dramatic, in* Wild at Heart, *they're instead poetic, they play with elements such as fire, which also appears in the song "My Love Went into Flames." Furthermore, as much as* Blue Velvet *was blue, as its title indicates, this film is red.*

DL: Red and yellow, absolutely. Fire is not really in the book, it came from the matches. It became an element that reunited Sailor and Lula, but that also destroyed their relationship. So I wanted it to be a constant between them, and it produced the extreme closeups of cigarettes and matches. Most of the elements linked to fire were in the script. I believe that the story, as the basic structure, is primary. But during the shooting certain things can take on greater importance than in the script. Every time the actors repeated a scene, when we were finished, a part of the text had been changed. Certain parts didn't work and we added new dialogue. It's never finished before the shooting is done, and the same goes for editing. The first version of *Wild at Heart* was very long. Duwayne Dunham, the editor, had to give it a new form. We had to find a way of telling so many stories at the same time. Many of the stories in the book did nothing to advance the main story. It would have been simple to take them out, but I didn't want to lose them. So we worked hard to fix the problem, in order to go from one place to another and to move among different areas without losing the central line, and, eventually, with trial and error, we reached the final version. But it was partly written and partly revealed during the shooting.

MC & HN: *While writing the screenplay, are you looking for concrete and physical elements that characterize your films, or at that moment are you only interested in the narration? Do you work on the visual conception of the film while you write the screenplay?*

DL: Yes, but in a way that's more abstract. On the set, you begin to see everything more clearly. The lamp that a production designer has just brought out can give you some ideas. For example, even though it wasn't used that much, there was a horse-radio, a beautiful piece in leather with a horse on top of the radio in the Iguana Motel. It's the sort of thing that comes from the western, from Texas, which is the reason that the production designer Patricia Norris had noticed it, and it became a symbol in that motel, a little character all its own. At the moment Lula touches it, it talks to her. Because of that horse, you know where you are.

MC & HN: *Are you already thinking of the editing when you add that kind of detail?*

DL: Sometimes, yes. For example, I took the nude dancer who starts moving when you press something: we shot it outside the context of the scene, and that allowed me to return to the end of the earlier scene, where Sailor presses the button and sets the dancer in motion. That fit perfectly during the editing. Some other transitions were conceived in the same way, like when Sailor says that he's ready to dance: he begins to shake, Lula also starts to move on the bed, the cushions begin jumping up and down, and the shot cuts to the dance. That transition was imagined earlier, but we found others afterwards, and sometimes they worked really well.

MC & HN: *Did you decide from the very beginning to start the film with the very violent scene on the stairs?*

DL: Originally, the first scene wasn't that one, but a scene—also very violent—of a motorcycle accident without a direct link to the story. But we fell behind the shooting schedule and I am sure that the producer was beginning to run short of money. Since that sequence was supposed to be shot by a second unit, we thought we would postpone the shooting, work at the editing, and then return to shooting, but by then we would know exactly what we needed and what we could do without. But in the middle of editing, Duwayne Dunham thought of starting the film with the character of Bob Ray Lemon. That seemed the thing to do. That scene had all the power needed for a start of the film, and it was also much more closely tied to the story than the scene we originally conceived. I remember that when I was a student of Frank Daniel, the Czechoslovakian professor at the American Film Institute, he explained that it was necessary to indicate to the spectator relatively early on what kind of film he was going to see, so that you can show him what direction you're going to take him.

MC & HN: *Sailor hits someone in only one other scene, but one where this time he is instead the victim . . .*
DL: But there too, in the first scene, he's more victim than anything else. He goes to prison. At the end of the story he's also a victim. Unless you don't figure out very quickly what's really going on, you may think that he has control of things, except that he doesn't do anything more than react to Marietta Pace (the role played by Diane Ladd).

MC & HN: *Even if you didn't shoot the accident that was supposed to serve as the story's opening, there are two other accidents that are totally independent of the story, but entirely in the spirit of the film. The first of them is very striking.*
DL: It wasn't in the novel, but it was suggested to me by the title: "Wild." I even envisioned putting in more accidents, but I think that now there's a good balance. I intended to include an accident where all the suitcases broke open so that clothes were strewn all over the road. I visualized that scene happening at night, and that image remained in my mind. Driving at night, and seeing, little by little, some pieces of clothing appear. . . . It's one of my favorite scenes in the film, and it took shape in stages, and the last was the music. You come across different sorts of emotions—fear, mystery, horror—then this girl comes out of nowhere; there's humor in the dialogue, a horrible humor, and a sadness that saturates everything. And the music lifts the scene to another dimension. It's very simple music, like the kind children love. It's a very good scene for Sailor and Lula, because it defines their relationship better, how they become closer.

MC & HN: *You use two very different types of music: on the one hand, that of Angelo Badalamenti, which is romantic, lyrical, and close to music of Italy, and on the other, rock and roll.*
DL: Angelo Badalamenti wrote more music for *Blue Velvet* than for this film, but *Wild at Heart* is composed more of preexisting music. Two songs were written, but only one, "Up in Flames," was used in the final cut. Koko Taylor, the blues singer from Chicago, is absolutely the one we needed. An entire story comes alive because of the sole fact that she sings a single word. It's terrific.

MC & HN: *What role did the music play in the conception of the film?*
DL: Again, it's necessary to remember the title: *Wild at Heart.* Music

plays an essential role. The central piece that expresses that quality is the very fast number by Power Mad, "Slaughterhouse," and I like it for its terrific power. With Richard Strauss, a piece from *Four Last Songs* is one thing that I heard in Germany and that comes into the film to introduce a different tone, to give much greater force to what's happening. But you can't insert just any piece of music, it's necessary to do a lot of experimenting during the entire process. At the point of mixing the sound, you always put in too much music, and the result just doesn't work. You end up having to remove certain musical tracks. At some points everything is extremely calm, you don't hear anything, and then at others there are twenty-five sounds all mixed together. But as we all know, contrast is what makes things work.

MC & HN: *Do you choose the musical pieces during the shooting or the editing?*

DL: I choose many of them before the shooting. One day, I would like to choose almost all of them beforehand, because very often the sound engineer "sends" the music to my earphones so that only I can hear the dialogue with the music. I can tell whether the tone of the dialogue fits the music. The same goes for some shots that have no dialogue: in listening to the music you can tell whether or not it's going to work.

MC & HN: *Was that also true when you shot Harry Dean Stanton in his car as he first takes to the road?*

DL: I heard a piece that I already knew, "Baby Please Don't Go Down to New Orleans," in the middle of shooting. There are radio stations that broadcast old tunes, music from the fifties and sixties, and also from the thirties or forties. And sometimes you hear a piece at just the right moment when you need it.

MC & HN: *The use of closeups is, more than in* Blue Velvet, *one of the characteristic features of* Wild at Heart.

DL: There were also a number in *Blue Velvet*, but the story was more traditional and the film was centered on a small number of characters until the very end. *Wild at Heart* is more atomized, it has more characters and more secondary, parallel storylines. I'm not a film buff, but I like the idea of B-films; Nicolas Cage and Laura Dern are in a way the characters of B-films.

MC & HN: Wild at Heart *is at the intersection of two genres: on the one hand, the gangster film, featuring a couple in flight, young, doomed people in love—as in* The Right to Live, They Live by Night, Bonnie and Clyde—

and, on the other hand, the family melodrama represented by Marietta, the uncle, or the father. Are you interested in playing with traditional genres, and not without a little irony?
DL: I haven't really thought about it, but humor and irony are linked to a sense of what is "larger than life." That's the way I see B-films: "larger than life," not very realistic. It's a world at once realistic, but a long way from the world as we know it.

MC & HN: *Is it the world of film noir?*
DL: Yes, especially because of the title, but not just because of the title. I know that it's possible to make a film where there's a fair amount of light all the way through, all in managing contrast and tension. But when you can work with things truly, thrillingly dark, it's not only dark, but intense.

MC & HN: *Is it because you conclude the film with a good witch (combined with "Love Me Tender" and a return to love) that earlier you have to go to extremes in showing a hand carried off by a dog, or a head that flies through the air? Does that supposedly prepare us for the unrealistic ending?*
DL: If you want to push things to the limit, you have to show viewers from the beginning what's allowed in order to be able do it later on. So it's entirely possible that a sawed-off shotgun can produce that effect, or that a dog that finds itself in back of a building will snap up that pretty hand and carry it off . . .

MC & HN: *The character of Marietta, who heightens the melodrama of the film, a little like a Shelley Winters or an Angela Lansbury, is a character who is typically American.*
DL: People in Europe see things that way, but believe me, if you ask some Americans whether they consider her a typical American mother, they will tell you no. Marietta is in the novel, and she is Diane Ladd. If someone else had played the role, it would not have evolved to the same level. That's because certain actresses seize the opportunity and are ready to go all out. So it was terrific working with Diane.

MC & HN: *She acts with her own daughter.*
DL: That worked out really well. Laura Dern is crazy in her own way, but she knows that her mother is too. They adore each other. They're real actresses.

MC & HN: *Did she sometimes improvise certain things?*
DL: When she was in her first scene, she was miles away from the text

that I'd written. She got the spirit of the scene perfectly, but she didn't recite a single word. So I took her aside and after that we worked very well together. She was bad at sticking to the dialogue, but she really loved to be seized by an emotion and to be carried away by it. It was quite something to contain all that energy.

MC & HN: *Willem Dafoe, who also has a great deal of energy, went a long way with the creation of his character.*
DL: Watching him work is a terrific experience. He is so controlled, so precise, there's not a single wasted emotion. What he did was fantastic. I don't know whether the scenes between him and Lula in the hotel room would have worked with two other actors. I think that the false teeth helped him with his conception of the character [Bobby Peru]. From the moment when he puts those teeth in, he talks a little differently, he discovers a certain kind of smile.

MC & HN: *In a certain way, the character of Bobby Peru incarnates all the spirit and style of the film, a mix of emotion and irony. He is totally dramatic, you believe what he tells you, and all at once he bursts out laughing. But it must have been difficult to maintain that balance: to come so close to caricature, all the while sustaining the emotion?*
DL: If you look at things only one way, whatever that might be, a film can become a potential disaster, and you won't be able to make it. I tried to be faithful to the original idea, and the feeling and images emerged as we went along.

MC & HN: *Wild at Heart has several "bad guys" who are all in one way or another extensions of the role of Dennis Hopper in* Blue Velvet: *Harry Dean Stanton, Willem Dafoe, J. E. Freeman, etc.*
DL: Harry Dean Stanton is not a "bad guy," he's a detective, he's the worst victim of Marietta, and one of the most moving characters since he's actually a pretty nice guy. J. E. Freeman was chosen for the role of Santos the day before shooting his first scene, and he fits perfectly into the world of the film. I love what he did. I've already told you about Willem Dafoe. And with Morgan Shepherd, who plays Mr. Reindeer, I'd worked with him on *Elephant Man*, where he has a small role in a scene in a pub. He's a crazy guy, and I want to work with him again. He was very keen to be part of a project that didn't work out some time ago. He has a strange look [*regard*]. And he has a very British accent, but with him there's a diabolical and very sweet side at the same time.

MC & HN: *How was the sequence constructed that brings together Reindeer and the girls?*
DL: It wasn't in the novel. It's a little scene that takes place in an elegant place, but beneath that you sense something awful the entire time. Even if things seem to flow and are beautiful, a feeling of horror emerges. It wasn't an indispensable scene for the story, but it created another world in my mind, and a glance into the life of Mr. Reindeer that makes you dream. And then the fire breaks out . . .

MC & HN: *The intimate link between the surface of things and what lies beneath was already at the center of* Blue Velvet.
DL: Yes, no doubt about it. But each of my films deals with that. Maybe I am obsessed with hidden things, maybe I am obsessed with this theme all the time. Scientists and private detectives observe the world and discover new things every day, but all the while they know that they're really far from knowing everything.

MC & HN: *But you're not a fan of realism on screen.*
DL: That's for sure. Even the filmmakers who believe in realism can't stick to the surface, they can't keep themselves from starting to dream. When you're shooting a particular scene and suddenly a shadow comes over the face of a young girl, that moment creates a sense that goes beyond the physical detail because of the context, because of what's happened earlier, because of sounds, etc. Then your mind begins to work. It's impossible to stick with appearances. I was just at a restaurant where there were two young Chinese women who were seated side by side, rather than face to face. It was a very expensive place and they were very elegant. I began to dream while watching them eat so very slowly. It was like a poem and I asked myself what was going on. Their faces moved in the same way with an extreme slowness, and they seemed even more strange in that setting. Nothing can stop you in a certain situation from asking yourself questions and from letting your mind wander. I think that the cinematic experience is like that. There's some kind of magic that happens if you get close to internal feelings.

MC & HN: *That's sort of the case in* Blue Velvet. *At the beginning, it focuses on a traditional investigation pursued by a man who discovers, little by little, a number of secrets, before finally discovering himself.*
DL: It's always more intriguing, and more exciting, when there are many levels. Many films, in my view—but I don't know whether I have

the right to comment, since I haven't seen any films for a very long time because of my work—only seem to deal with a single thing. Still, even when you strike only a single note on a keyboard, you hear harmonics. A film can also accomplish that—evoke a lot of things at the same time.

MC & HN: *Don't you think that current American cinema drastically lacks any mystery, that few films succeed, like yours, in getting to the other side of the mirror?*

DL: Here's how that happens. Let's say that ten people happen to be in an office. A man enters who's going to tell them a very abstract, very original story. He begins his story, and little by little the others ask some questions. He finds himself compelled to explain what he wants to say in words more and more precise because they don't understand. By the time he's finished, everyone in the room understands his story, but the story has been reduced to one thing. There are no more harmonics. And that's when they decide to finance the film. But they've killed the mystery. I think instead that it's good not to know too much about what you're going to do.

MC & HN: *Do you feel some affinity with other filmmakers, someone like Buñuel, for instance?*

DL: From what I've been told, I think I would love his films if I were to see them. But I only know his *Andalousian Dog* [*Un Chien Andalou*]. I really like Fellini, Bergman, Kubrick, Hitchcock, Tati, and *The Wizard of Oz*!

MC & HN: *The reference to* The Wizard of Oz *in* Wild at Heart *is not found in the original novel.*

DL: I think that the idea appeared when we meet up with Sailor, when he's just broken up with Lula, and then gets beaten up. At that moment he's decided to cling to the idea that he can get out whenever he wants. He's decided to stick with that idea even if he's wrong. It's a whole attitude he takes on for himself, and when he's attacked by the gang at the end, it seemed natural that the good witch comes to visit him. We have here a very macho character, very cool, who still treats Lula very well, like his equal. He never condescends to her at all in his gestures or words. And he shows the same composure in his rapport with the good witch. I think that the public likes that character trait in him.

MC & HN: *How do you explain the appearance of* The Wizard of Oz *in a number of contemporary films, from* Alice Doesn't Live Here Anymore *to* Zardoz?

DL: For me, that book really matters. There are also some allusions to it in *Blue Velvet* with the name of Dorothy, the red shoes, etc. *The Wizard of Oz* is a film with very great power, and I suppose that Martin Scorsese and John Boorman saw it, like me, during their childhood and that it made a very strong impression on them. And it's to be expected that it has stayed with us for the past several years and that we find its echoes in our films for such a long time after. *The Wizard of Oz* is like a dream and it has immense emotional power.

MC & HN: *You have a background in painting. In what ways does it influence your approach to directing?*
DL: I'm always a painter. It's necessary to consider two things: on the one hand, what's in front of the camera, and on the other, how to film it. I talk about that with Patricia Norris, my production designer, and Fred Elmes, my director of photography. We have an ideal concept at the beginning, we think about particular colors, but those things disintegrate quickly. When you look for locations and find yourself in particular places for a shoot, you can't begin to repaint the whole world. Sometimes you also find new ideas that are better. In any case, it's necessary to start somewhere. With Fred, when we read the script together, we talk about feelings, emotions, and about basic things like the cold and heat, what's clearly visible and what's not. We decide for each scene what we do or don't want to see, whether in a particular case it will be dark and hot, etc. We talk about fluorescent flashes, direct lighting, incandescent lights. What we have to do is highlight the ambience of each sequence.

MC & HN: *The beginning of* Blue Velvet, *for instance, creates a falsely light-hearted ambience with the white picket fence and the red roses . . .*
DL: The idea came to us from a book, *Good Times on Our Street*, and they give it to all American school children. It talks about happiness, everyday surroundings, and being good neighbors. For a young American who comes from a well-to-do family, paradise should be like the street where he lives. I was brought up in that kind of setting: wooden fences and old houses. I am sure that some horrible things happened behind all that, but in my childhood mindset, everything seemed serenely beautiful. Airplanes went slowly by in the sky, rubber toys floated in the water, meals seemed to last five years, and a nap seemed endless. Everything was pleasant, and *Good Times on Our Street* recreated that scenario. You learned to read with the book telling the adventures of Dick, Jane, and their dog Spot. Of course, that world now seems very far away, and I am sure that

schools have stopped using that book because now, probably no one can feel close to the atmosphere portrayed there.

MC & HN: *On the surface, it's also the world of* Twin Peaks.

DL: Certainly. It's a world you want to enter, because even though it's unsettling, at first it seems to be ideal somehow. The topic was proposed to me by my agent, Tony Krantz, who's also the agent for Mark Frost. Tony had already tried to get us to work together on television, because Mark had written a number of episodes for *Hill Street Blues*. Earlier, we were co-authors on a comedy, but neither of us was very keen to collaborate on a film for television. For me, I had reservations, if for no other reason than that no interesting idea had presented itself. And for Mark, he knew what a horror television could be. Even when it works, your time is not your own, it's a matter of working against the clock. Then we thought of a project that combined a police investigation with a soap opera. The idea of a story with episodes that went on for a long time appealed to me. We began to imagine the characters and, one after another, they appeared in the story, and little by little a world took form. That's how we took on the project of *Twin Peaks*, and Tony couldn't have been happier, so he sent us to ABC. They asked us for a script that we wrote in eight or nine days. It was the first episode, the pilot. Before I realized it, I found myself in Seattle in the middle of shooting! In twenty-one days of ultra-fast production in freezing weather, the film was in the can! I couldn't believe that I could produce ninety-three minutes of film in so short a time, even though the days were very long. ABC liked my work, but at the same time they were afraid. I am too close to *Twin Peaks* to know how it's different from other television shows, especially since I watch very little television. Everything that's "different" for television can potentially be a success or a disaster. And most of the time, it's a disaster. So the company should be careful about what it broadcasts, but fortunately *Twin Peaks* was a big success.

MC & HN: *What is your role for the other episodes of* Twin Peaks?

DL: I'm not as totally involved as when I write and direct a film. Mark and I, we supervise the evolution of the story. We read the scripts, make our notes, and see to it that things don't go too far off track. But at the same time, there are some limits to our control, there comes a time when you have to let the director take charge of the film. During postproduction, I offer my advice on the sound mix and the music.

MC & HN: *How many episodes will there be?*

DL: This year, in addition to the pilot, there were seven episodes, each forty-five minutes long (that is one hour of broadcast time with advertisements), and next year there will be thirteen.

MC & HN: *At the beginning of* Twin Peaks, *we are in a traditional soap opera. In a small town, someone is killed, a body is encountered on the shore, someone calls the sheriff, and then little by little the film distinguishes itself from* Dallas *or* Dynasty: *the mystery grows, some strange characters appear, the atmosphere darkens. And at the end of the pilot, we find ourselves in a completely different universe, twenty-five years later.*

DL: That ending was produced for the video version sold on the European market, and it offers a conclusion to the story. When I signed my contract, it was very thick, and I didn't know I was committing myself to that. It's my own fault if I didn't pay attention to what I was signing! Americans still believe somewhat stupidly that Europe is as far away as the planet Mars, and ABC thought that no one would ever hear about that "closed" [*fermée*] ending. In the middle of production, someone reminded me that I was supposed to shoot it. I already had an extremely tight working schedule, and I couldn't see how I would have the time to devote to filming the ending, let alone imagining it. Then all at once, strangely, an idea came to mind, and the production company gave me complete freedom, even though they were anxious for me shoot the ending so that the story had a conclusive feel to it. That took very little time, and we had an extra day of shooting in coming back to Los Angeles for the shots of the ending with the midget, Laura Palmer, the dream, and the dance. Personally, I love those four minutes of film. They reappear in another form that you'll see in the seventh episode and again in the thirteenth.

MC & HN: *How did you obtain that incomprehensible language that nonetheless resembles English?*

DL: We filmed everything backwards. The actors walked and talked in reverse until they reached the beginning of the sequence, and then we projected it normally.

MC & HN: *For a director like you who works a great deal on the soundtrack and the visual elements, television must present constraints with its "flat" sound and a reduced image.*

DL: I think that the sound of *Twin Peaks* is as good as it can be given the limits of television. In any case, we recorded it just as we would for a movie. For mixing the sound, they thought that the work would be much easier because it was for the small screen. But in fact we made the task more complicated for them! If you watch *Twin Peaks* on a big screen in a good auditorium, you'll feel its power even more. On television, the sound and image are so weak that you really lose a lot. When we watch a film on video or on television, we think we are watching the real thing even though it's a long way from the original! With a film, if it truly has a real dimension, it envelops you and you find yourself plunged into its world. It's very hard for you to escape it. But when you are in front of the television, the moment you turn your head you're no longer in the ambience.

MC & HN: *When you began your career, you had the reputation of working a great deal on sound with Alan Splet.*
DL: Sound is very important because it really is half the film. With film, the whole can be greater than the parts if you have the sound, the image, and sequence of scenes right. When I work on the sound, I want it to support the film and the emotions, but also, if possible, to reach something at a higher level. Until the sound is done right, you haven't really seen your film. But when that happens, some magical things start to take place.

MC & HN: *It would seem, in contrast with what you did in* Eraserhead, Blue Velvet, *or* Wild at Heart, *that you "restrain" yourself more with the mise en scène of* Twin Peaks. *Do you think that there are different languages for cinema and for television? In* Wild at Heart, *for instance, you can immediately engage the heart of the action and impose your vision.*
DL: I think that's true. When you know that you're working for television, you wear different glasses. Your head refuses to think about certain sexual things or certain violent scenes. You know that you can't approach certain areas, and you're aware of limits that shouldn't be crossed. But—and this is very strange—you still feel pleasure in working and you experience true contentment. There was practically never a moment during the shooting of *Twin Peaks* when I told myself that there were some things that I couldn't do. No doubt that's true because from the very start, I defined a limited space in which I had to work, but it was one that still allowed me to express myself. Traditionally, television is more narrative than visual, but I think that *Twin Peaks* compares well with film.

On the other hand, films transferred to video have proved that it's not necessary to shoot in closeups for the small screen. Of course films lose a lot when they're adapted to television, but if they're good, they still work very well. But once or twice I made a mistake in *Twin Peaks* by placing the camera too far away, so that the characters are the size of a ping pong ball!

MC & HN: *What have you been doing in the three years between* Blue Velvet *and* Wild at Heart?

DL: I tried to produce *Ronnie Rocket* and, one more time, *One Saliva Bubble*. I'd written *Ronnie Rocket* after *Eraserhead*. I really liked my idea, which was very abstract. It was sort of a comedy of the absurd. In a certain way it resembled *Eraserhead* with its strange and somber world. I failed to get it produced several times, particularly with Francis Coppola before his company Zoetrope went bankrupt. And another time with Dino De Laurentiis, before he also went bankrupt! But actually in the latter case, the reason wasn't financial. It was more that Dino really didn't understand the project and didn't feel attached to it. I sensed that there would be trouble if once it was done, the film didn't have the form I wanted. I would still like to produce *Ronnie Rocket*, but with the help of people who aren't looking to make big profits. It's a film that has a lot to do with the roots of rock and roll, even though it's not historically specific. It's as if you wanted a film about the '50s, I mean, the 2050s.... It unfolds in another world with lots of gigantic factories, like there used to be. Nowadays, factories are smaller, cleaner, with everything computerized. And that scares me. The casting was all set up with Isabella Rossellini and little Mike, the midget from *Twin Peaks*, who was to play Ronnie Rocket.

One Saliva Bubble was a nutty film, a sort of family comedy where nothing scary took place. There were a ton of substitutions, a little like in *Trading Places*, where a black man takes the place of a white man, and vice versa. I got the idea while on a plane trip, but I didn't realize at the time that twenty-five million films like that were being produced, and that's one of the reasons why I didn't make it. If the comedy of substitutions is a genre, why not make another one anyway? Steve Martin was very interested in one of the roles. In fact, he was supposed to play two roles. And another actor was supposed to play two roles, so there would be substitutions to the max!

MC & HN: *Isn't Kyle MacLachlan, who was in your first films and also in* Blue Velvet, *a kind of alter ego for you?*

DL: That's what they say. But it never crossed my mind. You could say that Nicolas Cage is too.

MC & HN: Twin Peaks *and* Blue Velvet *are a little like the world of Frank Capra turned upside down. The American dream become nightmare. What connection does that have with your childhood?*

DL: I think that at one time—and this must happen to everyone—I glimpsed the possibility of an ideal and perfect world. Little by little I saw how much that idea has deteriorated, how much the world has become more and more evil. My father, who is retired today, but who worked on research for the Department of Agriculture, did experiments on the diseases of forests, on insects, and he had huge forests at his disposal for his work. He was a wise man of the woods. My mother was a homemaker, but she also taught some languages.

MC & HN: *Where were you born?*
DL: I was born and then I lived for a while in Montana, where my father was raised on a ranch in the middle of wheat fields. A large part of my family on my father's side lives in that state. After that I lived in Idaho and the state of Washington. My mother is from Brooklyn. My parents met each other in a course on environmental science when they were both students at Duke University. As for me, I went to high school in Virginia, just next to Washington D.C.

MC & HN: *You finished your schooling when the age of rock and roll reached its peak.*
DL: Yes, you could say that, since that period lasted from 1955 until 1965. I was totally a part of all that.

MC & HN: *Your first artistic interest was in drawing.*
DL: I never really thought about movies during my youth. I didn't think about becoming a painter either, because for me, it was an activity of the past and I couldn't see how you could be a painter in the modern world. When I left Virginia to live in Washington, I met a friend whose father was a painter. I'd thought earlier that he was a house painter. But no, he was very much a painter who was an artist. I visited his studio and then thought that I could be like him. After that I studied in art institutes in Boston and then in Philadelphia. I didn't like my one-year experience at the Boston Museum School. But at the Pennsylvania Academy of Fine Arts there were some terrific teachers and a painter like James Havard, who studied there at the same time as I did. Everybody worked hard.

MC & HN: *Do you still paint, and with what general orientation?*
DL: Yes. I would say that I paint more in the expressionist vein with a sense of the strange. After I did *Blue Velvet*, a journalist, Christine McKenna, who wrote movie reviews but who had switched to doing art criticism, saw some of my drawings and paintings and encouraged me to find a gallery to exhibit them. I'd never wanted to do that because I didn't feel committed to painting to the point of going all the way and showing

my canvasses. But little by little I let myself be persuaded, and she introduced me to some merchants in Los Angeles. James Corcoran organized two exhibits for me, and since he's a friend of Leo Castelli, I also had an opening in New York. Recently pieces of mine were shown in Dallas. So I've had four exhibits in the past three years.

MC & HN: *When did you get to know the production designer and director Jack Fisk, who is one of your good friends?*
DL: We met each other in high school in Virginia, where we shared a studio. Then when I went to Boston, he went to study at Cooper Union in New York. Since he hated his experience in New York just as much I hated mine in Boston, we decided to enroll in Philadelphia. It's a city that I both hated and loved. Jack is my oldest friend, and I married his sister, and we had a child, Austin, before getting divorced.

MC & HN: *Knowing your work, we expect that you should be interested in the work of Terrence Malick, for whom Jack Fisk was production designer.*
DL: Actually, it's Alan Splet and I who introduced Jack Fisk to Terrence Malick while we were studying with Malick at the American Film Institute in Los Angeles. There are two producers who want to sign me up as director for *White Noise* since they have the rights for it, and they have two scripts right now by Terrence Malick, and I think Terry will return to the movies.

MC & HN: *Your first two short films,* The Grandmother *and* The Alphabet, *use animation techniques like pixilation. How much did your experience in graphic art prepare you for your work as filmmaker?*
DL: A lot, I think, but I didn't realize it at first. At first, I wanted the paintings to move, and I could make that happen with animation. I knew absolutely nothing about movies. I thought that a 16 mm camera was a certain type of camera and that they were all the same. When I wanted to rent one, I was shocked to discover that their prices varied enormously. So I decided to get the cheapest one, after talking things over with the people in this little shop in downtown Philadelphia, who hardly knew more about it than I did. Little by little they provided me with a certain amount of information, and I did some experiments until I made a one-minute film that I set up as a feedback loop showing six people getting sick. It was also the title of the film! It had a sculpted screen. It was half sculpture, half film, and overall a work of art in motion. That was the moment when I was taken by the magic of film, and I kept going after that without ever really stopping.

MC & HN: *You also have a third artistic activity: music.*
DL: Angelo Badalamenti is the one who introduced me to the world of music. He writes the music, and I do the words. We talk together about the atmosphere, the words influence the music and also the other way around. It's been one of the happiest experiences in my life. It was as if time had stopped. We created forty songs and we made an album with Julee Cruise. All these activities—writing the script, the visual composition, the music—they're all connected for me, and each one gives me ideas for the others. So working on the music can inspire me about the visuals.

MC & HN: *You made a short piece produced by French television for the series* France as Seen by Others *[La France vue par les étrangers].*
DL: Yes. That's called *The Cowboy and the Frenchman.* That was a great experience. That was when I met Harry Dean Stanton, Tracy Walters, and Michael Horse, an Indian who later had a role in *Twin Peaks*. We shot it in Los Angeles.

MC & HN: *What was your experience at the American Film Institute?*
DL: First they found me the tools I needed and a place to work. And the director of studies, Frank Daniel, helped me a lot with his analyses of film. He talked to us about the role of sound, background sound, and the repetition of certain noises. He had us make cards with coded names that enabled us to remember those elements and that corresponded to each scene. By the end we had seventy cards and the film was finished! That worked for me. For the five years I was at the American Film Institute, three were practically underground because I was no longer taking courses. At that point I worked in a separate place far away from everyone else, but they never kicked me out. I shot *Eraserhead* during those years, and the reason why it took so long is that I lacked money. The Institute was right there for me and helped all along. Sid Solo, the director of CFI laboratory in Hollywood, developed my negative for free. And I wasn't the only student who got that kind of treatment.

MC & HN: *Was there rivalry among the students?*
DL: Not really. I didn't talk to too many people at the Institute. Even today it's difficult for me talk about my own creative work with my colleagues. I remember reading a script by Terrence Malick for a short piece and liking it a lot. He's a fantastic writer. It's possible that there was a working group at AFI, but I didn't participate. I worked in my corner and ignored what others were doing. Overall it was a thrilling place. There

was something in the air. Fifteen of us entered the program, courses lasted for two years, and since I started during the second year after the Institute opened, there were thirty of us in the program.

MC & HN: *That was a period when in Europe we had the impression that there was a renaissance in Hollywood. Were you aware of that?*
DL: No. On the one hand, I was very ignorant about the movies, and on the other, what I liked were films like *Sunset Boulevard*, *Rear Window*, or the work of Jacques Tati, and I watched them during the shooting of *Eraserhead*. I had no sense at all that there was any renewal in Hollywood—just the opposite. Nothing seemed to be going on there! The only films of that time that struck me were by Kubrick and Scorsese.

MC & HN: *You once said that the first film you watched was* Wait Till the Sun Shines, Nellie, *by Henry King.*
DL: I don't want to see that film ever again. About five years ago it was broadcast on television. I watched a small part of it and I couldn't believe that it was so different from what I remembered. I immediately changed the channel. Still, I would like to know whether in watching it again I could recapture my state of mind as a child. When I was little I watched it at a drive-in movie with my parents. There was a scene that made a huge impression on me, where a button gets stuck in the throat of a little girl. I'm sure that it was a very short bit, and that you didn't see very much, but I can still remember the impression that I experienced of that button caught in that child's esophagus. Anyway, that's the first film that I remembered.

MC & HN: *Did you go to the movies as a child?*
DL: Practically never. In Idaho I went once in a while on Saturday afternoons because there was a theater at the end of the street. I liked to tell the stories of the films that I saw. They seemed very realistic to me, like for everybody, I guess. But I wasn't clearly destined for making movies. I really appreciated the music of Henry Mancini, and I remember *Summer Place* with Sandra Dee and Troy Donohue. It was fantastic to watch that kind of soap opera with your girlfriend. That made us dream!

MC & HN: *Did you prefer books to painting?*
DL: No. I didn't read books, and I didn't look at pictures. I saw life in one extreme closeup shot—in one, for instance, of saliva mingled with blood—or in long shots of a peaceful environment. I don't remember any more what I was thinking about then. It was never original, in any case. I didn't watch television, and I listened to music, but not religiously. The

only things that I really did were drawing, swimming, and also baseball, but not so that it was a really important activity. I liked the general atmosphere where I lived, and I daydreamed a lot because the world seemed a marvel to me. The first time that I had the impression of having a personal idea was when I returned to Philadelphia.

MC & HN: *Coming from graphic work and animation, what must have seemed new to you in your experience as director was your relationship with actors. Has that evolved along the way?*

DL: In one sense, yes, but I've always got along well with people. Some people have the kind of personality where it's terribly difficult for them to communicate, and that makes it a separate problem from film, because it's a medium where one deals with all sorts of individuals. I've never had that problem, even from the very beginning. Sometimes when I don't feel at ease with other people, I adjust myself to their point of view, and that pays off. I love to work with actors. Sometimes at the start I have difficulty explaining my ideas to them, but little by little we understand one other. It always works out that way.

MC & HN: *Do you have a preference—writing, directing, or editing?*

DL: Each stage for me is a joy and just as important for the final result. It's necessary to invest yourself completely at each phase, because otherwise you don't get anywhere.

An Interview with David Lynch

KRISTINE MCKENNA/1992

THE FOLLOWING conversation with David Lynch took place at his house in the Hollywood Hills on the morning of March 8, 1992. The day we spoke, Lynch had just returned to LA from New York where he'd been working with the composer Angelo Badalamenti on the music for the soon-to-be-released adaptation of his TV series *Twin Peaks*; the next day he was scheduled to leave for Berkeley where he'll spend months mixing the sound for the film. Lynch is perpetually on the go, and it's not surprising that his large multi-leveled house has the feeling of a dwelling where the occupant is away a good deal of the time. It's sparsely furnished (a few '50s style chairs, a low couch, and a coffee table), done in muted tones, and there's nothing on the walls (Lynch recently bought two photographs by his favorite photographer, Diane Arbus, but he hasn't hung them up). In the kitchen one finds Lynch's treasured cappuccino maker along with neat stacks of scripts, videos, and books. This is a house of a busy person—there's no evidence anywhere of anyone lounging around and relaxing.

The fact that it's Sunday morning doesn't prevent business calls from pouring in, and talking to Lynch between calls, one deduces that there's no down time in this man's life; he manages to cram an extraordinary amount of highly creative activity into each and every day. As can be seen in the following conversation, Lynch's creativity and his life are built on a solid structure of philosophical belief. One could make the case that it is this structure of belief that gives him the enormous vitality at the core of his diverse and ever expanding work.

From *David Lynch* (Colleción Imagen, 1992). Reprinted by permission of Institució Alfons el Magnànim.

KRISTINE MCKENNA: *Your paintings seem to depict the world from the perspective of a terror stricken child; is that an accurate assessment?*
DAVID LYNCH: Pretty much. I love child things because there's so much mystery when you're a child. When you're a child, something as simple as a tree doesn't make sense. You see it in the distance and it looks small, but as you go closer, it seems to grow—you haven't got a handle on the rules when you're a child. We think we understand the rules when we become adults, but what we really experienced is a narrowing of the imagination.

KM: *How do you explain the fact that you've retained such a clear grasp of a child' perspective?*
DL: I guess I got whacked hard in the mystery department when I was little. I found the world completely and totally fascinating then—it was like a dream. They say that people who think they had a happy childhood are blocking something out, but think I really had one. Of course I had the usual fears, like going to school—I knew there was some sort of problem there. But every other person sensed that problem too, so my fears were pretty normal.

KM: *You use these words,* mystery *and* fear; *what's the connection between the two?*
DL: There's always fear of the unknown where there's mystery. It's possible to achieve a state where you realize the truth of life and fear disappears, and a lot of people have reached that state, but next to none of them are on Earth. There's probably a few.

KM: *Would someone who'd achieve that degree of insight still be driven to do creative work?*
DL: They'd do a different kind of creative work that would totally be in accordance with the laws of nature. Their work would be devoted to helping people who weren't there yet and elevating the universe.

KM: *Are the laws of nature cruel?*
DL: Absolutely not—they just seem cruel because we see such a small fragment for the whole plan. We live in a world of opposites, of extreme evil and violence opposed to goodness and peace. It's that way here for a reason, but we have a hard time grasping what that reason is. In struggling to understand the reason, we learn about balance and there's a mysterious door right at that balance point. We can go through that door anytime we get together.

KM: *How old do you feel emotionally?*
DL: Between nine and seventeen most of the time, and sometimes around six. When you're six, you can see down the street and you're aware there may be another block, but the world is pretty much two blocks big.

KM: *One of your recent paintings,* So This Is Love, *seems to take a fairly dark view of love. The image centers on a lone figure with impossibly long legs that elevate his head into bleak empty space. An airplane splutters by his head pumping smoke into the night sky; can you talk a bit about this piece?*
DL: It's like a negative image of my childhood. In reality that sky would've been blue and Technicolor, and the plane would've been a large military plane that made a droning sound. The plane took a long time to cross the sky, and the sound it made was very serene. The world seemed to be more quiet when the plane was passing through the sky.

KM: *This is a pleasant memory for you, yet you've translated it into a dark image; why?*
DL: Because darkness has crept in since then. The darkness is realizations about the world and human nature and my own nature all combined into one ball of sludge.

KM: *Many of your paintings combine allusions to romantic love, physical wounding, and death; do you find something erotic about illness and decay?*
DL: Erotic? No, but illness and decay are a part of nature. Illness on a piece of steel is rust. If you throw a piece of paper out in the rain and come back in a few days, it'll have little molds on it, so it's like a magical thing happens. Illness is a very bad thing, but people design big buildings for illness and invent machinery and little tubes and all that kind of stuff. So just like in nature, a whole new thing rises up out of illness.

KM: *Do you fear the body?*
DL: No, but it's a strange thing. Its most important function appears to be carrying the mind from one place to another, but there are a lot of fun things that you can do with the body too. Of course, it can also be torture. I'm not into exercise so I worry about keeping my body in good enough shape to take everything else around.

KM: *What's the most frightening thing about your home?*
DL: It's a place where things can go wrong. When I was a child, home seemed claustrophobic to me but that wasn't because I had a bad family.

A home is like a nest—it's only useful for so long and then you can't wait to get out. Saying that all nests are only useful for a limited period doesn't mean all love dies with time, but love changes. I still love everyone I've ever loved.

KM: *I once heard love described as an intermingling of pity and desire; do you agree with that observation?*
DL: Not really. To lose love is like light and it's only a problem when there's an absence of it. Pure love asks for nothing back and it's more like a sensation or a vibration, but unfortunately most people don't understand pure love. We tend to put the responsibility onto another person and that doesn't work out too good.

KM: *Who taught you the most about visual art?*
DL: My first really important teacher was a guy named Bushnell Keeler who was the father of my good friend Toby Keeler. This was when I was fifteen and living in Virginia, and Bushnell was the first professional artist I ever met. I'd never heard of such a thing, and from that moment I wanted to be a painter—his life seemed like a miracle to me. The most important thing was that he had a studio and painted every day. He also turned me onto this book by Robert Henri called *The Art Spirit* that sort of became my bible, because that book made the rules for art life.

KM: *What was the first artwork that made an impression on you?*
DL: An exhibition of Francis Bacon's work that I saw at Marlborough Gallery in New York when I was eighteen. It was images of meat and cigarettes, and what struck me about them was the beauty of the paint and the balance and contrast in the pictures. It was like perfection.

KM: *Does art go through fertile and fallow periods?*
DL: Yeah, it must, and it seems to be in a kind of lean period now. The '80s were a good period because although all that money churning through caused a lot of goofball stuff to bob up, there was an excitement about painting for the first time in a long time.

KM: *Looking over your paintings of the past eight years, it seems your work is becoming increasingly minimal; would you agree with that?*
DL: Yes, and the reason for that is because I feel a yearning for purity. As my life becomes more complicated, I want my art to become more simple because everything in life revolves around trying to maintain a balance.

KM: *I also notice that the surfaces of your paintings are becoming more increasingly modeled and sculptural; was it a conscious decision to take the work in this direction?*
DL: Yes, I'd like to build them out even more. The idea of paint on a flat surface doesn't excite me so much right now. I like the idea of a field where someone's dumped some garbage—the garbage puffs up higher than the surface of the field, and I like that.

KM: *Have you ever spoken to a conservationist about how the mix of materials you use will age? (Lynch's paintings incorporate cardboard, cotton, Band-Aids, and medicinal ointment along with standard painting materials).*
DL: I don't care one bit how they age. Nature should go to work on these things—they're not finished really, and they'll look a lot better in fifty years.

KM: *If your paintings had sound what would it be like?*
DL: Different paintings would have different sounds. *So This Is Love* would have a muffled sound like talking through a glove. *A Bug Dreams* would be a really shrill 15,000-cycle piercing sound. *She Wasn't Fooling Anyone, She Was Hurt Bad* would be an extremely slow motion, muffled breaking glass sound.

KM: *I also see the work becoming increasingly rough and aggressive. The violence in your work used to be muted and now it's very overt; are you conscious of that?*
DL: I'd like to bite my paintings, but I can't because there's lead in the paint. Which means I'm kind of a chicken. I don't feel I've gotten in there yet, and the paintings still seem safe and tranquil—regardless of what I do, there's still something beautiful about them.

KM: *That you find your work tranquil and beautiful while most people find it disturbing suggests you're unusually comfortable with the dark side of your psyche; why is that?*
DL: I have no idea. I've always been that way. I've always liked both sides and believed that in order to appreciate one you have to know the other—the more darkness you can gather up, the more light you can see too.

KM: *What kinds of things function as seeds for paintings?*
DL: Inspiration is like a piece of fuzz—it kind of comes up and makes a desire and an image that causes me to want to paint it. Or I can be

going along and see an old Band-Aid in the street, and you know how an old Band-Aid is. It's got some dirt around the edges and the rubber part has formed some black little balls, and you see the stain of a little ointment and maybe some yellow dirt on it. It's in the gutter next to some dirt and a rock, and maybe a little twig. If you were to see a photograph of that not knowing what it was, it would be unbelievably beautiful.

KM: *What's your policy on color?*

DL: My policy is that I don't like it, maybe because I haven't learned to use it properly. Whatever the reason it doesn't thrill me—it looks cheap and goofball. Although I like to do brown and brown is a color. I also like earth colors and sometimes I use red and yellow—the red is used for blood a lot and the yellow is used for fire.

KM: *What about your painting is distinctly American?*

DL: The subject matter. A lot of my paintings come from memories of Boise, Idaho, and Spokane, Washington.

KM: *What aspect of the future do you find most disturbing?*

DL: The downhill spiral into chaos. I used to think that the president of the United States had a handle on the future and had some sort of control over what happened over my neighborhood but now we know that isn't true. We're in a time when you can really picture these really tall evil things running at night, just racing. The more freedom you give them, the more they come out and just race, and they're running in every direction now. Pretty soon there'll be so many of them that you can't stop them. It's really a critical time.

KM: *Has the violent aspect of the culture increased or did we just used to police it better?*

DL: It's way bigger now. Dark things have always existed but they used to be in a proper balance with good and life was slower. People lived in towns and small farms where they knew everybody and people didn't move around so much, so things were a little more peaceful. There were things that they were afraid of for sure, but now it's accelerated to where the anxiety level of the people is in the stratosphere. TV sped things up and caused people to hear way more bad news. Mass media overloaded people with more than they could handle, and drugs also had a lot to do with it. With drugs people can get so rich and whacked out and they've opened up a whole weird world. These things have created a modern kind of fear in America.

KM: *Have these things also played a role in the crumbling of the family structure?*
DL: Yeah, all these things are part of the same tension. If you put a jackhammer under a table, pretty soon all the stuff on it starts vibrating and breaking and flying off the table. People have no feeling of security about the future. If you have a job, you're lucky if it lasts until Friday. Macy's is bankrupt and nothing is sure anymore.

KM: *What's the proper course of action when everything around you is crumbling?*
DL: One change of attitude would change everything. If everyone realized that it could be a beautiful world and said let's not do these things anymore—let's have fun.

KM: *Will the world be better or worse in a hundred years time?*
DL: It'll be a much better place.

KM: *What's the most positive change that has occurred in your life in recent years?*
DL: I feel I can venture into any avenue I want. I remember not having enough money to buy canvas. And getting ideas for sculptures but not having any place to build them. It's still not 100 percent—I don't have a shop or darkroom—but I no longer feel restricted by external obstacles, and all the different directions I'm able to move in feed one another. The only material I have a shortage of now is time.

KM: *What's the most difficult aspect of the mass popularity you experienced with* Twin Peaks?
DL: That was pretty troubling. It's nice when people like something that you've done, but it's sort of like love that seems inevitable that the people reach the point when they've had enough of you, and they fall for the next thing. You're helpless to control that process and awareness of it is like a dull ache. It's not like a sharp pain—it's a little bit like heartache, and that heartache is about the fact that we're living in the "Home Alone" age. Art houses are dying. What we have instead are mall cinemas showing twelve pictures and those are the pictures people see. Television has lowered the level and made a certain thing popular, that TV thing moves fast, doesn't have a lot of substance, has a laugh track, and that's all.

KM: *You once made the comment "This is a lesson world and we're supposed to learn stuff"; why are we supposed to learn stuff?*

DL: So we can graduate. School is a good symbol for what we're going through. You graduate and go into another place that's so incredible that we can't even conceive it now. The human being has this potential to have this experience and it has nothing to do with gangs and cars. It's a whole beautiful thing that's completely above it. But you've got to get it together to have that world.

KM: *It's interesting that you have this well ordered, optimistic structure for belief, and yet you still see this great big darkness in existence; how do you explain that disparity?*
DL: It's like being locked in a building with ten maniacs. You know there's a door somewhere and there's a police station across the street where they'll take care of you, but you're still in the building. It doesn't matter what you know about the other places if you're still stuck in the building.

KM: *Do you pray?*
DL: Yes, I do.

KM: *Have you ever had a religious experience?*
DL: Yes I have. Several years ago I was at the LA County Museum of Art, and they had this show of sandstone carvings from India. I was there with my first wife and our daughter Jennifer and I wandered off and got separated from them. There was nobody around, just these carvings, and it was really quiet. I rounded a corner and my eyes went down the corridor and there was a pedestal at the very end. My eyes went up the pedestal and at the top was this head of a Buddha. When I looked at the head, white light shot out of it into my eyes and it was like boom! I was full of bliss. I've had other experiences like that.

KM: *When do you feel powerful?*
DL: Not too often. When you do something that works you have a happiness, but I don't know if it's a feeling of power. Power is a frightening thing and that's not what I'm interested in. I want to do certain things and make them right in my mind and that's it. The fact that you have to go out and get reviews and get theatres and galleries to show your work doesn't jive with what it's about for me. I get heartache out of that part of it.

KM: *What's your fondest memory of your father?*
DL: Him walking to work dressed in a suit and a ten-gallon cowboy hat. We lived in Virginia and it was so embarrassing to me at the time that he

wore this hat, but now I consider it totally cool. It wasn't like a regulation thing—it was a grey-green, forest service ten-gallon cowboy hat, and he'd put his hat on and walk outside the door. He wouldn't go by bus or car or anything, he'd just start walking and he'd walk several miles all the way across the George Washington Bridge into the city in that hat.

KM: *To what degree do we fictionalize our past?*
DL: We favor ourselves in all our memories. We make ourselves act better in the past and make better decisions, and we're nicer to people and we take more credit than we possibly deserve—we candy-coat it so crazy so we can go forward and live. An accurate memory of the past would be depressing, probably.

KM: *Why do we try to find meaning in life? Why is it so difficult to accept the possibility that existence is pointless?*
DL: Because there are so many clues and feelings in the world that it makes a mystery, and a mystery means there's a puzzle to be solved. Once you think like that you're hooked on probably finding a meaning, and there are many avenues in life where we're given little indications that the mystery can one day be solved. We get little proofs—not the big proof—but the little proofs that keep us searching.

KM: *What would the big proof be?*
DL: Total bliss consciousness.

KM: *What do you think happens after death?*
DL: It's like going to sleep after a day of activity. A lot of things happen in sleep and then you wake up and have another day of activity—that's how I see it. I don't know exactly where you go, but I've heard stories about what happens, and there's no denying that dying is the number one fear. We don't even know how long it takes to die. If that person has stopped breathing is that person still in the process of dying? How can we know when they're finished and it's OK to move them? Eastern religions say the soul needs a few days to exit the body, and I've heard that exiting the body is painful. You've gotta kind of pull yourself out of your earthly existence. It's like getting the pit out of a young peach. When George Burns dies, he'll be such an old peach that the pit won't be stuck. That pit will just pop right out there—this will be such a beautiful thing.

Twin Peaks: Fire Walk with Me: The Press Conference at Cannes 1992

S. MURRAY/1992

THE TWIN PEAKS: *Fire Walk with Me* press conference at Cannes featured director and co-writer David Lynch, co-writer Robert Engels, actor Michael J. Anderson (who plays the Man from Another Place), composer Angelo Badalamenti and French producer Jean-Claude Fleury from CIBY 2000.

As is often the case, the press conference was chaired by Henri Béhar, a French journalist and critic who, apart from his long association with Cannes, has just written (with Cari Beauchamp) a particularly witty and readable book on the festival, *Hollywood on the Riviera: The Inside Story of the Cannes Film Festival*.

The following transcription follows as closely as possible the actual press conference. Where questions were asked in French, this is noted, but only Henri Béhar's English translation is given. The text has been edited far less than is usual to keep as much of the flavour as possible. Obviously, questions posed by journalists whose first language is not English are not always grammatically straightforward; equally, David Lynch has an unusual way with English.

It is a requirement at all press conference that journalists identify themselves before asking a question, but in many cases names were not given; in others, the names were so mumbled transcription was impossible. Thus, for consistency's sake, all names are deleted. (Incidentally, the Australian journalist referred to at one point is not this writer but from ABC television.)

From *Cinema Papers* (no. 89, August 1992). Reprinted by permission.

If David Lynch seems less forthcoming than one might expect, the poor reception (of hissing and booing) when he entered may have been partly to blame. Apparently, though, Lynch was unaware of the negative response his film had just received at the press screening in the Grand Palais.

Q: *Mr. David Lynch, I have a two-part question to ask you. The first part is: When you started to make the film, what did you really want—need—to add to a series which has been all around the world? The second part is: For those people who did not know anything about* Twin Peaks *the series, do you think the film is understandable? From the beginning, we are supposed to know who the characters are.*

LYNCH: I happened to be in love with the world of *Twin Peaks* and the characters that exist there. I wanted to go back into the world before it started on the series and to see what was there, to actually see things that we had [only] heard about.

There is a danger, of course, that the more you know about anything, the more depth of appreciation you can get from it. [sic] But I think, although I have been wrong many times in the past, that someone could get very much from [the film] not having seen anything of the series.

There are things in there that they wouldn't understand as much as some others, who have seen the series. But abstractions are a good thing and they exist all around us anyway. They sometimes can conjure up a thrilling experience within the person.

Q: *Mr. Lynch, as you are now under contract [to CIBY 2000[1]], I want to know if you feel as free as before* Blue Velvet? *Didn't you have arguments . . . ?*
BÉHAR: *Are you asking whether CIBY 2000 was a tyrant?*
[Audience laughter followed by a conversation in French between the journalist who put the question and Béhar, who then translates the question.]

Q: *The question is to messieurs Fleury and Lynch. It is well known that you, Mr. Lynch, have signed a contract with CIBY 2000. Do you feel as free under the terms of this contract as you may have been on* Blue Velvet? *And M. Fleury, did you give David Lynch* carte blanche *and a free hand?*

---

1. CIBY has a three-picture deal with Lynch (and also financed Jane Campion's *The Piano*, now in postproduction). One must pronounce "2000" of CIBY 2000 in French to get the allusion [to director Cecil B. DeMille].

[Fleury responds in untranslated French, "Bien sure, . . .," the point being that Lynch and all the directors working within CIBY 2000 have a free hand.]

LYNCH: I don't *parlez vous*ing [sic] Français so well, but I feel very free, very free.

Q: Mr. David Lynch, many characters from the television series are not in this movie, like Audrey. Why?

LYNCH: There are different reasons. Some scenes were shot and they just didn't sit within the story. And some characters, even in the script, didn't find themselves in the story. It was a little bit of a sadness because I would have liked to have everybody there, but they didn't have a bearing on the life of Laura Palmer so much in her last week.

Q: Mr. Lynch, I really loved your film and I would like to ask two questions for you. The first question: What is reality for you?
[Laughter from audience and Lynch.]

BÉHAR: *In twenty-five words or less.*

LYNCH: I haven't got a clue what is reality. I'm sure I'll be surprised when I learn what it is.

Q: *My second question is whether we can consider your film an anti-drugs film?*

LYNCH: Well, um, you know, you could look at it that way if you would like to. [Laughter.]

Q: *[French] You have a very young following, Mr. Lynch. Are you not afraid to make drugs seem desirable? There is a line in the film which says, "All young Americans . . ."*

LYNCH: Half! . . . Half! [Laughter.]

Q: *"Half of the youth in America are on drugs."*

LYNCH: That was a little bit of a joke.

It is very dangerous. If we didn't want to upset anyone, we would make films about sewing, but even that could be dangerous. [Laughter.]

So it's hard to say. But I think, finally, in a film it is how the balance is and the feelings are.

Film exists because we can go and have experiences that would be pretty dangerous or strange for us in real life. We can go into a room and walk into a dream. It doesn't necessarily follow that you are going to go out and start shooting heroin or taking coke. You worry about it. But I think there has to be these contrasts and strong things within a film for the total experience.

Q: *I have a question for Mr. Lynch, and maybe one for Mr. Badalamenti. Congratulations on the film. I had the impression at the end of it that what I had been watching was perhaps an American nightmare, rather than the American dream. Can you comment on that?*
LYNCH: That is a good impression that you got. [Laughter.]

Q: *The life [?] of the American dream appears always in films. We are very aware of the idea of this. You are playing with the whole idea of family and social conscience. Are you trying to attack the American dream?*
LYNCH: No, I was trying to make the story of Teresa Banks [who is murdered at the start] and the last seven days of Laura Palmer. [Applause.]

Q: *Mr. Badalamenti, to me this film also has elements of horror, real gothic horror. In your writing of the score, did you consider that as an element of the film?*
BADALAMENTI: Actually, I think the scoring is more darkness than horror. We imply power through the darkness of the music. At least, that is what the intention was.

Q: *David Lynch, as a filmmaker, do you feel any responsibility for putting such violence in your movies?*
LYNCH: That is the same answer I'm going to give you that the other gentleman got into. I think that it is very dangerous [. . .] that we are attacking films for violence and not doing a whole lot in the world for violence. Film is a safe place to have experiences. Violence exists; it has a major part in a lot of fantastic stories. If [the film] was championing violence it would be one thing, but I don't think it is.

I believe in very strong films and I don't apologize for them one bit, as long as there is a balance to the thing.

Q: *[French] I like the film very much and I haven't seen the television series.*
LYNCH: Fantastic. I will have a lunch with you later on. [Laughter.]

Q: *[French] Question to the scriptwriter and to Mr. David Lynch. What influence did working with familiar characters have on the writing, the scoring and the directing?*
ENGELS: Writing for a film as opposed to writing for a television series didn't feel that much different. You're obviously not restrained by an hour and fourteen pages to an act. But other than that, it was the same

people and you have more time and can be more intense about these people.

BADALAMENTI: Musically speaking, it might be a shade broader and just a little larger than the approach on the television series. But very similar to the characters and the style.

LYNCH: What was the question?

[The question is repeated.]

LYNCH: It didn't affect it so very much at all. There are obviously some things we couldn't do on television that we did in the film, but I was always amazed at how much we could do in television. As well, we were shooting the whole series on film, editing it on film, and mixing it just like on film, so the differences were not so great.

Q: *Mr. Lynch, given [your responses to] some of the other questions this morning, and from talking to you in the past and at other press conferences on other films, I know that when people raise issues about the symbolism that we think we see in your films you like to let things slide. You have glib answers and you're very clever. A couple of examples of that this morning were when the Australian gentleman was asking about whether this was the American nightmare versus the American dream. I personally have great discomfort at the end of the film because of what I see as a sort of puritanical, religious, right-wing attitude to the end of the story. Now, I may be making this up in my own mind. The point is that I feel that we are not allowed to ask you these questions because we won't get answers. And I am wondering if it is because you won't talk about it or you don't want to think about it?*

LYNCH: I don't like to give my interpretations because . . . um, um . . . because if I wasn't around, you'd have to make up your own interpretations of what you see on the screen. And, ah, I have my own version of everything and when I'm working I answer them myself. But when it's over, you set it free and it's on its own and everyone is allowed to enjoy their own interpretation. And I'm against a kind of film that would make absolutely one interpretation available.

Q: *I think it is fair to say that everyone is in love with* Twin Peaks *[the series] except a few select idiots who have Nielson boxes in their homes back home. What can we expect for the future of* Twin Peaks *on television and could you also give us a brief description on what is happening with* Ronnie Rocket *and* One Saliva Bubble?

LYNCH: I can tell you probably for sure that *Twin Peaks* on television is gone. But, like I said earlier on, I love this world. The jury is out on whether or not we will ever be able to go in there again. But for me there are still open ends and clues, and I'd be excited to try and find out what could be going on.

Now, what was the other question?

Q: *What is happening with* Ronnie Rocket *and* One Saliva Bubble?
LYNCH: I'm not going to do *Ronnie Rocket*, or at least I'm not going to do it right away. I think I may be doing *One Saliva Bubble*, but I'm not one hundred percent on that. *One Saliva Bubble* is a very wacko, infantile, bad-humour kind of film.

Q: *I would like to hear the normal voice of Mr. Anderson. I was also wondering if you could explain the shooting of the dream sequence. The atmosphere of this dream is amazing.*
ANDERSON: Well, here's my normal voice. [Laughter.]

What was the second part about? Do you mean technically? We had someone reading the lines offstage frontwards and I would translate them backwards and we would film that backwards. Then, when we showed it forwards two negatives made a positive.

[Anderson then gives example of speaking backwards. Cheers.]

Q: *[French] Mr. Lynch, by retaking, reusing, characters from the series that you have made, is it either a lack of inspiration or you wanted some kind of time-out?*
LYNCH: Well, I think that there are some things in there which, in my opinion, are fairly original and, as I said before, I love the characters and the world. When we started writing this thing, we didn't think of it as rehashing some old thing. We thought about going back into a certain world we love and enjoying a story there. It was, for me, an incredible place to be.

Q: *Mr. Badalamenti, do you think you continue the tradition of Morricone?*
BADALAMENTI: That's quite a compliment.

BÉHAR: *Are you going to score ninety films a year?*
BADALAMENTI: No, I'm not that effusive. I like doing maybe three film scores a year and some television and Broadway. I try to pick my properties very carefully.

But Morricone is great, absolutely.

Q: *[Unintelligible question, which begins "Mr. Lynch, since micro-cosmos is [?] cosmos, what have you learned from micro-cosmos . . ."]*
[Lynch looks at Henri Béhar.]

BÉHAR: *Don't look at me! [Laughter.]*
LYNCH: What was that question once again?

Q: *The micro-cosmos is [???] cosmos, so what have you learned from this movie for your own [???] cosmos . . .*
LYNCH: I'm sorry, I can't help you with the answer. [Laughter.]

Q: *Another question: How do you choose actors you work with?*
LYNCH: Well, when you have a part you picture words said a certain way, you picture a certain look and you enter into a casting session with the idea of finding that person who will fill that role. And, little by little by little, the others are weeded out and the right person is right in front of you and away you go.

I don't read people or make them perform anything. I just talk to them. I also work with a person called Johanna Ray who brings me in very good people. It's just common sense of the right person for each role.

Q: *I am trying to write a thesis about your work and in your movies, except for Teresa Ray [?], the mother is always on [?] the dark side and in* Twin Peaks *it is the father. Is it because he has to draw some sexual relations with Laura or what?*
LYNCH: Again, I'll get into it with you some other way.

Q: *Which character in* Twin Peaks *is closest to you?*
LYNCH: Ah, I don't know . . . Gordon Cole [whom Lynch plays in the film].

Q: *I don't think you're deaf [like Gordon Cole].*
LYNCH: No, but sometimes, like this gentleman said back here, I pretend I'm deaf.

Q: *I have another question, about the score. There is a special part in* Twin Peaks *[the sex scene] which is like a part in* Wild at Heart *[the porno movie]. Is it the same?*
LYNCH: No.

Q: *The guitar?*
LYNCH: No.

BÉHAR: *How do you score a sex scene, Mr. Badalamenti?*
BADALAMENTI: With great interest [Laughter.] I think we just capture the mood of the scene and let the music flow with it.

Q: *Mr. Lynch, I have two questions. The first is that violent films are becoming more and more a normal thing in Hollywood. I would like to know how you feel about violence, especially in your films where the violence is mostly very explicit and particularly in* Twin Peaks, *I think, because it is shown in a very sadistic way.*

LYNCH: Well, I don't know why there is violence in American films; it's probably because there is a lot of violence everywhere in the air. And I think that when people get stories they pick up on whatever is around them and the story starts unfolding in your mind.

Like I said before, I believe in balance. I believe in violence, but I don't want to champion violence. I believe that a film should have contrasts, and I believe that a film is a place where you can go and have an experience, like reading a book.

Q: *But do you find it in a way sadistic? If you followed the television series, you know what happened to Laura Palmer and all you are waiting for in the film is the murder. That is basically the storyline: when is she going to die.*

LYNCH: And a lot of little things along the way, too. But you do know that she is probably going to die, yes.

Q: *My other question is: Do you feel inspired by the American B–movie generation such as the [???] films and the exploitation films of the 1960s and '70s? I find a lot of your work comes from that. Is that true?*

LYNCH: I don't know. I do believe to a certain extent in B films.

Q: *Mr. Lynch, what do you love in the world of* Twin Peaks?

LYNCH: I love the mood and the characters. I love the possibilities for stories. There's a magical thing that can take place in my mind in that world. It's inspiring to me.

Q: *[French] Mr. Lynch, is there an intention of parody in the way the sound effects are used?*

LYNCH: Ah, no.

Q: *I heard this question asked in Berlin of Mr. Scorsese. I would also like your opinion, Mr. Lynch. What do you have more pleasure shooting: horror scenes or suspense scenes?*

LYNCH: I like to shoot all different kind of scenes and that's part of the thing, the textures and the moods. Almost any kind of scene I just love to fall in there and try to make it as real as possible. I wouldn't choose one particular type of scene over something else. I like pretty much everything.

Q: *I would like to follow on from an earlier question about Mr. Lynch saying that he loves this world. If this is true, why do most of the characters have such miserable and fucked-up lives?*

LYNCH: I think there are opportunities for strange exchanges and interesting human motivations in this world. I would have to sit down maybe with a psychiatrist for a long time to tell you exactly why I like it, but I really do like it.

BÉHAR: *Mr. Lynch, when you decided to do a long film on Laura Palmer, was it because you felt you owed the actress for having spent the entire series as a corpse?*

LYNCH: No. Sheryl Lee, who plays Laura Palmer, was hired to be a dead girl laying [sic] on a beach [actually a river bank]. It turns out, at least in my opinion, she's an unbelievable actress, and there are things that she's done in this movie that are truly incredible. I haven't seen too many people get into a role and give it as much. So, the big news for me was this person hired to be a dead girl turns out to be a great actress and a perfect Laura Palmer.

Q: *Mr. Lynch, I know obviously you are a very busy man, but I was wondering if you took time out to see films. What sort of films have you seen lately and have you seen any sort of influence on those films that you consider has possibly come from your films?*

LYNCH: I'm not a real film buff. Unfortunately, I don't have time; I just don't go. And I become very nervous when I go to a film because I worry so much about the director and it is hard for me to digest my popcorn. [Laughter.]

So I can't tell you if anyone has been influenced by me.

Q: *Mr. Lynch and Robert Engels, late twentieth-century literacy means that not only are we able to read the written word but also read the screen. We are inundated with screen images and I was wondering if both of you are keenly aware of that fact when you both write and direct?*

ENGELS: I'm not sure what you're asking.

Q: *Today we are much more image literate than before. There is much more study of form going on. You can happily say that you are going to sit and read a film now without people going, "What's wrong with you?" And you make particularly dense projects. You can sit there and read a David Lynch film. I'm wondering if you come to it from the other end, thinking about this while you're doing it?*

LYNCH: There is a language of film which I have always said is the most magical thing. It's this festival which has been keeping this idea of cinema alive for forty-five years and that is why it's the best film festival in the world because it gets the language of film and celebrates it.

Q: *We heard that the film will be released first in Japan. Did the success of the television series in Japan put...?*
LYNCH: I think Jean-Claude [Fleury] would have to answer that. I know the series is extremely popular in Japan, but it is in other places as well. I don't know why they got it first.

Q: *Another question: Why did you decide to shoot the story of Laura Palmer? Do you think that with the shooting of this story as a film it will to a certain extent dismiss the mystery that was aroused around the world during your serial?*
LYNCH: I don't think so, no.

[Henri Béhar then asks Fleury in French why the film will open first in Japan. Fleury replies in French that it just happened that way; cinemas were available.]

Q: *Mr. Lynch, I have read that Kyle MacLachlan was really afraid to be only known by, and only famous for, this character Dale Cooper and that he was not very enthusiastic about playing in the movie. Is that true? And another question: Are you afraid to become known as the* Twin Peaks *master in the future?*
LYNCH: It is very tough for an actor, I think, to find a role that everyone loves them in and they want to break out and show they can do other things. I think that Kyle is finally realizing that he can do anything else he wants and that people love him as Dale Cooper so much he should be very happy about that.

In the very beginning, he was tired of doing the series, because we'd done thirty-two hours and he didn't know if he wanted to go in and do it again. But then finally he decided that he would and off he went. He didn't want to do *Blue Velvet*, either. He turned it down, then thought about it and changed his mind a couple of times.

It is a very tough thing to make a decision to buy into something for a year and have to go on the screen and all that. So, he had to think about it some.

Q: *[French] Without passing a moral judgment, many would probably define you as a very perverse director. Would you agree?*
LYNCH: I think perverse things are interesting and non-perverse things are interesting. I like contrasts, like I said. I like perversity and non-perversity; both things.

Q: *Let's say you're the campaign strategist for the Democratic or Republican party. You take the night off and go and see this movie. Would you come out of there thinking this was good for your campaign or bad, which may be another way of asking how you think Americans will see the film in terms of the political and social climate?*

LYNCH: Just as you see from this press conference, there have been many different interpretations and feelings about anything we see these days. You can't please all the people and everyone of those Democrats going to see the picture would come out with a different feeling, most likely. It's the same all the world over.

Q: *Mr. Lynch, I'm interested in the use of dead-pan humour in your work. There seems to be more of it in the series than in the movie. In the series, you encourage a complicity with the audience; they feel like they are in on something. That is part of why it was so popular. So why do you have less of it in the movie? And why is it that you are one of the few directors who wants everyone to have a separate opinion about your work?*

LYNCH: It isn't that everyone must have a completely separate one, but they have to have their own opinion.

There is less humour in this film because the story gets heavy after awhile. Humour has a place in a picture, but you have to know sort of intuitively where that place is and where it isn't. But Bob and I were laughing while we were writing many times, at various places.

ENGELS: It goes back to the story, I think. You pick out the story you are trying to tell. It's the same with characters that are in the series that aren't in the movie. We chose to tell this story and that's how it comes out.

LYNCH: I think humour is like electricity. You work with it but you don't understand how it works. It's an enigma.

Q: *David Lynch, could you tell me the purpose of the dream sequences in the film and in the series?*

LYNCH: No, ma'am. [Laughter.]

Q: *It is an integral part of the film. Why did you feel you wanted to use a sort of [???] reality?*

LYNCH: [Long pause.] Well, for me, and I think for pretty much everybody that's ever been, there's a feeling that there might be something like subatomic particles existing that we can't see and x-rays and maybe a few other things out there and that a little opening could exist and we could go somewhere else. And this kind of idea excites me.

BÉHAR: *Ladies and gentlemen, thank you very much.*

LYNCH: Thank you very much.

[Applause. Conference ends.]

Naked Lynch

GEOFF ANDREW/1992

THERE IS A PARADOX about David Lynch. If *Eraserhead, Blue Velvet, Wild at Heart,* and *Twin Peaks* have ensured his reputation as the brain behind some of America's weirdest films, he has tended to present himself as the epitome of ordinariness: a regular guy of uncommonly mundane habit, whose inspiration springs naturally from the depths of his unconscious, not from the intellect. But I suspect it's not that simple. Just as *Wild at Heart* appeared contrived—the weirdness a mannerist affectation as opposed to the genuinely disturbing oddity of his best work—so Lynch's banal persona sometimes seems calculated to emphasise his strangeness. Why, for example, when we meet in Cannes' Carlton Hotel, does he feel the need to don not only his now familiar dark suit and buttoned-up shirt (*sans cravate*, obviously), but the baseball cap as well? After all, he's only had to walk up one floor from his suite, and he doesn't even keep the millinery on during our half-hour together. It's almost as if he comes complete with uniform; but is there a sentient human being behind the obligatory threads?

I should admit that this impression is coloured partly by my feelings about *Twin Peaks: Fire Walk with Me*, the movie we're here to discuss. At its first press screening in the Palais des Festivals, anticipatory excitement soon turns to disappointment, so that any cheers over the end credits are swamped by cat-calls. Even more than *Wild at Heart*, the new film suggests a director simply going through his paces; indeed, as it proceeds to cover the last week of Laura Palmer's life (this after a lengthy prologue about a murder investigated a year earlier), the film appears to be a deeply cynical exercise, a blatant attempt to cash in on the success

---

From *Time Out London* (18 November 1992). Reprinted by permission.

of the TV series. None of it is properly thought through, let alone original or heartfelt; the overwhelming impression is that Lynch is churning out exactly what he imagines "Tweakies" will expect and no more. Sadly, the same can be said for the first half-hour episode of his upcoming TV series *On the Air*, a sitcom set in a poverty-row '50s television station, which not only reaffirms his ineptitude with outright comedy, but provokes the suspicion that he is slipping ever more depressingly into self-parody.

Small wonder, then, that he appears so listless when asked to explain and discuss *Fire Walk with Me*. Is this reticence just part of the Ordinary Joe pose? Perhaps, but nothing he says suggests that he is prepared, or even able, to examine and confront his work in any depth. Maybe he has fallen victim to the cult-worship and grown lazy, but the question remains the same. Is the inarticulacy an act? If so, it's boring and dumb; if not . . . well, judge for yourself.

GA: *Why make a movie-offshoot of the TV series?*
DL: I wanted to go back into the world of *Twin Peaks*. I felt very bad when the series ended. And rather than go forward, I fell in love with the idea of going back into the last week of Laura Palmer's life. It just caught hold of me and that was the seed of it.

GA: *But why make a film, rather than continue the series?*
DL: It just had to be a film.

GA: *So do you think there's an inherent difference between film and television?*
DL: No, not really. My experience was that television was for me little films. The frustrating part was that it moves so fast, you can't direct each one of them yourself. The main difference is the speed, the hunger of television; if you were extremely prepared upfront with a million episodes, it would be one thing—but that's never the case. With a film you can fall into it and concentrate on it.

GA: *Did the logistics of going back to the same subject—such as getting the right cast, sets, and so forth—present any problems?*
DL: Well, many things existed. Seattle and the surrounding area existed. So it came together pretty fast.

GA: *Would you have made the film had the series not been so successful?*
DL: I don't know. I think I would've. I love that world: there's something about trees and cars and a little town that gets me going.

GA: *But what is it that makes you love those things so much?*
DL: I just love that setting. It conjures up mysterious things in my head. I like the stories, characters, the possibilities of things that could happen in that setting.

GA: *So would you do another* Twin Peaks *film?*
DL: Yes. It could go on forever. I'd like to do different things as well, but I feel so comfortable in that world.

GA: *Is it good for an artist to feel that comfortable?*
DL: Well, let's say comfortable like inspired; not comfortable like sit back and watch the scenery. It's an inspiring place. There are mysteries there for me.

(Evidently, Lynch is not big on discussing motivation; time to check out if he's any happier with meaning.)

GA: *The film seems to imply that there are mysterious forces influencing our lives, strange gods watching over us. Do you believe that?*
DL: I don't know anything for sure, but I think there are a lot of things going on that we don't see, which make themselves known through feelings or strange ideas that pass through the mind. It's like picking up on stuff. Like when you go into a room where there's been an argument, you sense something's wrong. It's like radio waves going on all the time and you just need a receiver to listen to them—you can't see them, but you can pick them up at times.

GA: *Many of your films might be seen as accounts of moral and social breakdown; is that how you see the world?*
DL: I don't know, but I think that in every generation people are shocked by things that are going on. It's a relative sort of thing. But probably, you know, it's pretty bad these days.

GA: *So is there anything in particular that shocks or disturbs you?*
DL: Well, it's more of a sadness that so many people are in trouble of some sort.

GA: *Economically, or how?*
DL: In many ways. There seem to be people in trouble.

GA: *Why do you think that is?*
DL: I haven't got a clue. I don't know whether we're looking out for number one too much and pretending it's all gonna be okay, but it's gradually coming apart.

(So, he's not hot on meaning, either. Let's try tone and narrative method.)

GA: *Though your films often paint a harrowing portrait of life, they're also funny in parts. So how seriously should we take them?*
DL: Well, everyone takes things differently. I never say how someone is supposed to take something. When you read a book, you take it as you see it; that's the way with a film. A hundred people see it and have a hundred different takes on it. It's an amazing thing.

GA: *But do you take your films seriously?*
DL: Yes, they're serious to me. But it's not that there's a certain point where you can switch straight over to humour. Humour exists in the midst of serious things, or in the wrong place. It's the weirdest intersections in life. People get together that are very different and strange things are said, meanings are misunderstood. It's just the way it is.

GA: *Frankly, I had trouble making sense of the film's prologue section, in terms of the narrative leaps and the deductions being made about the murder. Does it all make sense to you?*
DL: It does and it doesn't. It's like opening a window and looking for a moment; then closing it and asking someone to explain an hour's worth of scenario when they've only seen a small bit. It was like impressions a detective might get—a prologue of sensations, of feelings, trying to capture something. The FBI don't have a clue what's happening, but they have their sensors going.

GA: *Did you worry that audiences might not understand what was happening?*
DL: I think some people might have that feeling, but not all the film is that way. Some things are just, you know, abstractions. There are people who analyse dreams for a profession, and yet each person having a dream could maybe make up a meaning for themselves. They could roll it around and that kind of thing.

GA: *Is one of your aims to show that plot-logic need not be important?*
DL: It is and it isn't. It would be the greatest thing if you could be left with some vagueness, some imagination at the end of a film, when so often you're robbed of the magic. That vagueness makes me dream, and I love it. Like, in a Bergman film there are so many things I don't understand, but they make me dream and thrill my soul. And it opens a window on sort of an infinite thing.

GA: *Would you say there are any very personal elements in your films?*
DL: You can't read anything into them that way. When you work you don't think that way. There's a channel open and you go with it. You check things with a certain part of yourself, try to be true to the ideas, and you go. Maybe there's a link to me personally—there probably is—but I don't know what it would be.

GA: *So you're an intuitive rather than analytical filmmaker?*
DL: Purely, yes.

Interview

CHRIS DOURIDAS/1997

CD: *I'm Chris Douridas, the* Morning Becomes Eclectic *on KCRW. Happy to have in the studio, David Lynch. Welcome.*
DL: Gracias. Good to be here, man.

CD: *You know,* Wild at Heart *was drawn from a preexisting novel by Barry Gifford, and now,* Lost Highway *is drawn from a novel by Barry Gifford but really just a couple of words from the book, right?*
DL: Two words, um ...

CD: *Two words!?*
DL: Barry Gifford wrote a book called *Night People*. Two characters mention going down the lost highway, and when I read those words "lost" and "highway," it made me dream, and it suggested possibilities, and I told that to Barry and he said, "Well, let's write something." And that started the ball rolling.

CD: *So the two of you just sat around and sort of let your minds fly free?*
DL: Right, we sat down, both sharing ideas that we'd been collecting, and neither one of us liked the other's ideas. And we sat there for quite a long time in silence, and then I told Barry an idea that had come to the me the last night of shooting *Fire Walk with Me*. And it was the videotapes and a couple. And Barry loved this idea, and when you focus on an idea, even though it's a fragment, it opens the door to other fragments that want to hook themselves to that idea and away we went.

CD: *So when you say focus on an idea, do you literally carry this with you through your day, around you as you live and work and move across the earth?*
DL: Exactly. Ideas, some of them, are very powerful and some of them

---

From the *Morning Becomes Eclectic* radio show, broadcast by KCRW (Los Angeles, CA) on 19 February 1997. Reprinted by permission of KCRW. Transcribed by Melissa Musser.

you fall in love with. And when you fall in love, you know, when you're in love, the focus is not a problem and the being in love and the idea create a magnet, and it pulls from this avenue, it pulls the rest.

CD: *Well, I was wondering if there was any kind of random quality to the writing of this film. And indeed there were—you brought two unrelated stories together to help propel you into this.*

DL: Yeah, there's always fragments that are strange because you don't know how they're going to arrange themselves. And so Barry and I were further down the road before we realized what it was that was happening; and so it's a surprise. It's like being inside an experience and it tells you how to go.

CD: *Makes me think of Bowie's idea of cutting up words and phrases and putting them together to make a song, a lyric.*

DL: Right. There's a lot of serendipity. You can set things up for accidents and many times it will trigger a brand new thing and accidents have helped me a lot.

CD: *So you've actually described this as a Moebius strip, which is a phrase I wasn't familiar with until this morning.*

DL: Right.

CD: *This is a scientific term, a term in mathematics from what I understand, to describe an object when the inside surface becomes the outside surface. Sort of like Escher, an Escher drawing.*

DL: It twists in on itself and comes back to the beginning. And this idea of a Moebius strip is not something we were thinking about in the beginning, but it presented itself.

CD: *I see. So it conjured that up toward the end.*

DL: Exactly right.

CD: *Now was there more written than what we saw up on the screen?*

DL: Always a script is a blueprint. And you think very seriously that this is what you are going to be making, but the process continues. Always new things come in, small fragments or large changes, you know, happen along the way. Always it's talking. Always you're checking back to the original idea, but the film wants to be a certain way, and it's not finished till it's finished. So, you just follow your intuition.

CD: *Well, that's the key word there, intuition. I mean as you double check what you're doing as you're building the film, as you go back and look at what you're up to, it's always about the intuitive, isn't it?*

DL: Exactly right. It's a feeling of knowing what is correct. And it sounds abstract but it's really fairly simple.

CD: *So has it ever happened where you shoot too much, and there's just too much information there, and you have to pull things away from the audience, and say, "Well, this is too much, we have to give room for their own intuition."*

DL: When the film is finally cut together and you see it as a whole, more often than not, it doesn't work. And always before even working with fragments, pieces of this a whole scene but it's not the whole. Then, when you see the whole and it's not working, it's another series of experiments to get the whole thing to work together and then there's the mixing, sounds and music, and that alters things and . . .

CD: *. . . And can save you!*

DL: It can do magic. But it's not foolproof. It's always feeling your way.

CD: *Now, when you see the film on the screen in its final form, how close is it to the film you felt in your head, that you saw in your own head before the whole thing sorted and it took shape?*

DL: In a lot of ways it's very, very close. But usually, it's more beautiful. It's better than what you first imagined. Some scenes may be almost exactly and other things, because of finding locations that weren't exactly the locations in your mind, you know, there's differences. But the mood and feeling, and this since you have those original ideas to check back on, is usually fairly close, but you know, because it wants to be the way it is, there's always a feeling, a difference than what you first imagined it as well.

CD: *What about the viscosity of it? Do you govern yourself? Do you put a govern on yourself, "This is too intense, I can't go where I want to go"?*

DL: That's part of the intuition; it is an experiment in many ways, and you can see that this is not enough, that this is too much, and that this is just perfect. It's finding your way and taking advantage of accidents and setting up a situation where they can occur, and so when you translate an idea into a medium, the medium plays a part, and that's really beautiful, to see what cinema can do with the ideas, and you feel your way through.

CD: *The lens of the medium. Now, do you double check your intuition with anybody, or is it simply yourself that you rely on for that?*

DL: There's many people that can give you ideas and suggestions, and you'd be a fool to turn down a good idea. And you have to throw out the bad. But all these things should filter through one filtering system so that the whole thing has a chance to hold together. Films by committees, you know—I'm sure there's exceptions to this—generally speaking they just don't hold together.

CD: *And it's sort of that narrative form, that layering down of too much information for the audience that you've been backing away from. I mean, when we look at* Twin Peaks, *the show built itself on this large and great mystery. Once it was unfolded the show sort of lost its momentum. Was that in some way a lesson for you, that we can't give the audience too much information? We can't . . .*

DL: You can give them information but not the wrong information. In the case of *Twin Peaks*, Mark Frost and I never intended to solve the murder of Laura Palmer—it may recede into the background, but it needed to be there because that was the mystery that enabled everything to happen. And once it was gone, it was over, and the show just drifted. So human beings love mysteries. I love a mystery that at the end of the mystery allows you room to dream. Continue the dream.

CD: *For a long time people expected that you were a guy that had a troubled childhood. That you grew up in some sort of mad environment, when in fact the opposite is true, and sort of the opposite has come out since then that you had a pretty perfect childhood growing up.*

DL: Trent could've named his song, "The Perfect Childhood." You know when you're. . . . No matter what type of childhood you have, there's a feeling that you're sensing more than what you're seeing in front of you. That's one of the things I remember from being young. A lot of information comes to us, not in the form of words or pictures, it's a feeling in the air.

CD: *Do you remember when you first had that feeling?*

DL: I think very early on, but I think I was living in Spokane, Washington.

CD: *I think at one point you had said it was the study of science. That when a kid goes through that they start to discover there's an inevitability to life.*

DL: Science . . . you know, in a way scientists are detectives and we are all detectives. And you start someplace, and the mystery leads you deeper either into the material world or an emotional world and we're searching and adding up information and it's just the way it is.

CD: *I guess at some point you do learn growing up that there is a probability of something not to be what it appears, and that is a recurring theme in your work. It's heightened, because of course of the medium, but it does sort of reflect that quality of life, that essence of life.*

DL: Exactly right.

CD: *Now there's another thing. You've described your youth as you were the guy that didn't really have the lights on upstairs or something like that, and there was this turning point where you started to make these realizations. That sort of ducktails with your descent, or I shouldn't say descent, but exploration of painting and artistic creative pursuits.*

DL: Right, I might have been storing up information, but in terms of painting I was pretty naive. Hadn't been getting a lot of information to speed up the evolution of ideas. And it was Philadelphia, Pennsylvania, that kicked in, you know, a kind of original thinking. It felt original, it felt like I was finding something on my own. And Philadelphia at that time was a very strange city, and sometimes a person needs an environment; the environment can be so powerful to kick in ideas and even fear can be a motivation.

CD: *Well, yeah, there's a wonderful quote from you. "Once you're exposed to fearful things you begin to worry that the peaceful, happy life could vanish or be threatened."*

DL: This is something I think we all understand.

CD: *Well, it's a fascinating juxtaposition of that innocence and naiveté with the man who knew too much, for example.*

DL: Exactly.

CD: *There's a song that is in the film ["Song to the Siren"] but not on the soundtrack, from This Mortal Coil, that I understand you have a long history with.*

DL: Right, I heard the song in the '80s and I'm not sure whether it was '85, but I really pretty desperately wanted to use it in *Blue Velvet*, and it was tied up in some sort of legal thing, or it was either that or something involving a lot of money, and we couldn't get it. And it broke my heart, but on the other hand not having This Mortal Coil's "Song to the Siren" led me to Angelo Badalamenti and Angelo, you know, I've worked with ever since. Angelo really brought me into the world of music, right into the middle of it.

CD: *So this not being able to use "Song to the Siren" led you to go to an alternative.*
DL: Exactly, the alternative was "Mysteries of Love" that Angelo wrote and I fell in love with. I didn't think I would—I thought, there's a million songs, how can Angelo write something that is going to take the place of this? And it was strange. It took the place of it, and continued this great, great relationship I have with Angelo.

CD: *And when* Lost Highway *came around there was another opportunity to use the track.*
DL: Right. I'd been waiting and waiting, and there it was, and it's definitely high on my list as one of the all time most beautiful songs.

CD: *How come it didn't end up on the soundtrack?*
DL: Ivo, the producer, was happy for it to be in the film, but it's something very emotional to Ivo and he didn't want to exploit it any further.

CD: *Well, that much you have in common, the power of song has a place with you as well.*
DL: Exactly right.

[Intermission, "Song to the Siren" and Marilyn Manson's cover of "I Put a Spell on You" is played.]

CD: *Marilyn Manson's "I Put a Spell on You"—what a great cover that is.*
DL: A great cover.

CD: *Marilyn Manson, another gift to the world from Trent Reznor.*
DL: Exactly right. Marilyn is a guy who I think is sitting on a very modern thing and getting bigger every day.

CD: *Yeah, he turns up in* Lost Highway *in a little cameo.*
DL: Exactly right.

CD: *So, Marilyn Manson is one contribution of Trent Reznor, but also he's been on tour with David Bowie, there's that connection. He's transformed I think an aspect of film culture, soundtrack medium, to a new level. And he can connect to thirteen-year-olds.*
DL: Amazing.

CD: *A lot going on there, yeah. The film I understand was actually shot, in part, at one of your houses, right?*
DL: Right.

CD: *Is this true that you own three houses all next to each other?*

DL: That's true, I've been very fortunate. During preproduction I got a hold of this third house, and we were able to destroy portions of it and build it back to work with the story. So it's almost like being on a sound stage, but you can go outside as well.

CD: *And you lived at this location?*

DL: Right.

CD: *For some time now?*

DL: Right.

CD: *This is not unusual for you, for you to actually live at the sets where you're making your films.*

DL: Well, you would live there mentally, but it's very nice to live there physically.

CD: *I mean, physically you've lived at* Eraserhead.

DL: Yeah, I lived in Henry's apartment for a good number of years, and you feel the mood, and you live it, eat it, and breathe it, and you can imagine each day more of the outer world doesn't in reality exist, but it just reinforces the mood and helps seep into the film.

CD: *You get to know the environment intimately.*

DL: Right.

CD: *You can explore and exploit it.*

DL: Exactly right.

CD: *Now in a perfect world if you didn't have the bothers of everyday life and had a film before you that you wanted to accomplish, what would be the process? I mean, what is the typical process in a perfect world for you?*

DL: Well, in a perfect world, because there's so much pleasure involved with entering another world and experiencing it, that aspect of *Eraserhead* would be great, that living in the sets, or living in the location, to experience it and to slow down the filmmaking process a little bit. Sometimes it goes so fast that you get what you need, but you haven't really enjoyed sitting in Fred Madison's living room for a moment and thinking. I mean, I got that opportunity, but you know what I mean.

CD: *Fred Madison being the lead character.*

DL: Fred Madison being the lead character in *Lost Highway*. So I think it's pretty important that you have a very deep experience of the environment.

CD: *So would you say that most films that we actually see are glimpses of what the original idea was?*
DL: I wouldn't say that. I think there's a lot of people out there realizing their ideas and . . .

CD: *. . . taking them to their furthest . . .*
DL: Yes, I think people, you know, like they say, no one sets out to make a bad film.

CD: *Of course.*
DL: And it's a lot of work. Those who have been through the process know that. It's just that I'm sure people would agree the deeper you can go into the world, the better it is for the film.

CD: *Well, you said the joy of filmmaking is in part relating to the fact you are creating an environment and a world you have total control over. That you leave reality for awhile and you create this other environment that you have dominion over.*
DL: Right. And then married to that is what film and sound and music can do in translating the ideas happening in this environment, and the medium of film is so powerful it is an experiment, and it is so much farther to go, this beautiful medium. And so it's just beautiful to see how it can work on ideas that are concrete or abstract.

CD: *And at this point you're sort of exploring those fringe . . . well, you're just sort of pushing the envelope at this time in your life.*
DL: Well, it's all in the world of human behavior, which is a wide range as we all know. There's so many possibilities in this beautiful thing of humans behaving in this world. And that has a long way to go being explored.

CD: *Like how much of our brains we're not using, right?*
DL: Exactly.

CD: *You are credited on the film as sound designer as well. What does that mean? What did you actually do?*
DL: Well, you always work with other people. And we had some great people, you know, working on sounds. But every single thing you as a director are involved in, it has to be a certain way in your mind to work with the whole. It's critical, and it's based on a feel. And so it's working with people to get all these different sounds to be correct, and also taking advantage of serendipity and accidents. So it's a group effort but passing through one filter.

CD: *And it's not typically an aspect of a director's job. What you were doing was more involved?*

DL: Well, I'm sitting at the board. I'm actually on the board mixing music, but I think, as in the case of everyone on the crew, after awhile everyone tuned into that one original doorway that Barry and I experienced, and pretty soon things start going right in tune with those original ideas and so you move as one.

CD: *We got a call from somebody who brought up the name Alan Splet, who was a sound designer. And when we mentioned his name to you, you smiled.*

DL: Alan was one of my very best friends. He's passed away, and Alan and I, you know, met in Philadelphia, and he and I worked on the sound for *The Grandmother* and became great friends, and I worked with Alan through *Blue Velvet*, and never would do anything without Al. One of the most sensitive human beings with a tremendous love of sound and music.

CD: *I would imagine he would've had a great deal of impact on how you sat at the board on* Lost Highway.

DL: Exactly right.

CD: *Now, we already know the work of Angelo Badalamenti, and you've been longtime collaborators, and he, as you said earlier this morning, brought you into the world of music. What do you mean by that exactly?*

DL: Well, I've always been interested in sound effects that approach music, and maybe obey some of the same rules—they are music. But I never got deep into working with a composer and having that experience of being able to fall into the world of music, and Angelo invited me into that world and encouraged it, and many great experiences have come out of that.

CD: *Well, there's actually a new bit of experience you've brought with you this morning that is essentially a demo of sorts?*

DL: It's a demo, yeah.

CD: *This is a woman . . .*

DL: Her name is Jocelyn West, she's from England, plays the fiddle and sings.

CD: *So you guys, together, you and Angelo . . .*

DL: She came in for a five-minute meeting, it lasted seven hours, and we ended up with this song, "And Still." I wrote the lyrics with Artie Polemisis's wife. Artie runs the studio in New York, his wife Estelle and I wrote the lyrics.

[Intermission, "And Still" is played.]

CD: *It's called "And Still," Jocelyn West. This is from a demo produced by, David Lynch, I guess, and Angelo Badalamenti, music by Angelo?*
DL: Right.

CD: *And no sign of when this will be surfacing I guess.*
DL: No sign.

CD: *Working in the studio with a musician or a singer must be similar to working with an actor in front of a camera.*
DL: It's very similar, and through strange dialogue or things passing through the air, a hand gesture, you find your way. A dialogue between me and Angelo sends us going, and when a minute follows and another, maybe even time disappears, and suddenly there is something.

CD: *And it's that way with your actors? I mean you sort of guide them in a broad sense?*
DL: Well, at first with an actor you start one place and you talk, you rehearse, you talk, you rehearse, and little by little you're coming closer to that place where you're united with the original ideas, that same doorway, and then you're rolling.

CD: *How much rehearsal goes into these scenes?*
DL: In the case of *Lost Highway*, I rehearsed with Balthazar [Getty], Bill Pullman and Patricia Arquette—it would be nice longer, but it was two weeks of rehearsal before we started shooting.

CD: *How about Robert Blake?*
DL: Robert Blake required no rehearsal.

CD: *It's one of the most—I don't have words to describe the fear he conjures up in this film.*
DL: People are going nuts over Robert Blake.

CD: *Where did you dig him up? Where's he been?*
DL: He's been here, and you know, he's got the stuff; there's no two ways about it.

CD: *Since he was two!*
DL: Since he was three, I think he's been acting. He's a great guy and has a thousand stories.

CD: *Well, what else is going on with you? You've been doing a comic strip for some time, "The Angriest Dog in the World." Are you still...*
DL: No, they pulled the plug on "The Angriest Dog in the World."

CD: *How long ago was that?*
DL: That was in '92! It went for nine years, and it had a good run.

CD: *I just thought it wasn't in Los Angeles anymore, and it was elsewhere, or something.*
DL: Right... No, it died the death.

CD: *Well, any other mediums that you have...*
DL: I'm painting, you know, still. I've always been painting. I had a show in Paris recently, and a show in Japan.

CD: *When is it going to come to Los Angeles?*
DL: I've got a gallery here, the Cone Turner Gallery. I had a show there a year and a half ago, maybe two years ago, and I don't know when I'll have another show, but you know, I'm deeply, deeply in love with the world of painting.

CD: *Now what about this idea of kits?*
DL: Kits started in London. I bought a fish and cut it up... like an airplane kit that you buy and assemble the parts.

CD: *Now you got a fish where, at the fish market?*
DL: At the fish market. And I took it home, and then I...

CD: *...dismembered it.*
DL: ...assembled it, took it home to disassemble it, photograph it, to make it look like something one could put together and enjoy.

CD: *So that, you call a Fish Kit?*
DL: A Fish Kit. And then I did a Chicken Kit in Mexico.

CD: *So there are two of these kits in existence.*
DL: Yeah, there's a Duck Kit but it didn't turn out too well.

CD: *Hmm... How did it not turn out well?*
DL: The photograph—there were so many parts and it didn't quite catch the details of the small parts.

CD: *That's a complicated animal!*
DL: Yeah, a duck, it's a... well, one of the most beautiful animals.

CD: *Now you've actually compared the art of filmmaking to . . .*
DL: A duck. Nature is a great teacher, and many of the things that happen in nature can guide you in your other avenues.

CD: *Now I understand there was a coffee table book you were putting together of collected visual works reflecting your interest in—dental hygiene?*
DL: Well, I was very interested in dental hygiene because as a kid, you know . . . soft, bad teeth and always visiting the dentist. I have a dentist now, Dr. Chin in Santa Monica, who I think is the world's greatest dentist.

CD: *There goes an ad!*
DL: O.K., I'm sorry, but he's fantastic. I enjoy the dental—the different machines and textures of dentistry, and so I did some photos to reflect that enjoyment.

CD: *So where to from here in terms of the film work?*
DL: I'm now in the sad spot of having to try to find the next thing, you know, to catch an idea, and it's frustrating because I don't know when that will happen. So, I wish that I could start a film right away.

CD: *You've described this catching of an idea in a similar fashion to the way songwriters who come through here describe the way they'll catch a song. Sometimes—as I've quoted Tom Waits before, I'll do it again—songs are like cartoon characters, sometimes you don't really get the songs at all, you get their underwear, you know, you get the song's underwear, you're trying to grab it . . .*
DL: Right . . . well, there's many ways to say the same thing. Everybody relies on ideas. Ideas are the most important things. Every single thing in the world that was made by anyone started with an idea. So to catch one that is powerful enough to fall in love with, it is one of the most beautiful experiences. It's like being jolted with electricity and knowledge at the same time.

CD: *Is there anything you've learned that helps you to be more receptive to these chance occurrences?*
DL: Well, you know, I'm a meditator, and the idea of that is to expand consciousness by clearing the machines of consciousness, which is the nervous system, and the greater the consciousness—I think in the analogy of fishing—the deeper your hook can go to catch the bigger ideas. And it's very important to get down in there. Sitting comfortably,

in a chair, drifting off, not trying to manipulate what's in front of you, sometimes you can drop into a beautiful area or bounce up to a higher one—whichever way you want to see it—into a beautiful area and catch ideas.

CD: *Is there any medium you haven't explored that you have an interest in? Radio, for example?*

DL: I've never explored radio, but seeing you here in this environment is pretty inspiring.

CD: *Well, if you come up with any ideas you want to try out on KCRW let us know.*

DL: You got a deal.

CD: *Thanks so much for joining us.*

DL: Chris, it was really a pleasure.

CD: *David Lynch, the* Morning Becomes Eclectic *on KCRW. This is one that's sort of another work in progress.*

DL: It's a demo done with Don Valzone, Andy Armor, Dave Jurike, and Steve Hodges.

CD: *We'll hear as much of it as we can.*

DL: O.K., thanks a lot, Chris.

CD: *David Lynch.*

The World Reveals Itself

KATHRIN SPOHR/1997

SEX, VIOLENCE, and madness prevail: With his films, David Lynch has painted a cryptic picture of the States. He sees *Eraserhead* (1976), *Blue Velvet* (1986), *Wild at Heart* (1990) and his current project *Lost Highway* all as "travelogues from Hell." Hardly any other director is as controversial. And hardly any other has so rejuvenated U.S. cinema. Art vs. kitsch? Lynch does not believe they are opposites. After all, he loves crossing borders: "Design and music, art and architecture—they belong together." And he has been designing furniture for years. Secretly. Now he reveals all, in the first interview he has granted a design journal.

FORM: *You're internationally renowned as a film director, actor, and creator of the meanwhile legendary* Twin Peaks *TV series. But your passion lies not only with cinema and television. You've composed music with Angelo Badalamenti. You're a writer. And a painter . . . Recently, your pictures were on show in Paris. And now we find out that you've been designing furniture for some time. What else can we expect to find you doing?*
DAVID LYNCH: Don't worry. I don't want to appear like some all-round talent. Not at all. I just inevitably get involved with different things.

I started out being a painter. And like many painters I was looking for a new challenge. Because it is not easy to make money with art. After all, just to build canvas stretchers, and stretch a canvas you get involved with a lot of tools. And one thing always leads to another: Pretty soon I was building things.

It's a special outlook. You build your own world. And, in my case, my father always had a workshop in the house, and I was taught how to use

From *Form* (no. 158, February 1997). Reprinted by permission of Kathrin Spohr and *Form*.

tools and spent a lot of time in the shop building things, so it all started at a young age.

FORM: *So furniture design is nothing new for you?*
DL: Right. I've always been interested in it.

FORM: *Is there a particular element that connects all of your creative activities?*
DL: Well, film brings most mediums together. Painting, building furniture, or working with Angelo in music is like an avenue and is initially it's own thing. Sure, you can get lost in those specific things completely. And if you get an idea for some table or some piece of furniture, it's pretty thrilling.

FORM: *In April, you are presenting a collection at the world's most important and famous furniture exhibition, the Salone del Mobile in Milan. The furniture will be produced. Are you planning a second career as a designer?*
DL: Yes . . . I've got many ideas.

FORM: *And when did you start designing furniture?*
DL: Well, when I started I never really thought of myself as a furniture designer. I would just get an idea and build something.

In art school I started building things based on my own designs. And then things kind of went from there.

But now, I'd like to get hooked up with a company that could produce my stuff. When somebody is interested in following through, then ideas really start flowing, and you need an outlet, and people to back you.

FORM: *You actually started building things while a student in the sixties?*
DL: Yes, right. During the decade of change . . .

FORM: *Well, what about the tables on show in Milan. How old are they?*
DL: The "Espresso Table" is about five years old. The others are newer.

FORM: *People often associate violence, some special desires, and nightmares with your movies. In this context, it seems to be a far cry to design.*
DL: That could be, but films, paintings, furniture, etc. are all based on ideas. You get an idea. And then you're hooked.

Not to forget: I love building. And building is as important as designing, because many times design grows as one is building.

FORM: *It's not very common for directors to design furniture for their movies themselves.*

DL: Could be. But sometimes I see a need for a certain piece of furniture in a certain place. It'd take too much time to search for a specific piece. And it's more fun for me to build it on my own.

FORM: *Have you ever attempted to sell your furniture?*
DL: Well, years ago I sold my first little table to Skank World, on Beverly Drive. Skank World is a small place featuring fifties design and furniture—I love the place. But people don't normally go there to buy new furniture. So, it didn't work out. But since then I haven't worked on selling my furniture again. Till now, that is.

FORM: *Are you looking to have your designs produced in large numbers?*
DL: No. First a small series, but not a limited edition. I hope the series will generate sales and become larger.

FORM: *Some of your tables are very small. It seems as if they are only large enough for one purpose at one special time. The Steel Block Table, for example, looks as if there's only a space for an espresso cup, or some glasses. Another table is for one coffee mug and an ashtray. What's the secret behind these miniature tables?*
DL: To my mind, most tables are too big and they're too high. They shrink the size of the room and eat into space and cause unpleasant mental activity.

FORM: *Have you considered how the public in Milan may interpret your furniture?*
DL: No, not a bit. (laughs).

FORM: *It's obvious from your movies that wood attracts you. In your office there is a perfectly equipped carpentry workshop. At the premiere of* Lost Highway *here in Los Angeles you held a speech in which wood functioned as a metaphor for quality of content in films. How did you come up with such an association?*
DL: Well, wood is a very special material, and since the dawn of time people have been chopping down these trees and working with wood. Most wood will take a nail and not split apart. And wood can be cut with a saw and carved with chisels and smoothed. It has this beautiful grain, there's something that goes right to your soul.

FORM: *Isn't such praise of wood and handicrafts a little anachronistic nowadays?*
DL: I've always been interested in industrial structures and materials.

Plastic has a place and it's really a cool thing. But it's two or three steps removed from something that's organic. So, wood talks to you and you can relate to it. It's such a pleasant material and so user-friendly, really. There're so many different types of wood—quite amazing. Wood is more than just a material.

FORM: *What role does architecture play in your movies?*

DL: Architecture or space is all around us. But capturing space in a really pleasing way is an art form in its own right. And there're very few people who can do it. Most houses, generally speaking, and especially the modern U.S. approach, more or less destroy something inside.

They're devoid of design. I think they suck happiness away from people, and it's really hard to live in those kind of places.

I always go by ideas. The idea for the red room in *Twin Peaks* just popped into my head. The floor has the same pattern as the floor in the lobby of Henry Spencer's apartment in *Eraserhead*. I liked that pattern.

FORM: *While watching* The Elephant Man, *I was struck by a scene in which the Elephant Man constructs a perfect model of a church. Did you design the church?*

DL: No, Stewart Craig, the production designer, made it. It was based on Victorian cardboard kits they used to sell and a church near the London Hospital.

FORM: *You wrote the screenplay to* Lost Highway *together with Barry Gifford. And you said that* Lost Highway *is "a world where time is dangerously out of control." How is this idea expressed in the set design?*

DL: The film deals with time: it starts at one place and moves forward or backwards, or stands still, relatively speaking. But time marches on and films compact time, or prolong time in different ways. There are sequences built with time in mind, as is the music. So, I guess it really probably has more to do with the story and the editing than with the elements and the set design.

FORM: *In your screenplay there's no mention of the set design at all. When do you usually start to put such ideas to paper?*

DL: They never go on paper. When you get an idea many things come with the idea, most things. And pictures form in your mind, and those pictures and the mood that comes, and the light, and many things you remember and you stay as true to those things as you can. When you're working on a location you might have pictured a different place in your mind, so you look around for the closest thing to it that you can find.

FORM: *During* Eraserhead *you were living in the rooms in which you shot the film; in* Lost Highway *your house is part of the scenery. Why do you prefer to use your private space?*
DL: If you love the world of the movie so much, you want to be in the middle of things. So, it's great if, while shooting a film, you're always living in the places, and spend as much time there as possible. That way, the world reveals itself more.

FORM: *And, as far as I know, your house was designed by Lloyd Wright, son of Frank Lloyd Wright.*
DL: Correct. Lloyd Wright designed the house that I live in, the Beverly Johnson House, in the sixties. Lloyd Wright's son, Eric Wright, supervised the building work for his father. Twenty-five years later, Eric designed a pool and a poolhouse on the property in the spirit of his father's work.

FORM: *And you believe that your house has an influence on your work?*
DL: Wright is a great architect. The house has quite a feel of pure Japanese architecture, but also of American modernity, a bit of both. The whole space is just pleasing, gives me a good feeling. So it affects my whole life to live inside of it. And then, sometimes I see things, shapes or something that would go inside of it and that leads to furniture or film.

FORM: *In your house things are very carefully arranged. You've designed boxes which conceal the phone and the video system. Why do you hide these devices? Do you find technology somehow threatening?*
DL: It's a double-edged sword. Technology doesn't threaten me in general. It could, though. It all depends on how it's used. But if it leads to a better standard of living then I think it's really O.K.

FORM: *So why do you hide your video system, for example?*
DL: Well, I could hide everything to keep rooms as pure as possible. You have electronic equipment that works, it's state of the art stuff, but the boxes it comes in are really boring. A lot of thought has gone into the front, but not into the other sides.

FORM: *Perhaps those sides are more interesting for precisely that reason. They aren't designed as consciously as the front.*
DL: But they're always more boring.

FORM: *You've said that your ideas very often occur in the form of daydreams. Is the Beverly Johnson House the house of your dreams?*
DL: It's a beautiful place. Architecture is something to always think

about. Design influences my life. I need pleasing spaces. Often my mind drifts in that direction, but I'm not an architect. Although I really appreciate the great architects, and the difference a great design can make to a person.

FORM: *Who are the architects you admire most?*
DL: From Bauhaus, all the students of the Bauhaus School, and Pierre Chareau, he did the House of Glass in Paris, Ludwig Mies van de Rohe, all the Wright family, Rudolph Michael Schindler and Richard Neutra. I like really beautifully designed, minimal things.

FORM: *Did you ever dream of furniture?*
DL: I daydream of furniture, yes.

FORM: *Do you think the spirit of the so-called, "American dream" produces a special kind of furniture?*
DL: Different cultures produce certain things for one reason or another. But a great design is recognized everywhere.

FORM: *You say you were inspired by Ray and Charles Eames. What is it that you appreciate most about their work?*
DL: The design. I love Ray and Charles Eames, yes.

FORM: *Their entire oeuvre?*
DL: Yes, I like their designs.

FORM: *Did you ever meet the Eamses?*
DL: I had lunch with Charles Eames, he came to the American Film Institute in 1970 or '71 and took part in a lunch with all of the students. And I sat at his table. He was one of the most intelligent, down to earth, greatest persons I've ever met. He was just a pure, kind of happy person, somehow childlike, enjoying life. The kind of guy you'd like right away.

FORM: *Vladimir Kagan, the New York designer, is also a source of inspiration for you.*
DL: He's very old now, maybe around eighty. He was kind of famous in the fifties, and his designs are coming back into vogue now, as is the work of Charlotte Perriand, who worked together with Le Corbusier and Pierre Jeanneret. They're getting recognition again. And rightly so.

FORM: *In Europe, incidentally, the work of the Eamses is more admired than it is in the U.S. Any idea why?*
DL: Because Europeans appreciate the finer things.

FORM: *Do you like German design?*
DL: Yes. German design is usually very pure, and sparse, and solid and functional. And those are exactly the features I like.

FORM: *In other words, you like the technical aspects of German design?*
DL: No, in many cases the look and materials. The Germans are known for very good craftsmanship, and so if the thing is built, you know it's going to work. That's for sure.

FORM: *For many years now, you have worked with Patricia Norris. She designs your productions. Does she influence your own design work?*
DL: She is production designer and in charge of the costume design. With regard to the costumes, I hardly ever say anything to her, the things just blow right out of her. But when it comes to set design. Well, we always talk about everything.

I try to get her in tune with the thing I'm tuning into and so the thing flows, and then we just keep a constant dialogue going. But the design of each and everything is important if the whole film is to hold together.

FORM: *Are there any other architects or designers involved?*
DL: No. Only her.

FORM: *Are you able to compromise when the locations or interiors that you imagined for your set simply can't be found?*
DL: No. There's no compromise possible. You keep looking until you find the place that will work for the story. And that holds for the objects, too. Many places are painted or rearranged, new furniture is brought in. You can't make compromises. Compromises kill the film.

Highway to Hell

STEPHEN PIZZELLO/1997

ON A SUNNY DECEMBER day in the Hollywood Hills, David Lynch sits in a deck chair on the outdoor patio of his filmmaking headquarters, a two-story modernist building that houses the aptly named Asymmetrical Productions. He is surrounded by the tools of the painter's trade: an oversized wooden easel, drippy paint cans, a scattered selection of brushes. Resting against a nearby wall is an unfinished example of his oeuvre: a large chunk of roast beef adhered to a canvas with an acrylic glaze, flanked on either side by the similarly embalmed corpses of a tiny frog and sparrow. Scratching at the salt-and-pepper stubble on his unshaven chin, Lynch appraises his creation. "That roast beef has gone through a strange metamorphosis," he says, folding his arms. "It was bigger when I started, but one day a squirrel came by and took a big hunk out of it. I'm kinda workin' with it."

The line is classic Lynch, a collision of avant-garde eccentricity and folksy good humor. It's quotes such as this that have led media pundits to lampoon the director as some sort of cinematic idiot savant—the weird but brilliant neighborhood kid who occasionally comes over to show off something repulsive that he's dug up in his backyard. But the David Lynch that I encounter is clearly no fool; he is well aware of his image, and is most likely its canny architect. This is, after all, the man responsible for *Eraserhead*, the ultimate midnight movie; the director who unleashed Dennis Hopper's psychotic alter ego, Frank Booth, upon unsuspecting audiences in *Blue Velvet;* the same David Lynch who once staged a one-man home invasion of the entire nation, swamping suburbia's tele-

---

From *American Cinematographer* (March 1997). Reprinted by permission.

vision sets with the outlandish images of *Twin Peaks*. He is, in short, the high llama of existential horror, hero to all who find life to be just a little bit *strange*.

Still, for someone who at various points in his career has been branded "the Czar of Bizarre," "the Wizard of Weird," and "the psychopathic Norman Rockwell," Lynch seems a pleasant enough fellow. When asked to explain how his rather unique thought processes conspire to conjure up his cinematic visions, the director assumes a sincerely thoughtful expression. "Everything sort of follows my initial ideas," he offers. "As soon as I get an idea, I get a picture and a feeling, and I can even hear sounds. The mood and the visuals are very strong. Every single idea I have comes with these things. One moment they're outside of my consciousness, and the next moment they come in with all of this power."

But what is it that triggers these transcendent states? "Sometimes if I listen to music, the ideas really flow," Lynch offers. "It's like the music changes into something else, and I see scenes unfolding. Or I might just be sitting quietly in a chair and *Bing!*—an idea will hit me. At other times, I might be walking down the street when I see something that's meaningful and inspires another scene. On anything that you start, fragments of ideas run together and hook themselves up like a train. Those first fragments become a magnet for everything else you need. You may remember something from the past that's perfect, or you may discover a brand-new thing. Eventually, you get little sequences going.

"Before you think of anything, the whole landscape is open," he concludes. "But once you start falling in love with certain ideas, the road you're on becomes very narrow. If you concentrate, ideas will come to that narrow road and finish it.

To this point in his career, Lynch has led movie audiences down some very twisted roads indeed. This time around, with the help of cinematographer Peter Deming (*Evil Dead 2*, *Hollywood Shuffle*, *House Party*, *Drop Dead Fred*, *My Cousin Vinny*, and the upcoming comedy *Austin Powers: International Man of Mystery*), he has unleashed *Lost Highway*, a neo-noir nightmare that plays like an unholy marriage of *Body Heat* and *Altered States*. Violent, non-linear, and shockingly odd, the film may baffle and even offend many viewers, but it certainly reaffirms Lynch's considerable talents as a visualist.

The plot, such as it is, tracks the strange tale of Fred Madison (Bill Pullman), a jazz saxophonist whose marriage to a dour, raven-tressed sex kitten (Patricia Arquette) is decidedly on the rocks. Shortly after someone begins breaking into the couple's home and videotaping them as they sleep, the wife is murdered, and Fred is ushered to an amenity-free suite in the Graybar Hotel (a.k.a. prison).

The setup is textbook film noir, but things soon takes a sharp turn toward the surreal. While languishing in his cell, Madison suddenly and inexplicably morphs into a teenaged garage mechanic named Pete (Balthazar Getty). Released from the clink by the baffled authorities, who tail his every move, Pete soon finds himself lusting after the sultry blonde moll (Patricia Arquette again) of a short-tempered crime boss (Robert Loggia). His infatuation gets him in dutch with the gangster, who subsequently employs a full arsenal of scare tactics—such as introducing the youthful grease monkey to a truly bizarre mystery man (Robert Blake) who has no eyebrows and the apparent ability to be in two places at once.

All of this, of course, must be seen to be believed, which is no doubt part of Lynch's master plan. Early press notes for the film described it simply as "a psychogenic fugue," and the director himself offers no further hints about the movie's true meaning. "The unit publicist was reading up on certain mental disorders during production, and she came upon this true condition called 'psychogenic fugue,' which is where a person gives up himself, his world, his family—everything about himself—and takes on another identity," Lynch relates. "That's Fred Madison completely. I love the term *psychogenic fugue*. In a way, the musical term *fugue* fits perfectly, because the film has one theme, and then another theme takes over. To me, jazz is the closest thing to insanity that there is in music."

Some viewers may prescribe a straitjacket for Lynch after experiencing *Lost Highway*, but adventurous filmgoers will be treated to a torrent of dazzling images that defy indifference: a pitch-dark hallway that looms like a tenebrous abyss; Pullman's transformation into Getty, a sequence which seems inspired by a tab of bad acid; an opulent mansion that serves as a proscenium for porn; a nocturnal interlude of dusty desert coitus caught in the headlights of a car.

Like most of *Lost Highway*, these scenes have the febrile quality of a dream. By his own assertion, Lynch is "not an intellectual thinker," but an instinctual artist whose primarily motivations are mood, texture, and emotion. "Film noir has a mood that everyone can feel," he says. "It's people in trouble, at night, with a little bit of wind and the right kind of music. It's a beautiful thing."

In order to interpret Lynch's existential directives, his closest collaborators must attune themselves to his singular mindset. Lynch's longtime production/costume designer, Patricia Norris, says that she and the director have developed a strong creative kinship after years of working together. "We both have the same idea of what 'ugly' is—in terms of both decor and people," Norris submits. "All rooms come out of people, and if you understand who the characters are, you understand how they live. Most decorating conveys what's not written, and gives you a sense of the people. In *Lost Highway*, for example, the porno guy's mansion is really awful-looking—over the top and in bad taste. Everything is too big, and it looks as if he probably had someone else furnish it for him. We took a very different approach to the Madisons' house, because we wanted their relationship to be mysterious and nebulous. We decorated their place very sparingly with the kind of jazzy, fifties-style 'atomic furniture' that David favors; the look was basically 'a phone and an ashtray.'"

Although cinematographer Deming has not worked with Lynch for nearly as long as Norris, he benefitted from his prior experiences with the director on television commercials, the short-lived television series *On the Air*, and the HBO omnibus *Hotel Room*. "David's not a big fan of prep; he doesn't like to be pinned down too much," Deming says. "Before shooting began on this film, we only talked specifically about two scenes: the first involved the hallway in Fred Madison's house, and the other was the love scene in the desert. We discussed different levels of *dark*—dark, 'next door to dark,' gradations like that. To figure out exactly what he meant, I would reference things we had done together, or other work he had done. The colors David was most interested in were browns, yellows, and reds. We wound up shooting a lot of the film with a chocolate #1 filter, which helped me get the look that David wanted. The lab felt that it was the most difficult filter to reproduce in timing.

"In testing, I ran into a bit of a problem using the chocolate filter at night," he submits. "The filter factor was a stop and a third, and it just ate up the shadows; you couldn't see into the shadow areas at all. Knowing the way David likes darkness, the chocolate filter was too much of a wild card when we were shooting at the low end of the exposure curve. We tried using chocolate gels on the lights, but that also proved to be a little too thick.

"What I ended up doing was having Ron Scott, the timer at CFI, time in the effect to the scene. I'd give him two gray scales: one normal and one with the filter in the camera. He would match the normal one to the filtered one and apply that correction to the whole scene in varying densities. It wasn't my preferred way of doing things, but in the long run I think it was better because it gave the night scenes a slightly different look, even scene to scene. David grew to like the workprint he had watched for six months, and he didn't want to change that. I did one timing for the movie which was fairly consistent with the chocolate look we had designed for the day work, but it wasn't really happening, so we went back to what we had in the workprint to a large degree, improving it in places where it wasn't quite right. We wound up with a movie that has a different and nonuniform look."

Working in true anamorphic widescreen (2.40:1), Deming shot most of the film on Eastman Kodak's 5293 and 5298 stocks, and always deployed a Fogal stocking behind his lenses. He says that his choice of stocks was dictated by practical considerations and plain common sense. "Even when we were outside, we would somehow always end up shooting late in the day or under trees," he submits. "With the chocolate filter and some 85 correction, I really couldn't get away with anything but 93—which was fine, because I like the 93 a lot. Normally, I shot 93 when I had enough light. I used the 98 for anything that took place at night. I might have done things differently if this hadn't been an anamorphic film, but with anamorphic you have to get at least a 2.8 whenever you can to make it look really nice. Sometimes we were a little below 2.8, and on one or two occasions we had to shoot wide-open. I would shoot 93 more at night on a flat [1.85] movie, when you can shoot with a lower stop."

Deming says that his biggest challenge on the show was trying to accommodate Lynch's love of dark, inky visuals. "It was a struggle," he concedes. "I know what David likes; if he had his way, everything would be a little bit underexposed and murky, which is murder for me. On this film, I often found myself riding the bottom edge of the film's latitude. I didn't want to overexpose the images and print them down, because they would have had too much contrast. I wanted the overall look to be low-contrast in relation to the day work at the Madison house and in the rest of the movie."

Scenes within the Madisons' home—a practical location with low, seven- to eight-foot ceilings—posed a number of logistical difficulties. Although the filmmakers were able to alter the structure a great deal—by replacing the living room's large picture window with two very small vertical windows, and adding a skylight—the house's cramped interior forced Deming to plot out some very economical lighting setups. "It was one of those situations, particularly in the daytime, in which we just put lights where we could," the director of photography relates. "For daylight scenes, we were coming *in* from the outside, primarily with HMI Pars.

We also bounced light down through the skylight. Most of our fill lights were Kino Flo banks, which allowed us to keep down the obvious shadows on the walls. The bedroom was a little different. We used a Dino on a Condor outside because there was a good-sized window we could work with, but there was only one day scene in the bedroom."

Night scenes at the house further complicated matters for the crew. "Usually in a setup like that you would work off practical light sources," Deming says. "That's what we did most of the time, although there were scenes without any visible practical fixtures; in those cases you just put something up and hope it's not too bright and obvious. For the night stuff we used a lot of paper lanterns. When you're shooting anamorphic, you normally have a lot of room below the frame line; usually you have room above as well, but not at the house we were using. We'd hide lights and hang them and jam them in corners where we could. Sometimes we would pin bounce material and shoot a light through the shot; because there was no smoke you wouldn't know it. My gaffer, Michael Laviolette, made a hard internal rig for the lanterns that took two 500-watt Photofloods. So we were dealing with a 1K light which, even with heavy diffusion on a lantern, was a lot of light in a small place like that. The lanterns were made out of pretty thick paper. Sometimes when we were dealing with a bigger set we would use an 8' x 8' light grid and a 12' x 12' muslin."

For certain key scenes, super-minimal lighting schemes were employed to great effect. A particularly impressive example of this strategy is the filmmakers' sepulchral rendering of the Madison home's main hallway, which has a foreboding quality reminiscent of the work of one of Lynch's favorite painters, Francis Bacon. Achieving this look required some deft interplay between the various crewmembers.

"Fortunately, the hallway was a setting we could control, even though we were shooting at a real house," says Deming. "Patty Norris and her crew physically altered the structure, making the hallway as long as possible. She also helped me by putting Bill Pullman in dark clothes, and by painting the walls a color that wouldn't reflect too much light. To cap things off, we hung a black curtain over the windows at the end of the hall."

Because the building's ceilings were so low, Deming opted to light the space primarily with a single, slightly diffused 2K zip light suspended directly above the camera. He used cutters and black wrap to perfect the angle of the light, relying on the high-speed 98 film stock to do the rest. "The 98 can really pick up details in the dark, so I knew that we were in trouble if the end of the hallway didn't disappear to the naked eye," says Deming. "David feels that a murky black darkness is scarier than a completely black darkness; he wanted this particular hallway to be a slightly brownish black that would swallow characters up. After we had finished the shot and sent it to the lab, I called the color timer and told him, 'As Bill Pullman walks down the hall, he should vanish completely, because if I see him down there I'm never going to hear the end of it.'"

The utilization of Kino Flos lent an eerie ambience to other sequences in the house. In one shot, Bill Pullman steps into a hallway so dark that he seems to be walking through a wall. A single Kino Flo created the mere hint of depth along the sides of the hallway entrance. The next scene shows Pullman gazing at his reflection in a mirror within the tomb-like confines of a small room. "The spot where David hung the mirror was only about six feet high," Deming says. "We put a Kino Flo up above, gelled it with chocolate and cut it severely. It was the only thing I could use to keep Bill from looking too ghoulish. We shot that the first day, and when it came up in dailies I thought it was underexposed. After the lights in the screening room came up, I said to David, 'We need to do that mirror shot again.' He looked at me as if I were crazy and replied, 'No way, I love that shot!'"

The filmmakers veered toward the opposite end of the photographic spectrum while shooting a hallway scene set within the opulent mansion of a porn-peddling hustler (embodied to oily perfection by Michael Massee). As a disoriented Balthazar Getty stumbles along the passageway, it begins to spin kaleidoscopically amid a barrage of lightning effects provided by two large, old-fashioned carbon-arc machines. "Lightning is an issue that's very close to David's heart," says Deming. "He doesn't like electronic lightning machines, because the look they create is very clean. With carbon arcs, there's a certain color-shift in the flashes; they sort of warm up and cool off. In this particular scene, one of the units we used was bouncing off two mirrors aimed at the end of the hail, and the other was positioned above a skylight. We had the camera and another smaller lightning box on a doorway dolly, and we tracked backwards as Balthazar walked toward us. I had a tiny eyelight on him, and the camera was attached to a tilting Dutch head.

"To make everything spin, we used a Mesmerizer; it's an aspherical element that clips onto the end of the lens, and you can rotate it. When you use it with a flat lens, the image will squeeze and get wider as you spin it. As we were dollying, I was Dutching the camera and spinning the Mesmerizer; all the while, David was blaring the piece of music that would accompany the scene in the finished film, which allowed us to take our camera cues directly from the music."

Equally spectacular is a later shot of actors Getty and Arquette engaging in their nocturnal desert love scene, illuminated only by the white-hot headlights of a car. "That situation involved things you're taught never to do—front-lighting and overexposing," says Deming. "When we talked about the love scene in prep, David said he wanted the actors to be glowing. He didn't want to see any details except their eyes, noses, mouths, and hair. We lit them with tungsten Pars which were supposed to simulate the headlights of their car, and we overexposed by about six-and-a-half stops. The final effect is very surreal; David knew it was not the 'technically correct' way to do things, but it worked for the movie."

The cinematographer notes that Lynch often comes up with his most inspired cinematic riffs on the set, sometimes while a sequence is being shot. "A lot of ideas would come up on the day of filming, after he'd gotten together with the actors and blocked out the scene," Deming asserts. "There's always a certain amount of logistical preparation, but when you're working with David you have to be ready for anything."

Lynch confirms that he encourages his crews to transcend the technical and logistical tenets of traditional film production. Intent on creating motion pictures with primal impact, he allows his fantasies free reign, and frequently improvises in order to commit them to film. "When you first get an idea, you're imagining it, but eventually you're out there in the real world," the director notes. "There are little holes and blurs in the imagination, and it's not totally complete. But when an actress arrives on the set in her costume, you suddenly have a concrete element, and a whole new bunch of things can happen. You can be painfully aware that something's wrong, and you have to fix it. Or you can be blown away by something odd that happens. The crew might be hanging a lighting fixture that's flopped over and blowing light where it's not supposed to be, but I might see it, grab Pete and say, 'Look at that.' Even if it's not right for the scene we're doing, we sometimes save the idea and use it later. Little things like that always happen, and it's useful to store them away."

The director recalls that such a moment arose during the filming of a scene set in Fred Madison's prison cell, just prior to the character's hellish transmutation. "I wanted Fred Madison's face to go completely out of focus," says Lynch. "We had a black screen hanging behind Bill Pullman, and the camera had to be locked off for the scene. I told Pete to start de-focusing the lens, but he couldn't get the image as far out of focus as I wanted; he had reached the end of the lens. I said, 'Well, we've got a problem.' He replied, 'The only thing we can do is to take the lens out.' So I said, 'Okay, take it out.' He popped the lens on and off the camera as we did the shot, and it looked beautiful! We dubbed that technique 'whacking,' and after that I started going a bit whack-happy—but only when it suited the picture."

Surprisingly, Pullman's mindbending metamorphosis into Getty was not accomplished via computer-generated special effects, but rather with a careful combination of in-camera techniques and cutting-room trickery. The film's editor, Mary Sweeney (who also co-produced *Lost Highway*), reveals that a makeup effects expert constructed a special "fake Fred head" that was covered with slimy artificial brain matter and then carefully intercut with shots of the real Bill Pullman. She explains, "That sequence was completely designed by David, and we constructed it in the editing room, working entirely from elements he had shot on film."

In-camera trickery added adrenalin to other sections of the movie as well. For an operatic shot of a burning shack, the crew deployed four cameras: the Panavision Platinum that served as A-camera throughout production; the Panavision Gold II B-camera; a Mitchell owned by Lynch (with a mount that Panavision had converted to accept the company's Primo lenses); and an extra camera body for a Steadicam. The fiery destruction of the ramshackle structure was filmed at four different speeds: 24 fps, 30 fps, 48 fps, and in reverse at 96 fps with the Mitchell. "We just turned all of the cameras on and let it rip," Deming recalls. "I think one of the tighter shots done at 48 was later slowed down in post, but the footage in the film is primarily the stuff we shot overcranked in reverse."

Lynch's Mitchell was also used to record the moment when Getty's mechanic first sets eyes on the gangster's buxom girlfriend, who strolls through a garage interior and out into bright sunlight. Once again, the camera's speed control was set to 96 fps. "That shot presented a bit of a problem for me," says Deming, "because when you operate the Mitchell it doesn't unsqueeze the shot, so you're looking at really thin people. To shoot that fast with the filtration we were using I had to go to a higher-speed stock, and I knew that its limited latitude would make the exterior at the end of the shot blow out completely. I talked to David about it, but he just said, 'Great, the dreamier and weirder you can make it look, the better.' As a result, the exterior part of the sequence is white-hot, and I think we even timed it up to be brighter. In addition, the shot we used had a little flicker from the dancing of the light—the camera wasn't a sync model. When I saw the shot in dailies, I said, 'We should redo that,' but David vetoed me again! I told the same thing to the timer, and he said, 'Doing it over would be a big mistake.' He knew that it worked for the picture."

The filmmakers later used undercranked cameras to capture two "super-speed" car chases—one involving the crime kingpin, Mr. Eddy, and a climactic scene in which Fred Madison is tracked across the desert by a fleet of police cars. "For the first chase, we shot all of the stuff with the actors during the show, and then went back on the last day of shooting to get the second-unit footage. We tried a bunch of different speeds—from 20 fps down to six and even four. I didn't want Mary Sweeney to have to go in later, dupe everything and speed it up, because David and I both like to stay away from opticals whenever possible. In fact, most of the film's dissolves and fades are A/B roll and not opticals. It's hard to get people to do that these days, but David appreciates the quality of it, which is really nice for me.

"We did the final chase sequence three times, with two cameras outfitted with different lenses and running at slightly different frame rates—24 and 12 fps. In this case, some of the footage *was* sped up and blown up in post, and I think Mary and David also double- and triple-printed parts of it to make the tone more aggressive. While we were shooting that chase, we put Fred's car on a process trailer being towed by a tractor-trailer generator. We had the usual lighting inside the car, which wasn't much—probably Kino Flos. We also set up two carbon-arc lightning machines on scissor arcs, two 4K Xenons aimed into Mylar, two strobes, and a couple of smaller lighting units, like Pars dimming up and down. All of this stuff was working while we were driving down the road at night in the middle of the desert. From a mile away it must have been quite a sight!"

Lynch understands full well that the visceral and often oblique visions presented in *Lost Highway* may frustrate and even antagonize audiences, but he has often said that he prefers his pictures to remain open to many interpretations. "Stories have tangents; they open up and become different things," the director maintains. "You can still have a structure, but you should leave room to dream. If you stay true to your ideas, film-making becomes an inside-out, honest kind of process. And if it's an honest thing for you, there's a chance that people will feel that, even if it's abstract."

The *Icon* Profile: David Lynch

CHRIS RODLEY/1997

ERASERHEAD MARKED him as a freak, *The Elephant Man* clarified him as an artist. *Dune* made him look like a fluke. *Blue Velvet* cemented his place in cinema history. *Twin Peaks* catapulted him into mythology. *Twin Peaks: Fire Walk with Me* crushed his reputation. *Lost Highway*, his first film in over four years, could resurrect or bury him.

"Yes Ma'am!" David Lynch enthusiastically shouts in response to an important question: Does he want another coffee? Lynch has a theory about cups of joe: "If you turn away from them for one second, they go cold on you." Simultaneously comic, superstitious, even faintly sinister, the observation is typically Lynchian—it points to a recognizable truth. His ability to expose hidden meaning in the familiar or everyday seems instinctual, as natural to him as it is strange to others. When Mel Brooks famously dubbed Lynch "Jimmy Stewart from Mars," it was incisive shorthand for a complex puzzle. Lynch's work, at times deeply disturbing and darkly hilarious, is even more troubling against the back of his golly-gosh, folksy, clean-cut American persona.

"Eagle Scout, Missoula, Montana" is how Lynch chose to characterize himself to the press in 1990 the year his delirious road movie *Wild at Heart* won the international film community's greatest honor: the Palme d'Or at Cannes. The same year, TV audiences worldwide were enthralled with the mystery of who killed Laura Palmer in *Twin Peaks*. The small-screen series was created by Lynch with Mark Frost. It garnered fourteen

From *Icon* (April 1997). Reprinted by permission of Chris Rodley.

Emmy nominations and won Lynch the covers of *Time* and the *New York Times Magazine*.

"I think that David is the Eagle Scout from Missoula, Montana, who found some tools in his dad's garage," observes Laura Dern, star of *Wild at Heart* and *Blue Velvet*. "He's the neighborhood boy who always asks, 'Hey! Whatchya doing?' He probably started to paint some things, and decided he could paint in front of the camera." One of the boys in Lynch's neighborhood was Toby Keeler; Lynch was working on his Eagle Scout merit badges when they first met in 1960. "They just don't give those away," Keeler says. "I think that David achieved the highest level possible, though he doesn't like to talk about it. Even today his ability to make something out of nothing comes from the old motto, 'Be Prepared.' Despite friendship that has spanned thirty-seven years, Keeler says, "I have no idea where David's dark side comes from. He likes to portray himself as the straightest guy in the world, and obviously he's not."

Sitting in his beloved workshop, surrounded by heavy machinery, tools, and a stack of pictures ready to be placed in crates (for an upcoming tour of his paintings and photographs), Lynch is clearly at home. But talking about his work has always filled him with trepidation. He fears that words will only reduce his films to a single, literal meaning. Lynch's own four-word bio is indicative of an ever playful but essentially private personality—one of which defies easy description.

Actress and model Isabella Rossellini was Lynch's lover when practically every American magazine sought his famous, but toned up looks for their covers. In *Blue Velvet*, he cast her as the disturbed Dorothy Vallens, the masochistic victim of Dennis Hopper's sadistic Frank Booth. "A lot of people thought that *Blue Velvet* was sick, but for me, it was David's research of the good and the bad," Rossellini says. "There is an incredible gentleness and a conflict between good and evil in him that is so moving. It's absolutely the core of his art, and it makes him a profoundly moral person. He's also great fun. I mean, humor beyond the beyond! I laughed a lot in the years that I was with him. He doesn't make himself into a character. He's just from Montana." Dennis Hopper revels in the contradiction. "He's so straight it's hard to realize that he has such a sick and twisted mind," Hopper says with an evil laugh. "Dear David!"

Lynch is intrigued by what others see as paradox: "We all have at least two sides. The world we live in is a world of opposites. And the trick is to reconcile those opposing things." Lynch's unflinching cinematic engagement with his dark side seems dangerously public for one so private. However, the potential paradox masks a strange innocence. "I've always liked both sides," he says. "In order to appreciate one you have to know the other. The more darkness you can gather up, the more light you can see too." The self-portrait *I See Myself* (1992) depicts a strange half-white, half-black figure. If the white side is a regular guy sitting here in his painting studio, drinking more coffee and smoking another American Spirit cigarette, is the black side less pleasant? "Well, it has to be that way," he says and then laughs. "I don't know why but um, er, I don't quite know what to say about that."

Currently, Lynch is bracing himself for the release of his first movie in over four years, *Lost Highway*. The media attention that inevitably accompanies such an event disturbs him because he has been both praised and vilified in the past. "I like to have a film go out, but not have me go out," he admits. "Respect for, you know, the work—that's success for me."

Mary Sweeney, Lynch's "sweetheart" of many years and the mother of their five-year-old son, Riley, is also the editor and producer of *Lost Highway*. She's experienced Lynch's demons first-hand. "He tries to hold success at arm's length because good reviews are as destructive as bad ones if you start listening to them," she says. "Once you're on the cover of *Time*, it'll take you two years to recover." Rossellini says it's yet another example of Lynch's duality. "I think David is concerned very much with success, and hates himself for it," she says. "He admires the independence of the artist, and yet knows that without a certain amount of success his freedom would be taken away. But he won't do *anything* for success. He wants to be successful with his own imagery. I think that David was probably born like that, with vivid images in his head. As an office employee he would probably just be staring out the window, entertained by the images that his brain flashes to him. He wouldn't be good at anything else. His imagination is too strong."

The man possessed of such an imagination was "born like that" in 1946 in the small valley town of Missoula, Montana. Surrounded by lakes, mountains, and Native American reservations, Missoula boasts 30,000 inhabitants (smaller than Twin Peaks). His parents, Donald and Sunny, met at Duke University during an outdoor biology class. Sunny had been a language tutor and Don was a research scientist for the Department of Agriculture, both important factors in the making of David Lynch.

Despite what one might conclude from the dark, familial nightmares that trigger so many of Lynch's film narratives, his own childhood memories are of a carefree, idyllic past. "The only thing that disturbs me is that many psychopaths say they had a very happy childhood," he says.

"There's some line I read about the longing for the euphoria of forgotten childhood dreams. And it was like a dream. Airplanes passed by slowly in the sky. Rubber toys floated on the water. Meals seemed to last five years and nap time seemed endless. And the world was so small. I can't remember being able to see more than a couple of blocks. And those couple of blocks were huge. So all the details were blown out of proportion. Blue skies, picket fences, green grass, cherry trees. Middle America as it's supposed to be."

But if Lynch is inclined to romanticize, idealize or even construct an innocent halcyon past, at the time he was only too aware of it's other aspect. "But on the cherry tree there's pitch oozing out—some of it's black, some of it's yellow, and there are millions of red ants crawling all over it," he says. "I discovered that if one looks a little closer at the beautiful world, there's always red ants underneath."

Peggy Reavey, who married him in 1967 when they were both attending the Pennsylvania Academy of Fine Arts in Philadelphia, remembers well the young art student. "The first time I saw him was in the cafeteria," she says. "I just thought he was very beautiful. He looked like an angel to me." But Reavey, also a painter (Lynch purchased several of her recent pictures and included them in his *Lost Highway*), would soon discover that what was hiding beneath his angelic surface. "He was a person who was fascinated with anything dark. He told stories about his childhood on Park Circle Drive—all these idyllic rabbit-hunting stories. And yet he seemed determined to puncture artificiality by revealing all this darkness."

Never to be content with appearances is one of the foundations of Lynch's world view. It was through nature that he first encountered darkness beneath the surface. "My father had huge forests at his disposal to experiment on, so I was exposed to insects, disease, and growth in an organic sort of world," he says. "And it sort of thrilled me. A *National Geographic* photo of a garden is just the most beautiful thing. But there are a lot of things attacking a garden. There's a lot of slaughter and death, worms and grubs. A lot of stuff going on. It's a torment."

The Lynch family, which included a younger brother and sister, was an itinerant one. They moved with each government transfer: from Missoula to Sandpoint, Idaho, to Spokane, Washington, to Durham, North Carolina, to Boise, Idaho, and finally to Alexandria, Virginia. By then Lynch was fourteen years old. He cherishes the vivid memories of his father walking to work in a ten-gallon hat. "It was so embarrassing to me at the time that he wore this hat, but now I consider it totally cool," he says.

"It was a grey-green forest service, ten-gallon cowboy hat, and he'd put it on and walk out the door. He wouldn't go in a bus, a car or anything, he'd just walk several miles, all the way across the George Washington Bridge into the city in that hat."

It's Lynch's mental snapshots, such as his image of his sister Margaret, that at once captivate and deflect. "She was afraid of green peas," he says. "I think it had to do with the consistency and strengths of the outer surface, then the softness of what was inside when you broke the outer membrane. It was a big thing in our family. She'd have to hide them."

While the interpretation is probably exactly how Lynch perceives it, the story is a consistent construct. It's an edited version of a past that presents his memories in a way that conveys a greater truth. It also aims to arrest one's desire to pry further. Why didn't his parents simply stop giving Margaret peas? "Well," he says, "it was a thing about vegetables." That they're good for you? "Yes." But not if you're scared of them. "No, it's not so good. You have to try different vegetables. Something has to work!"

His family's peripatetic lifestyle offers clues to a highly developed, eccentric sense of place in Lynch's work and to the innocent, outsider quality of his cinematic alter egos. "When you're uprooted, you have to start all over again," he says. "It's hard if you're on the outside. It forces you to want to get on the inside. It's a shock to the system. But shocks are sometimes good. You get a little bit more aware. I had lots of friends, but I loved being alone and looking at ants swarming in the garden."

As a child, Lynch was always drawing and painting. "One thing I thank my mother for is that she refused to give me coloring books, because it's like a restricting thing," he says. "I mostly drew ammunition and pistols and airplanes because the war was just over, and it was, I guess, in the air still. Browning automatic water-cooled submachine guns were a favorite." But he had no ideas about a future in the arts. In fact he claims to have had little idea about anything: "I was, like, not thinking at all—zero original thoughts."

But in Alexandria, when Lynch was in the ninth grade, everything suddenly changed. "I met my friend Toby Keeler in the front yard of my girlfriend Linda Styles's house," he says. "Toby did two things: He told me that his stepfather (Bushnell Keeler) was a painter, which completely changed my life, and he stole my girlfriend."

From that moment that Lynch met Toby's stepfather, he dedicated himself completely to the "art life." He attended classes at Corcoran School of Art in Washington on Saturdays and rented studio space from Keeler, who became mentor to Lynch. "He was really a cool guy," remembers Lynch, "not part of the painting world really. Yet he was, you know, devoting his life to it, and it thrilled my soul. He also turned me onto a book by Robert Henri called *The Art Spirit* that sort of became my bible. It helped me decide my course in painting—100 percent right there." Toby Keeler confirms the change in Lynch. "When he found out about art and painting, he was possessed by it," Keeler says. "His time with Bush was very private. He was an artist and I wasn't. In many ways, he had a better relationship with my stepfather than I had at the time."

Lynch all but dropped out of school to paint, spending time in the studio instead of in class. Fortunately his parents seemed to accept this situation. But when Lynch didn't make the grades his brother and sister were achieving, Bushnell Keeler sprang to his defense. After high school, a year at the Boston Museum School was abandoned in favor of a three-year trip to Europe with fellow art student Jack Fisk. The plan was to study with the Austrian expressionist painter, Oskar Kokoshka. "I was nineteen, and my thoughts weren't my own," he says. "They were other people's. There was nothing wrong with that school, but a school is like a house—it's the people in the house that can be a problem. I was not inspired at all in that place. In fact it was tearing me down."

The trip, which was thwarted by the nonappearance of Kokoschka, lasted only fifteen days. When Lynch returned, he was financially cut off by his parents, who were now living in Walnut Creek, California. He went to live with Bushnell Keeler back in Alexandria, and to pay his way, he agreed to help paint the Keeler house. "David started in this second-story bathroom and he used a paintbrush that had a one-inch head on it!" says Toby Keeler. "A teeny little brush. He spent three days painting this bathroom and probably a day painting a radiator. He got into every single nook and cranny, and painted that thing better than when it was new. It took him forever. My mother still laughs today when she thinks of David in that bathroom."

Lynch's father and Bushnell Keeler eventually colluded in a plan to trick Lynch into applying for a scholarship at the Pennsylvania Academy of Fine Arts. "They conspired to make life miserable for me," says Lynch, recalling that Keeler was suddenly too busy for him. "I applied and unbeknownst to me until recently, Bushnell called and gave them the hard sell on me. He told them I had 'the stuff.'" Lynch was accepted and the Academy was a turning point for his painting. "I don't know what prompted it, but he suddenly started doing very dark things," says Peggy Reavey. "Big black canvases." In particular, she remembers a large picture called *The Bride*. "This painting was a real breakthrough in my opinion.

It sounds awful, but it's of an abstracted figure of a bride aborting herself. It was very beautiful and not repulsive in any way. It was hauntingly disturbing and beautifully painted."

Living in Philadelphia filled Lynch with both wonders and horror, and its influence seems to have had a lasting impression on him. It's clear that cities have always disturbed his equilibrium. "When I visited Brooklyn as a kid, it scared the hell out of me," he says. "In the subway I remember a wind from the approaching train, then a smell and a sound. I had a taste of horror every time I went." Lynch's urban angst is not a press release invention, but a form of sensory panic that has survived beyond childhood. "He was so frightened of New York City," explains Reavey, "I'd have to accompany him. He wouldn't go alone." But Lynch does love a story, absurdity, and the power of surreal imagery. "I visited my grandfather in New York, when he owned an apartment building with no kitchens," he says. "A woman was cooking an egg on an iron. That really worried me."

"It all started for me in Philadelphia because it's old enough, and it's got enough things in the air to really work on itself. It's decaying but it's fantastically beautiful, filled with violence, hate, and filth." That's how Lynch describes the backdrop for his breakthrough from painting to film. It came one day while working in the Academy. "I'm looking at this figure in this painting, and I hear like a little wind, and I see a little movement," he says. "I had a wish that it would really be able to move, you know, some little bit. And that was it."

The eventual outcome of his transcendental moment was Lynch's final year project, *Six Men Getting Sick*. It's a one-minute animation loop projected onto a molded screen made from six casts of his own head. Lynch knew nothing about film or photography, but that didn't stop him. "He had such audacity," Reavey recalls. On one occasion Lynch thought he could build a perpetual motion machine and went to the Franklin Institute to tell them so. "He'd just go straight to the top, and tell people, 'I think I know how to build a perpetual motion machine. I'm an art student,'" she says. "Einstein couldn't do it, of course, but people do what he says, so they let him in! He was utterly earnest. And this guy, very nicely, explained why his plan wouldn't work, and we trooped out to have a cup of coffee."

While Lynch's physics didn't win any prizes, his moving paintings did. He shared the Academy's prize that year, and was given $1,000 by a wealthy fellow student, H. Barton Wasserman, to make a similar piece for him. That project turned out to be a technical disaster, but Wasserman generously told him to use the remaining money to make something else.

Lynch shot his first film *The Alphabet*. It was an unsettling four-minute animation and live action piece about the horrors of learning and being a nonverbal person. "He hates words," says Isabella Rossellini. "David isn't very verbal. His films aren't that literal, they're more of a sensory experience." Remembering Lynch's preferred, highly codified form of communication makes Reavey laugh. "I was with David in his preverbal stage," she says. "He didn't talk the way a lot of people do about their work. He would make noises, open his arms wide and make a sound like the wind."

Lynch's subsequent success has forced him to communicate, but he still sees words as potential destroyers of magic and an enemy to real understanding. Toby Keeler knows the drill: "I asked him once,'What's *Wild at Heart* about David?' He said, 'Well, it's about one hour and forty-five minutes.'"

For the young Lynch in Philadelphia, the most significant break of his career was about to come. He was married to Reavey and had the responsibility of an unplanned daughter (Jennifer). Money was tight, and the future looked bleak. He had become obsessed with film, and his future hung on a small grant application to the American Film Institute to make his second short, *The Grandmother*. "I got a thing through the mail about the first wave of winners: Stan Brakhage, Bruce Connor, names that I was starting to hear about," he says. "They were like solid independent, avant-garde, cutting-edge filmmakers. I said, 'There's no fucking way!' So I gave up thinking about it. But I always said to Peggy when I left the house, 'Call me if anything exciting happens, and I'll call you if anything exciting happens.'"

It did. The AFI offered Lynch a grant of $5,000. "I took this phone call that changed my life," he says. "And now I'm floating, you know, and like so pressed to the ceiling with happiness! Everyone should have that feeling. The only way you appreciate it is to be so desperately down."

According to Lynch, nothing since has ever made that much difference or been so important, not even that call that offered him the $45 million *Dune*. To say the rest is history (or in Lynch's world, fate) is to ignore the fact that talent is not usually enough. He moved to Los Angeles to become a full-time student at the new AFI film center. He began a five-year period of work on *Eraserhead*—a film inspired by the city from which he had just escaped. "It's my *Philadelphia Story*," he says. "It just doesn't have Jimmy Stewart in it."

Listening to Lynch describe the movie's disorientated hero Henry (played by Jack Nance, who died on December 30, 1996) is an uncanny experience: his description is a tantalizingly evocative self-portrait. "Henry is very sure that something is happening, but he doesn't understand it at all," he says. "He watches things very, very carefully, because he's trying to figure them out. He might study the corner of a pie container, just because it's in his line of sight. He might wonder why he sat where he did. Everything is new. It might be frightening, but it could be a key to something."

Lynch obviously felt (and still feels) close to Henry. But it is the character's sudden discovery that he has fathered a premature baby and his attempts to deal with the harsh and fearful realities of parenthood that critics and friends alike have seen as particularly autobiographical. "I guess one of the main misconceptions of late," says Lynch's daughter, Jennifer, "is the prime idea for *Eraserhead* came out of my birth, because David—in no uncertain terms—did not want a family."

Lynch had dedicated himself to the "art life" and, as he puts it, wanted to have "as little baggage as possible, because in the beginning, you're climbing." It seems likely that the originality of *Eraserhead* caused people to assume that it must be based on personal experience. "I was born with club feet," explains Jennifer, "and people have made insinuations about it because the baby in *Eraserhead* was deformed. But I don't think David credits that directly as where *Eraserhead* comes from."

During the film's five-year production period, Lynch went back to menial work, including a paper route and a part-time plumbing job for which he apparently developed an affection. "It's satisfying thing to direct water successfully," he says. Reavey remembers those times well. "He was so dedicated. It could be pretty exhausting. He always had the sense that things were possible—a strong sense of entitlement." But their marriage failed to survive Lynch's intense commitment to his new passion. "It's a lot of work being with David Lynch," she says "Our friendship continued, I just quit the job!"

Despite his parting with Reavey, happy memories remain uppermost in Lynch's mind. "I like mounds of dirt," he says. "I really like mounds of dirt. When we were doing *Eraserhead*, Peggy and I lived in a single house in L.A. with Jennifer, and it had a circular wooden dining table. On her birthday Peggy went out and Jennifer and I started carrying buckets of dirt. And we made a pile about four feet high on the dining room table, covered a whole thing in just a mountain of dirt. Then we dug little tunnels in it, put little clay abstract figures in front of the tunnels. And

Peggy, bless her heart, was over the moon about it when she came home. So we left it there for months. It ate the surface of the wood on the table because it began to go to work organically. So the veneer was pretty much toasted."

When *Eraserhead* was finally screened publicly, Lynch recalls how John Waters helped to spread awareness. "One of his films was opening, and John had already established himself as the underground rebel," Lynch says. "So he did this Q&A and he didn't talk about his film. He just told people to go and see *Eraserhead*." Lynch's debut feature played seventeen cities on a regular basis. At the Nuart Cinema in L.A. it screened one night a week for four years. That meant four years on the marquee. The word *Eraserhead* got around.

If one determining, external factor remained in Lynch's rise to recognition and success, it was the attention of Stuart Cornfeld, a young producer working for Mel Brooks. Cornfeld was at the Nuart the first night on a tip-off from a tutor at the AFI. Nearly twenty years later he still enthuses wildly about the experience. "I was just 100 percent blown away," he says. "I thought it was the greatest thing I'd ever seen. It was such a cleansing experience. I just wanted to see his next movie."

After *Eraserhead*, Lynch married Mary Fisk, with whom he would have a son, Austin. At the time he wasn't exactly bombarded with offers. But he was writing a script called *Ronnie Rocket* ("It's about electricity and a three-foot guy with red hair"), building sheds ("Whenever you can build a shed, you've got it made"), and going every day at 2:30 p.m. to Bob's Big Boy Diner to consume chocolate shakes and coffee. "I discovered that sugar makes me happy and inspires me," he says. "I'd get so wound up that I had to rush home and write. Sugar is granulated happiness. It's a friend." Then came an all-important Cornfeld phone call, offering what was to be Lynch's follow up—the multi-Oscar-nominated *The Elephant Man*. "I literally went around the house repeating his name: 'Stuart Cornfeld, Stuart Cornfeld, Stuart Corn-Feld.' And it made me happy," he says. "Looking back now, I can see why."

Cornfeld got Mel Brooks's company, Brooksfilms, behind the project, although Brooks initially suggested Alan Parker. Once Brooks saw *Eraserhead*, he was sold. Brooks calls it "the best film I've ever seen about what it's like to have kids!" But since it was the first independent production for his company, he had to sell the idea of the story, and Lynch, to others.

"Mel was totally aggressive," Cornfeld says, recalling a meeting with Freddie Silverman at NBC. "Freddie says, 'So who is this David Lynch?' Mel says, 'That just shows you what a fucking idiot you are!'" Even when

Silverman asked if he could read the script, Brooks wouldn't budge. Cornfeld was amazed: "Mel says, 'What the fuck do you mean let you read it? Are you telling me that you know more about what makes a successful motion picture than I do?' He wouldn't give the guy anything." Still NBC wound up giving $4 million in pre-sale money.

Lynch was protected by Brooks's confidence in him, even when it came to screening the movie for Paramount Pictures, the eventual distributor. "Michael Eisner and Barry Diller were at Paramount then," recalls Cornfeld. "They were 'Gee, it's a great film, but we think you should get rid of the elephant at the beginning and the woman at the end.' And Mel said, 'We are involved in a business venture. We screened the film for you to bring you up to date as to the status of the business venture. Do not misconstrue this as our soliciting the input of raging primitives,' and he slammed the phone down!"

Patricia Arquette, star of *Lost Highway*, believes that Lynch's movies "are not understood in their time. Most people make movies for the immediate audience—what the country's in the mood for. With David's movies, you have to go back and watch them five years later to see that you're catching up with them." When asked where he gets his ideas, Lynch laughs, "I'm like a radio! But I'm a bad radio, so sometimes the parts don't hook together." Then more seriously, he says, "Ideas are the best things going. They're almost like gifts. Something is seen and known and felt all at once, and along comes a burst of enthusiasm and you fall in love with it. It's unbelievable that you could get ideas, and that someone could give you money to make a film."

"He sits in a chair and he stares at a blank wall," says Rossellini. "That's how he gets ideas. I know they come from deep within him. A lot of people do therapy. He does a lot of meditation." According to Mary Sweeney, "He's not finding stories, except in his own head. He likes to come up with something new. He likes to be modern. That's the main motivation. Luckily he's got a mind that just percolates. He's wisely shy of big budgets—because of *Dune*—but also because he's a modest person."

The specter of *Dune* has stalked Lynch's career ever since he agreed to do it. At the age of thirty-five and with only two films to his credit, he embarked on what was destined to be a dangerously unwieldy project. The sheer scale or production (seventy-five sets, four thousand costumes, and three years in the making) was far beyond anything Lynch has experienced before or since.

"That picture cut me off at the knees, maybe even a little higher," says Lynch of his experience with the sci-fi megaflop for Dino De Laurentiis' company, DEG. "I went pretty insane on that picture. Little by little I was making compromises. It was like, 'We have to watch David. If he goes in the direction of *Eraserhead*, we're dead in the water,' so I had to be restrained. I just fell into this middle world. It was a sad place to be." Lynch was intrigued by the project and the main character of Paul as "the sleeper who must awaken and become something he was supposed to become." With no final cut clause in his contract, *Dune* was a lesson well learned.

Personal and professional redemption rarely manifest themselves as clearly as Lynch's *Blue Velvet*. "To hear what people were saying about me after *Dune* could have completely destroyed my confidence and happiness," he says. "You need to be happy to make stuff." Lynch returned to earth and, more importantly, to his own dreams for what most critics claim was his masterwork. On seeing *Blue Velvet* for the first time, David Thompson, author of the encyclopedic and incisive *Biographical Dictionary of Film* says, "The occasion stood as the last moment of transcendence I had felt at the movies—until *The Piano*."

Whatever its artistic merits, the film is crucial to understanding Lynch's view of the human condition and of himself. Good and evil were never more polarized, and equilibrium never more painful or difficult to attain. The Oedipal battle between Jeffrey (MacLachlan again, this time in buttoned up Lynchian attire) and Dennis Hopper's preverbal Frank Booth (he can only express himself with one word: "Fuck!") is clearly a struggle between two sides of the same person. The conflict points to an important aspect of Lynch's character. "He's quite a religious person," says Rossellini, "quite spiritual. His visions are more to do with the way meditation makes him perceive the world. He has the conflicts of the great priests."

Sweeney recalls the time when four psychoanalysts went to work on Lynch on the basis of *Blue Velvet*. "Some of them said he was definitely abused as a child which, knowing his parents, I found pretty offensive." Lynch is apparently able to borrow or sense the experiences of others and infuse them with meaning. "Like everyone, he suffered his share of pain and fear in childhood," concludes Peggy Reavey. "But these particular stories help to express those feelings, even though they aren't exactly what happened."

Understanding Lynch also means recognizing a fierce independence in his life and his work. *Blue Velvet* was financed by De Laurentiis's company. In some respects it was a payoff for *Dune*, but Lynch had to agree to cut the budget, and his fee, in half before the project could go ahead.

"I don't think there's any reason to make a film if you can't make it the way you want to make it," Lynch says seriously. "It would be like a death and what would be the point?" In this respect, Lynch has been inspirational to a generation of younger filmmakers. "He's the maverick. That's his niche," says Bob Engels, a key writer on *Twin Peaks* (both the series and the movie). "He'll never go overground again. If Hollywood thought they could get him to do *Guns of Navarone*, they would. You'd get a different take on the same old story. But David doesn't want to do the same old story."

Twin Peaks ("a TV show about free-floating guilt that people just responded to," according to Engels) confirmed Lynch's maverick status. It also cemented an important professional relationship with composer Angelo Badalamenti. On the writing of the Laura Palmer theme, Badalementi explains their technique. "David would say that the music should begin very dark and slow. He said imagine you are in the alone in the woods at night and you hear only the sound of wind and possibly the soft cry of an animal. I'd start playing and David would say, 'That's it, that's it! Now keep playing for a minute, but get ready for a change because now you see a beautiful girl. She's coming out from behind a tree, she's all alone and troubled, so now go into a beautiful melody that climbs ever so slowly until it reaches a climax. Let it tear your heart out.' Not a single note was ever changed."

"A burst of fate," is how Lynch explains the surge of creative energy and success that by 1990 had propelled him into the forefront of the media. "But sometimes fate doesn't open the door. The light is red. And so, if you're given the opportunity to do something else, something else, something else, you do it. But you're heading for a big fall."

His big fall came in 1992 with the release of *Twin Peaks: Fire Walk with Me*. After a vicious roasting at Cannes (the same festival that only two years earlier blessed *Wild at Heart*), Lynch's movie prequel to the now canceled TV series was a critical and financial disaster. "I couldn't even get arrested that year!" Lynch says with a laugh. "I just had a bad smell. Some planets must have been out or something."

Lynch embraces fate in his professional and personal life. "It's like they say: 'And this too will pass,'" he says. "It was a beautiful experience in a way. When you're down, when you've been kicked down in the street and then kicked a few more times until you're bleeding and your teeth are out, then you only have up to go. You get reborn again, and expectations aren't so great because they've taken you away. It's beautiful to be down there. It's so beautiful!"

In the four years that Lynch has been absent from the big screen, he'd been busy, but until recently he was unable to get a feature project green-lighted. One stalled script from this time was *Dream of the Bovine*, which co-writer Bob Engels describes as: "three guys, who used to be cows, living in Van Nuys and trying to assimilate their lives." Finally the European-based company CIBY 2000, with whom Lynch has a three-picture deal (*Twin Peaks: Fire Walk with Me* was the first), agreed to go ahead with *Lost Highway*.

It helps to remember that Lynch started with painting, a medium that has never relaxed its grip on him. The black agitated surfaces of his canvases recall images of childhood (Band-Aids and cotton wool) and more recently, darker themes (sandwich meat and the skeletons of dead animals) have always indicated a troubled mind. "I'm lost in darkness and confusion," he says. Like "Eagle Scout, Missoula, Montana" it's easily said, but just as accurate. "I think he will always feel lost and confused in the darkness," says Rossellini. "He likes it and he hates it." "What he's talking about when he says that," clarifies Sweeney, "is how crazy the world is. How far away from good people have moved, and how far from enlightenment we are." "He s a sunny, optimistic person, but sensitive to all the darkness in an intuitive and uncanny way," Reavey laughs affectionately. "God bless him," she says. "I love it when he says stuff like that!"

The Road to Hell

DOMINIC WELLS/1997

"OH, MY," SAYS David Lynch, as he walks into the Paris hotel suite. "Look at you all lollygagging around."
Lollygagging?
Stranger still than Lynch's time-warp vernacular is the way he invests the word with the shocked awe a ten-year-old might display on interrupting his older sister shagging the college football team. Now, it might seem slightly unusual to find an assortment of film PRs together with Lynch's own fourteen-year-old son, your humble scribe, and shoestring video humorist Adam (or was it Joe?), all sprawled on the bed munching snacks and watching the cult duo's hysterical spoof *Toytrainspotting*, but more bacchanalian orgies have been known. And it's a bit rich coming from a man responsible for some of the most shocking scenes ever committed to film.

Lynch's debut feature, *Eraserhead*, is so called because the hero gets decapitated and his head made into pencils. His stab at a blockbuster, *Dune*, features a bloated, pus-faced pervert, Baron Harkonnen, pulling out plugs attached to the hearts of his boy victims at the moment of orgasm. *Blue Velvet* starts with a severed ear and gets much worse, and in *Twin Peaks* he turned supernatural evil, serial-killing, and incest into prime-time soap. In *Wild at Heart*, he cut graphic scenes of torture only after a hundred people had walked out of a test screening. But mostly, he uses the *un*seen, a heightened banality coupled with an extraordinary use of sound, to create a terror of the unknown. *The X Files* would never have happened without *Twin Peaks*.

So it's with some anticipation that the film-going public is *lollygag-*

From *Time Out London* (13 August 1997). Reprinted by permission.

ging around, awaiting his first movie in four years, *Lost Highway*. It is extraordinary, almost a compendium of Lynch's obsessions. It's also near-incomprehensible. Not so much a "whodunnit" as a "whatthefuckwasallthatabout?" it still gives the impression that behind the string of striking images there might just possibly be a narrative thread. I'll try to help you out on that score, but first, there's the problem that an interview with David Lynch is famously as mysterious. He won't talk about his private life, and he won't talk about his work. Since neither of us are football fans, that leaves us, for the moment, with his diet tips. So David, I ask, emboldened at being poured some Damn Fine Coffee by the man himself. Find any good doughnuts in Paris?

"I'm off the doughnuts," is the response that will shock *Twin Peaks* fans to the core. "I'm off bread and potatoes. On a diet, yeah. Of protein, vegetables, fruit, many good things. But you can't combine it with things that trigger your insulin level to go up. When your insulin level goes up, it forms a hand, and the hand grabs the fat, and puts it in your body." Miming this, he makes it so sinister that I haven't eaten a doughnut since. He's lost twenty-two pounds; quite something from the man who used to call sugar "granulated happiness."

Next up, kids: he's got a son of four-and-a-half; the fourteen-year-old on the bed next door; and a twenty-eight-year-old daughter, Jennifer. So far, so ordinary. Except that Lynch's first film, *Eraserhead*, made over a seven-year period, was about a father terrorised by a mutant baby that cried like a sheep and dissolved when its swaddling clothes were unwrapped. "Jennifer was eight when it was finished," says Lynch. "She saw it. She was right there. Yeah, I think she got it."

Jennifer Lynch subsequently wrote and directed *Boxing Helena*, about a woman whose limbs are cut off one by one by her adoring boyfriend to keep her by his side. Kim Basinger lost a multi-million-dollar lawsuit after walking off the project. Money well spent. Jennifer was quoted as saying that her dad found the film offensive (yes, it was that bad), something Lynch denies: "But it should perhaps have been a small film that found its way. The way it turned out, it just set her up for a fall."

Which is just where Lynch himself is often headed. Just two years after *Wild at Heart* was the toast of Cannes, winning the Palme d'Or, his *Twin Peaks: Fire Walk with Me* was booed and reviled. At the same time, his second attempt at TV, *On the Air*, was pulled after a few painfully unfunny episodes. Can *Lost Highway* put him back on the map?

Typically, Lynch leaves mundane cartography to reviewers and the public to worry about. Instead, he's driven right off the road to make the darkest, strangest film of his strange and dark career. The first third is slow and sombre and pregnant with menace, as Bill Pullman and Patricia Arquette, married but separated by invisible walls, receive anonymous videotapes each morning that penetrate further and further into their house. Then we're in another film entirely as Bill Pullman, on Death Row for the bloody butchery of his wife, metamorphoses in a police cell into young Balthazar Getty—why, we never really know—and is released by his baffled gaolers into a bright, '50s-styled world where Patricia Arquette is also transformed, into a blonde-haired gangster's moll who sucks him into danger, lust, and finally murder again. Things are further confused by a man known only in the credits as Mystery Man, Lynch's most disturbing creation since Dennis Hopper in *Blue Velvet*, who also has a habit of being in two places at once. The film ends, in an infernal time-loop, exactly where it began.

That's about all the plot that can be described. Along the way there's hot sex and distant sex; a head-wound of heroic proportions; and a gratuitously weird but very funny sequence in which crime boss Robert Loggia pistol-whips a tailgating driver while lecturing him on the highway code. If you can be arsed, you can spend a good couple of hours with your cinema date debating what on earth is going on. Alternatively, you can pick up what tips you can from the following ...

Try and ask Lynch anything about what the film means, and he'll say things like: "It's good to talk about some things, and some things it's good not to talk about. I love more than to intellectually understand something, to feel an understanding of something." Right. Thanks a lot, Dave. So if you won't say anything, here's what we'll do: I'll tell you what I think this movie means, and you can tell me if I'm hot or cold. Okay? Okay.

Here goes the big one. Kyle MacLachlan once said that, when playing Agent Dale Cooper, he imagined him as Jeffrey from *Blue Velvet* grown up. Maybe the Bill Pullman character isn't a different *person* from the Getty character; maybe he's just the grown-up version? That's why the second half seems so '50s, because it indicates a shift back in time. And while Getty and Jeffrey both lusted after these doomed mystery women, Pullman has actually married her, and found that life with her isn't all it's cracked up to be, because marriage is sometimes a matter of distance rather than coming together.

Lynch nods like a dog in a car's back window, almost rocking his head off during the bit about marrying the mystery woman. Is it my imagination, or are we both thinking of his now terminated relationship with Isabella Rossellini, whom he met while casting the part of Jeffrey's doomed siren in *Blue Velvet*? But all he'll say is: "Very good." So, does that mean warm-ish? "Yes, that's very good." But you've nothing to add to that? "No." Jesus!

Back to split personalities. There's an old proverb about how the devil enters the world through a mirror . . . (Lynch looks blank.) In *Twin Peaks* death is literally through the looking-glass, where people talk backwards. All your films deal with the duality of good and evil, often fought out internally. The Mystery Man in *Lost Highway* seems, like Frank Booth in *Blue Velvet*, a straightforward embodiment of evil, the dark side. (Lynch cocks his head like a bird to indicate "cold.") Um. Or is he a Creature From The Id, summoned up from Bill Pullman's subconscious? (Lynch nods at last.) Is that warm? "Yeah."

One bit I really liked was where Getty transforms back into Pullman, when they're making love in front of the car headlights in a bright, white light, like at the end of *Fire Walk with Me* where the angel descends. So is this a kind of angelic visitation? (He's nodding, saying uh-huh, but as if he's expecting more.) So I don't know where that goes exactly . . . (Lynch laughs, and doesn't help out.)

You've said before you believe in reincarnation. Is it anything to do with Karma, the wheel of life, with rebirth? "It could be." Then, evasively: "You know there's, ah, all sorts of symbols of beautiful transformations, like the cocoon into the butterfly. So it makes you wonder, you know, what is this transformation we're going through?"

Lynch is trying to stray off the subject, which means I'm on to something. So is there life after death? "Aaah, I think so. I think it's a continuum." So what's it like? (Laughter.) Not a room with red curtains and people talking backwards, then? "That would be kinda beautiful to me."

But the black, depressing thing about *Lost Highway* is that Bill Pullman can never die. He's trapped in this time loop, doomed to repeat his murders and mistakes forever and ever. "Well, maybe not forever *and* ever, but you can see how it would be a struggle. Yeah, that's it." (Lynch looks uneasy. He's given away too much!)

So it *is* that Buddhist notion of reincarnation, that you can only get off the wheel to Nirvana after thousands of years? "Exactly." So there is light? Pullman could be released if the film carried on? "Oh yeah. Sure. It's a fragment of the story. It's not so much a circle as like a spiral that comes around, the next loop a little bit higher than the one that precedes it."

So there you have it. Or not, depending on which particular red herring you're inclined to fish from what Lynch thinks of as the "ocean of ideas." But hey! There's a million stories in the naked city that is David Lynch's mind; it may be even he doesn't know which is the true one. When he paints, apparently, he paints with his eyes closed. . . .

But I still have to pin Lynch down on a couple of things that make people doubt his motives. What about including Richard Pryor, the great comedian currently laid low with muscular sclerosis, in his gallery of grotesques as a wheelchair-bound garage-owner? For the first and only time, Lynch gets quite narked. "Now why should I want to make fun of Richard Pryor? And why *shouldn't* he be in the film? Richard Pryor is a great guy. He's in a wheelchair, and he can't play a huge role, but I really wanted to work with him. I saw him in a show, and I fell in love with him. He was just talking about himself and his life, and I said I really wanted to work with this guy. He did the scripted scenes, and then I put him on the phone in the office of the garage, introduced a mental concept, and let him go for nine minutes. He was amazing. A fragment of that is in the film. That's the kind of thinking . . . it's really sick and twisted. It's really them that are imagining these things, so they're the sick and twisted ones just to come up with that concept."

Equally sick and twisted, according to him, are the accusations of misogyny and pornography that have dogged him ever since *Blue Velvet*. I have up my sleeve a copy of a 1980 book of *film noir* reviews by Barry Gifford, author of *Wild at Heart* and co-scripter of *Lost Highway* itself, in which he describes *Blue Velvet* thus: "One cut above a snuff movie. A kind of academic porn. I can never imagine things as depraved as those that occur here, and I've always thought I could get pretty low in that department. Pornography, as such, simply bores me. So this movie isn't for me, yet it seems somehow important and worth discussing." With friends like that, who needs enemies?

"He says it's not for him?" Lynch responds when I read it to him. "I'll never work with him again." He's joking, of course. . . .

Lost Highway will certainly reopen the debate. It features Patricia Arquette fucked from behind and made to strip at gunpoint, only to discover that she enjoys it. Lynch would counter that that's just the way the character happens to be. Certainly, his male characters are even more passive, and no less sexually screwed up. It's more that Lynch's own sexuality was imprinted in the '50s, with his fetishistic fondness for sweater girls in high-heeled shoes with lipstick like a gash of blood. It does seem suspicious that a man who "stepped out" with Ingrid Bergman's daughter for several years should also have cast Natalie Wood's daughter in *Lost Highway*—and, it must be said, dressed her in a tight '50s sweater which is conspicuously removed in the back of a car. Was it because he used to fancy her mum?

"I fancied Natalie Wood, sure, but that's not why Natasha was hired. I met her and suddenly realised I'd met her eighteen years before. I didn't actually see her then, but her mother was eight months pregnant. It was when I first went to the American Film Institute, and they had a big party one evening, and Natalie Wood came out on the verandah."

So it's back to your cycle of life and birth?

"Exactly right."

Later, I travel to the exhibition of Lynch's recent paintings and photographs at a swanky Paris gallery. The canvases mix words and images, wood and insects buried under paint, but the photos really disturb. Dozens of close-up snaps of high- heeled shoes, legs, bottoms, breasts; women's body parts disassociated from their faces. There's one full-length shot of a girl lying on a sofa, and then, lastly, the sofa with no girl, only a puff of smoke. Magic? Or abduction? The display reminds me of something, and it takes a while to work out what: it looks just like the wall of a serial killer—that bit in the movies when the police burst into his bedroom just before he's about to make his final kill elsewhere. . . .

Perhaps it's just as well that Lynch continues to make his extraordinary movies.

I Want a Dream When I Go to a Film

MICHAEL SRAGOW/1999

I KNOW WHERE David Lynch lives—a three-piece concrete compound in the Hollywood Hills—but I can't describe the layout. When I arrived on Friday morning I inadvertently went up a back stairs and ran into him and two assistants in a kitchen, where he was getting his necessary coffee. We swiftly moved into not a carport, but what I would call an art-port—a cluttered office next to an open-air studio for painting. He is currently working on a diptych; his materials include abused baby dolls.

The instant impression Lynch gives is a mix of intensity, kindness, and enthusiasm. With fingers fluttering like an ant's antennae (as if responding to vibrations at his core), he immediately begins to talk about his predilection for minimalism, and his belief that abstraction in movies intensifies an audience's participation. That belief bleeds into his conversation, where he loves to use words as simple as "thing" and as cosmic as "beautiful." I don't think he's coy or evasive, and when he exclaims "That's great!" for anything that delights him, whether a clear day or a fresh cup of coffee, it isn't a put-on. He wants to protect his own sublime feelings *and* communicate them to you without vulgarizing them. Watching Lynch gesture with his hands is the aesthetic equivalent of seeing Carlton Fisk nudge his left field shot into home-run territory in Game 6 of the '75 World Series.

Similarly, Lynch's buttoned-up white shirt and rolled-up chinos seem less a trademark outfit than a way of deflecting attention from anything except art and the potential materials for art. When he's engaged he's like a human tuning fork—he must sense my sincerity when I tell him that

From *Salon.com* (28 October 1999). Reprinted by permission of Salon Media Group, Inc.

I love the subject of our conversation, his latest film, *The Straight Story*. It's based on the true tale of Alvin Straight, a seventy-three-year-old resident of Laurens, Iowa, who in 1994 hitched a makeshift trailer to a riding lawnmower and trekked over three hundred miles to see his estranged brother in Mount Zion, Wisconsin. Lynch's treatment of the material is open and multilayered; his teamwork with his star, Richard Farnsworth, is empathic and total. Together they have made the rare "movie for all ages" that's also a movie for the ages. It's more about the importance of acquiring wisdom than dispensing it—even for Alvin Straight, who's lived three score and thirteen years.

Farnsworth, now eighty, gives new meaning to the phrase "face value": Entire silent epics pour out of his eyes. And that mature enfant terrible Lynch, now fifty-three, knows just what to do with them. Like Lynch's darker, weirder dreams—say, *Blue Velvet* or TV's *Twin Peaks*—*The Straight Story* gives off the thrill of discovery from the get-go. Anyone sensitive to mood, sound, and sensation, and to the complex presences of Farnsworth, Sissy Spacek as Alvin's daughter Rose, and Harry Dean Stanton as his brother Lyle, will find themselves shaken and honestly uplifted. *The Straight Story* is a testament to following one's own light to the end—and making movies the same way.

Of course, legends have sprouted around Lynch's roving individuality. How he bopped around from state to state as a kid (his dad was a research scientist for the Department of Agriculture) and from art school to art school as a young adult. How a traumatic stint of urban life in Philadelphia while attending the Pennsylvania Academy of Fine Arts affected him as profoundly as child labor did Charles Dickens. And how, for five years, he turned the stables at L.A.'s American Film Institute into his living quarters and the studio for his debut feature, *Eraserhead* (1976). No director alive has a more distinctive signature than the man who went on to make *The Elephant Man* (1980), *Blue Velvet* (1986), and *Twin Peaks* (1989)—popular masterworks with a nonpareil mix of fabulism, eroticism, terror, and cheek.

But Lynch is the first to tell you that much of his art derives from inspired collaboration. "A lot of the time, life is combos," he says when reminiscing about his late pal Alan Splet, the genius sound designer of his major films up through *Blue Velvet*. *The Straight Story* is no exception. To name the most obvious and important example: The woman who found the story, then co-wrote, co-produced, and edited the movie is Mary Sweeney, Lynch's longtime companion. Continuing the movie's family theme, Lynch was happy to be able to invite his parents to the premiere of this film, and his kid sister, too, a financial advisor in Coronado, California. (His younger brother was busy in Washington state, where he's responsible for the electrical wiring in prisons.) "My mother and father were not allowed to see most of my films—actually, I think my father has seen all of them, and that the last one, *Lost Highway*, really disturbed him."

Now that a proposed wild L.A. noir for ABC TV, *Mulholland Drive*, has gone into limbo, Lynch has been devoting himself to painting and to making music with his *Straight Story* sound mixer, John Neff, in an elegant studio down the hill from his painting digs. The painting and the music-making are for Lynch catalytic and elating activities that won't necessarily produce anything for public consumption. "I'm not a musician, but I love the world of music; I play the guitar but I play it upside down and wrong-way," he says. "But the music talks to me, does something good for me, and it's good to work with John; we've almost got ten songs. Like the painting, it could go somewhere but that's not what it's about."

Lynch doesn't see many contemporary films—"sometimes they just seem to be, you know, what they are." But he's reading *A Personal Journey with Martin Scorsese through American Movies* (the book that came out of the director's idiosyncratic documentary series) and Antoine de Baecque and Serge Toubiana's Truffaut biography ("a great book—I can't believe Truffaut's early life"). And he says "there are films I would see every other day if I had the time: *8½*, Kubrick's *Lolita*, *Sunset Boulevard*, *Hour of the Wolf* from Bergman, *Rear Window* from Hitchcock, *Mr. Hulot's Holiday* or *My Uncle* from Jacques Tati, or *The Godfather*. I want a dream when I go to a film. I see *8½* and it makes me dream for a month afterward; or *Sunset Boulevard* or *Lolita*. There's an abstract thing in there that just thrills my soul. Something in between the lines that film can do in a language of its own—a language that says things that can't be put into words."

MS: *In the script to* The Straight Story, *which has just been published, there are a lot of what seem to be obvious "movie" scenes that aren't in the finished film—scenes, say, of police stopping Alvin, or of Alvin having a hard time maneuvering because of his physical ailments.*

DL: A film isn't finished until it's finished. It's always talking to you, and it's an action and reaction thing all along, to the first perfect answer print. You add a part, and suddenly something else is affected. So it never fails that some of the scenes you think will never go are gone—and another thing that didn't seem so important, even a fragment, is saving the day.

One thing everyone should do before they say their film is finished is see it with, probably, twenty people or more (although it could just be one person). Your objectivity comes roaring back in because you're seeing it through their eyes now and that can save your film. It's a critical screening, to test it—and you don't have to have cards filled out, you just have to sit with it and feel it and you'll know what to do. Now, that's a rough screening. The film is working, and working, and all of a sudden it's not working. You can feel it even with people who've gone through the film with you, just from being in a roomful of people.

What gets me—and I've been thinking about this—is that the film is always the same when you've finished it. You know, there are variations from theater to theater, in the acoustics and in the brightness (because of the bulbs in the projectors), but the frames are all there, and the sound goes with it. Still, every screening is always different from one to another. This dialogue between audiences and picture is a fascinating thing. Circles seem to start going between them. The more abstract the film, the more audiences give—they fill in spaces, add in their own feelings. You have the same picture but a different result because of the mix in the crowd. In that way the film is never really finished.

MS: *When Alvin finally arrives at his brother's house he hollers "Lyle" twice—once he just calls out, the second time he sounds worried, like he fears he might have come too late. I just lose it when I hear that second time. It seemed to me like the sort of inspiration that happens with the director and the actor on the set. Sure enough, the script just has one "Lyle."*

DL: These things are gifts, in a way. When something just happens that's *normal* like that, it's so beautiful. What kills *me* is when Richard does this—[Lynch inhales sharply, in a strangled sob]—before the very end. I go crazy when I hear it. I would start crying in the editing room, standing behind Mary when we were working. I think the film really affects men. There's a thing about grandfathers and fathers alive in it—and brothers, too—and it gets you. It gets me.

MS: *Your father was a research scientist for the Department of Agriculture. You were born in Missoula, Montana, and lived in Sandpoint, Idaho; Spokane, Washington; Durham, North Carolina; Boise, Idaho; and Alexandria, Virginia. Your background wasn't too distant, geographically, from the people in this movie.*

DL: My dad was talking to Richard at the premiere, and they've heard of a lot of the same people, and know at least some of the same people. Richard spent a lot of time up at Glacier National Park at one point in his life, and that's a place where I went as a kid, there and all through the Pacific Northwest. It wasn't part of a cowboy life for me, but it was for my father, a generation before. He rode a horse to school—a one-room schoolhouse, that kind of thing. My granddad wore cowboy boots and was a wheat rancher and to me was just the coolest guy. Very cool. He would wear these really beautiful Western suits—and string ties and cowboy boots, really polished. He always drove Buicks. And he wore these special gloves, real thin leather gloves, when he drove. And he drove really slow—which I really loved. I hate riding fast. Sitting with my grandfather I got a lot of feelings I would never be able to articulate. But small children can feel so much, and they don't forget. And this goes in the bank—these relationships you have that are pretty profound but are never really spoken.

MS: *Your granddad's loving Buicks, and Alvin Straight's attachment to his Rehds and John Deere riding mowers—they're not exactly the same thing, but they seem linked. You've said the film is about man and nature, but it's also about man and his machines.*

DL: I've got pictures of my grandfather and his tractors, with these giant metal wheels and these big spikes sticking out of them, and he and his men with these giant canvas gloves and oil cans, and the scene looks more like a machine shop than a farm or a ranch. These machines were incredibly important to them.

MS: *And these machines, like the ones in the movie, have character. Something that has disappeared from contemporary design, which makes everything look the same.*

DL: Yes, the character of the machine is gone. I don't know when it happened, but it probably goes back to computers—when manufacturers started to design everything to be aerodynamically correct, and to use vacuum-formed models and everything like that. You can see why they did it—it makes perfect sense, and in some ways it's safer, and it could be really good. But then you see a 1958 Corvette Sting Ray, and you almost *die* to see what it was and what it's come to. You don't have any joy ever getting in a car, not the same joy anyway. There might be some cars that are still pretty cool but they're few and far between. I've got a 1971 Mercedes that is pretty beautiful, a two-door; I'm waiting to get an American car that I would love to drive, but it hasn't happened.

MS: *In the film it's not just cars or Alvin's mowers. It's Alvin and his daughter Rose sitting by the humming grain elevators at night, this gorgeous looming image. You provide a feeling for the rural landscape that isn't conventionally soft or pastoral.*

DL: It's not like you picture Pittsburgh in the smokestack-industry days—it's not about belching fire. But these people rely on a lot of machinery, and some of it's huge. When you go to a big John Deere dealership and see what's there, it's pretty impressive. And then there are these big grain elevators, and a lot of railroad tracks right next to them—it's an industry. But then it's also so organic. It's miles and miles and miles of fields and very few people. What you really feel is man and nature.

MS: *You mentioned that the film "talks" to you. How does a script talk to you?*

DL: When you read a script or read a book, you're picturing it and feeling it and being moved forward with it. A whole bunch of things start happening inside and those are what you have to remember and translate into film. One moment the idea doesn't exist for you, the next moment that idea comes into your conscious mind and explodes and you know the whole thing. Mary heard about this trip in 1994 when the press covered Alvin's journey. Millions of people read that story, but she got this fixation. And she was talking to me about it, and talking to me about it, and I knew she wanted to do something with it, and I was thinking, that's fine. In 1998, four years later, she got the rights to that story, and I'm still thinking that's fine for Mary. And she and John Roach started working on a script together. They went on the trip, they met Alvin's family and a lot of people. And as soon as they finished the script they gave it to me. I knew Mary wanted me to direct it, but I never really thought it was going to happen. Then I read the script and that was the end of it. It wasn't one thing that decided me, it was the whole thing. When I get an idea or read a script or a book that I love, the next thing I do automatically is "feel the air." And on *The Straight Story* the air married with the script and I knew I was going to do it.

MS: *"Feel the air." Having seen the film twice, I'm inclined to take that literally, as your reaction to the atmosphere in the story.*

DL: It's just a feeling of what's happening in the world right now—a note, a chord, something like that in the air. It seems to be accurate but there's no way to prove that it's accurate. It's a big thing, but also sort of subtle. "Zeitgeist"—is that what someone called it? It's the spirit of the time, and it's constantly changing, and it's fed by everybody. And you see if what you've read or fallen in love with jibes with that. It doesn't necessarily mean that the result will be commercially successful. It just means that you feel the timing is right.

MS: *Is it true that at Cannes you said you felt the potential or the need to make more gentle movies?*
DL: No, not a need—that would be a wrong reason to do a picture. I just loved the screenplay and wanted to make it when this thing in the air supported that.

MS: *Well, I was really conscious of the air* within *the movie—from the opening shots of the wind rustling through the fields and the leaves. In all your films, sound helps the audience feel what you see, and in this film I thought it also helped us understand the characters.*
DL: It's like talking is the tip of an iceberg. There's a whole bunch you can't say, but you *know*. And in a movie you want to carry that other thing. The story may be talking to you, but if an intuition is going, you just want to go with that. When you're working with actors you may not say so much, with words. But you're looking at the person's eyes *and* you're saying something *and* moving your hands in a certain way, and you can see some recognition suddenly appear. Then you go and do the scene again and it has now jumped, and is getting closer to this unspoken thing, which is much bigger, which is what's important. But how it happens is anybody's guess.

MS: *There certainly seem to be a lot of connections in the script that would set your instincts going—and not just your grandfather, and driving slow. I've even read that you like sitting in chairs the way these characters do.*
DL: I love sitting in chairs!

MS: *But there's not as much weather for you to react to while you sit in L.A.!*
DL: No, there's not a lot of change in the weather, but there's good weather. And there's a certain light in L.A. I came to L.A. in 1970 from Philadelphia, and I arrived in L.A. at 11:30 at night. My destination was Sunset and San Vicente. The Whiskey a Go Go was right there; I turned left and went down two blocks on San Vicente and that's where I was going to stay until I found a place. So when I woke up in the morning it was the first time I saw the light. And it was so bright and it made me so happy! I couldn't believe how bright it was! So I sort of fell in love with L.A. right there. And I like the idea in L.A. where you can go inside but you can then just walk outside and there's no change in temperature—it's just an inside-outside life.

There's something about sitting in a chair and just letting your mind wander. It gets harder and harder to do, but it's real important, because you don't know what you're going to wander into. And you can't try to control the wandering. You need time to think about mundane or absurd things or junk before you start getting down into something that could be useful. It doesn't always happen that something useful kicks in, but it *wouldn't* happen if you didn't give it a chance.

MS: *I imagine you can't do that during the making of a film.*
DL: No, then you're in a different mode, much more fast, action and reaction. A new idea could come in but it has to do with the dialogue you're having at that moment and you've got to make sure it feels correct before you leave that moment. So it's real intense, not like the period in between films.

MS: *What made you picture Richard Farnsworth in the role?*
DL: It's a thing coming *through* him that I think is unique. He's kind of an amazing person. He's smart but he's innocent and he's an adult but he's childlike. He *feels* what he says; and as he says what he says you see exactly what he's saying.

MS: *His emotional reactions become physical, like when the guy who sells him the John Deere mower tells him he's always been a smart man until now, and he cracks up—for just a second all his dignity crumbles, humorously.*
DL: That's exactly right. You can see how things strike him a certain way. Richard could really identify with this character and this dialogue beyond what people usually say; this is one of the most perfect marriages of material and actor that I can think of.

MS: *Did you consider character actors playing older than they are?*
DL: Some actors could do that but it's riskier. There's a lot to say about an old guy playing an old guy—they're going to bring twenty or thirty years more, or fifteen years more, to it. And their face is going to be their face. Richard is just perfect.

MS: *This is the first time you've worked with the director of photography, Freddie Francis, since* Dune *in 1984. Had you tried to work with him again before this?*
DL: No, we just remained friends. I always say—"Freddie's like a father to me. It's no wonder I left home!" [Laughter] Freddie is a crusty guy with a great sense of humor and he's always putting me down but loving me. He was a real big supporter of mine on *The Elephant Man*. On

Eraserhead there were like five people on the crew at the most; *The Elephant Man* was my first sort of regular feature and Freddie helped me out a lot. Anyway, after *Dune*, he was in England and I was going off in different directions and working with people like Fred Elmes, who had done *Eraserhead*. But when it turned out *The Straight Story* was coming along, I just felt it was perfect for Freddie to do. It was partly because he's one of the world's greatest D.P.'s, and partly because I wanted to work with him again, and partly because of his age. He's eighty-two. He was a little bit worried about really long hours in the beginning, so he asked me if we could keep it to ten hours. Ten hours of shooting means travel time on top of that. That's not a killer schedule—twelve hours plus travel is what it usually comes down to, and travel can be a long time, if you're out and far away from base camp. But Freddie never slowed down. We worked a lot of days longer than that, and it was the younger guys who were falling before Freddie was.

I was hoping for a camaraderie on the set with Freddie and Richard, which happened; it helps Freddie to look over and see Richard and it helps Richard to look over and see Freddie. Richard looks over and sees a thirty-five-year-old hotshot D.P., it's different; I wanted it more like a family going down the road.

MS: *However you two did it, the film does have an astonishing look.*
DL: The camera just kind of caught what was there. Out on the road there's just really one light, and that's the sun. But you can travel the road south, or north, or east, or west. The land is flat, especially in the beginning of the film, and the roads are blocked out in mile squares, they don't go diagonally. But it's beautiful to see the way the light plays going south or north or right into the sun; you can pump a little bit of light into a face but you can't go up against the sun. There are fewer choices than if you were building a set and lighting it. You go by what is there and then you get down into subtle little things based on a feeling, and that's your shot.

MS: *The whole movie is about a certain kind of American individuality. To use a California phrase, Alvin creates his own space wherever he goes. When he hunkers down in the yard of the Riordans, the people who help him fix his mower, he brings out a chair for the man of the house and says, "Now you're a guest in your own backyard." You give us a sense of the audacity of plunking down a house in the midst of these expanses; there's that incredible shot of Alvin waiting through a storm in an abandoned barn or granary, and he's both protected from the storm and seemingly submerged in it.*

DL: I love the idea of man and nature. So I love the image of a house and a person in this huge expanse of nature with clouds roiling and this kind of stuff. It's sort of what it's all about. And just that one image is about a lot of what's going on.

MS: *Although you follow the script closely, you also seem to have responded directly to what's happening on the locations—like when the businesswoman Alvin meets on the road complains about constantly hitting deer, and looks around, and wonders, as we do, where they come from.*
DL: We picked that location for the scene, and it was a surreal spot. But the day we shot, this strange, powerful wind and weather came up, and that just added a whole other thing to it—you couldn't choose that, it just happened for us. Film can clean up a room better than a vacuum cleaner almost—you really have to have a messy room for it to look messy on film, and you really have to have some nasty weather for it to register. But that day there was just a mood, with the clouds, that added to the surreal quality of the landscape.

MS: *Your tendency to heighten the abstract saves the film from any hint of sentimentality. When we first see Rose staring at the ball rolling in front of her lawn and the young boy going after it, it's just a pattern—we have no idea that she's lost her own children. The kid doesn't look at her, yet the combination of the visual and dramatic minimalism and Sissy Spacek's haunted face tugs at you. It seems like the epitome of how you want the movie to work.*
DL: It's like what I said about the dialogue between a picture and the audience. Watching a movie we're like detectives—we only need a little bit of something and then we'll add in the rest, no problem. The portrait of Rose—it's like in music, where you're going along, and a theme comes in. But it's only the introduction; the theme is beautiful but the rest of the music goes away from it. Then the music builds, and that theme comes back, almost in the same way, but joins with something else. And now it can destroy you.

MS: *This is also the first time that you worked with Sissy Spacek—and with her husband, Jack Fisk, as your production designer—even though they're both old friends of yours.*
DL: Jack is my *best* friend. We met in the ninth grade in Virginia. And we've been friends ever since. We were the only two in our school, with a graduating class of 750, who went to art school. Jack met Sissy when they were doing *Badlands* in '72 or '73; he brought Sissy to the stables I was setting up, when I was starting to make *Eraserhead*. I have always thought

Sissy was one of the greatest actresses; but it never happened that I was working on a film where a part was right for her, until this. And I was so thankful, I just wouldn't have wanted anyone else. So it finally happened. And I never worked with Jack as a production designer; I always worked with Patty Norris. But for the first time since before *Blue Velvet*, Patty Norris said it was OK for her to just do costumes. It wasn't easy for her to say that, but this was perfect for Jack, so it happened.

MS: *The way Sissy does the daughter's stop-and-go speech pattern—it never makes us laugh at her, but we do laugh, because her character almost seems to enjoy how she can focus and finish her thought no matter who interrupts.*
DL: Playing someone who is a little outside the norm and making it real is always a delicate thing. Where that becomes secondary to a thing inside the person. And Sissy just dances along the high wire and makes it look simple.

MS: *With Jack and Sissy along, it must have been even more like "a family going down the road."*
DL: All different ages traveling together, and it was beautiful. It was like the film. It took the same amount of time, we traveled the same roads, so there was another whole thing going on outside the film, behind the camera.

MS: *One story that seems to get into all your movies is* Dr. Jekyll and Mr. Hyde.
DL: Well, Alvin changed—he was another person and he changed.

MS: *And he compares the traumatic breakup with his brother to Cain and Abel—who are not that far, in a way, from Jekyll and Hyde.*
DL: And he meets up with twins—but they're pretty much the same.

MS: *The other story that always recurs for you is* The Wizard of Oz—*and though I know this is supposed to be a different sort of movie, I thought it entered in here too. When Alvin advises the teenage runaway to go back to her family, it's just like the scene where the fake swami (Frank Morgan) persuades Dorothy (Judy Garland) to go home.*
DL: Yes! Yeah! It really is. But I never thought about that.

MS: *And the whole movie is about a guy who offers, throughout the movie, the real wisdom that the Wizard does only at the end.*
DL: Good deal! I never thought of that. I'm sure that Mary and John didn't think about that. But maybe there's something about *The Wizard of Oz* that's in every film—it's that kind of a story.

MS: *You do run the risk of seeming as if you're dispensing a lot of little morals.*

DL: The way I see it, it's not so much little morals, as it is about teachers and students. And that, too, is a circle, because a student has to be receptive or the teacher can't teach. And the teacher has to be intuitive and give the thing at the right moment for the student to jump. And that causes a question in the student and an answer in the teacher and suddenly there's this thing happening—and that occurs in everybody's life.

MS: *And the film isn't trying to make Alvin's way everybody's way—it's about doing something on your own terms and coming into full maturity and awareness at age seventy-three.*

DL: Exactly. The way the trip is taken is extremely important—it's a good thing that Alvin did, to do it a certain way, to let someone know how much it means.

MS: *Some lines resonate on their own—like Alvin saying, "I'm not dead yet." But others are really tricky and two-edged, like when he tells the two young cyclists he's talking to, Steve and Rat, that the worst part of being old is "remembering when you're young."*

DL: Precisely. It's almost as if Rat goes out of his body and looks at himself for the first time. Talking with Alvin was not meaning much to him until then; to the other kid, Steve, it was meaning more. You can't know what it's like to be old until you're old, but you can get a feeling from it. So there's some of that going on there. And then, for Alvin: You can look back on when you were young as a good thing, and now it's different, or you can remember the things you did when you were young that you're paying for, or that you will.

MS: *And that pays off when Alvin and that old friend of the Riordans, Verlyn, trade horror stories—or exchange secrets—from the Second World War.*

DL: There's a bunch of things going on there, too. Because Verlyn tells his story first, and it's deeply disturbing. So for Alvin to tell his story is almost like a gift to Verlyn. Now, when Verlyn goes home, he won't feel bad and think, Jeez, I told Alvin this terrible thing and he just sat there. Instead, Alvin shares with him and puts himself in the same horrible, vulnerable memory spot. And, in a way, that's beautiful.

MS: *We've all been inundated with heroic clichés about the World War II generation. But here there's no inflation; the emphasis is on the emotional and psychological cost of the war.*

DL: It's just monumental that they lived with death and fear for so long, and no one else will ever know, really. But, again, you can get a feel from them. And Alvin and Verlyn can share an understanding more than they can with anybody else.

MS: *This is so much the opposite of a generation-gap movie. It's great, it's real, that Verlyn is the one who immediately gets what Alvin's going through and says, "You've come a long way." But the Riordans are terrific people in this wonderful middle period of their lives. Every generation is respected, and every age of life.*

DL: Each stage of life gives you something different. And it gets more and more internal as it goes along. The older you get, you kind of go into yourself; you don't start great big new projects, you don't do all the things you did at earlier stages. There's a lot of reflecting on the past, you kick into a different mode, and certain things that seemed real important don't seem that way anymore.

MS: *My wife and I have an ongoing debate about the relative safety of the city and the country. I always say I'm more afraid of the country, because if there's a serial killer out there he'll probably come to your house. But the countryside is peaceful in this film. Is that your Midwest fantasy?*

DL: It's not a fantasy—and that's the strangest part of it. Once I went with Mary to Wisconsin; she's from Madison. And I go to Madison and I start meeting her family and friends, and people in the store, and I think nobody can be this nice; someone is having some sort of fun, some sort of joke. Then I realize, no, it's true. And I think it has something to do with land and farms and the fact that there's fewer people and they get to rely on one another. And this reliance has to do with survival—they don't have any problems helping somebody, because they know that next day they could need help. Alvin did this trip and he didn't have anything bad happen to him, people did take him in and were rooting for him. You say that this is an American movie, but I'm convinced that there are people in every land who have the stuff to do that. It's certainly an American theme, but there are characters with this strength in them everyplace.

David Lynch: A 180-Degree Turnaround

MICHAEL HENRY/1999

MICHAEL HENRY: The Straight Story *is the first of your films for which you didn't write the script. What originally appealed to you in the project?*
DAVID LYNCH: The script! I live with Mary [Sweeney]. And I knew that she was fascinated by that story since 1994. She talked to me about it a lot. I loved the idea of this guy who gets on his lawnmower and goes to meet his brother on the other side of the state border. But I never imagined that one day it would become one of my films. Then, in 1998, when she obtained the rights for the story, Mary began to gather the relevant material. She and her partner John Roach retraced the trip of Alvin Straight, meeting his family and close friends. I followed their progress. All of a sudden, they completed the script and Mary gave it to me to read. At the beginning, I said to myself: there's very little chance that I'll like this enough to want to direct it. I even asked myself what I would really be able to tell them. . . . And from the moment that I began reading, all my misgivings disappeared. My imagination began to work and I felt the emotion that emerged from the material.

MH: *Does the script contain many visual descriptions?*
DL: Enough to start a film rolling inside my head while I was reading. What struck me was the simplicity, the purity of the story: it's about a man, all alone, and we learn quite a few things about him, and in the end, he teaches us quite a bit about life. That touched me. I thought that a film could communicate those qualities without tricks or distractions. I really like—and I do it from time to time, especially in *Elephant Man*—to create a pure emotion with images and sound. The screenplay by Mary and John permitted me to create exactly that kind of emotion.

From *Positif* (November 1999), translated from French. Reprinted by permission.

MH: *The film opens and closes, like the ending of* Elephant Man, *with the star-filled sky.*

DL: The stars are important because, when they were kids, the two brothers contemplated them together on summer nights. The stars were that and even more. I couldn't pass that up.

MH: *There's a terrific dissolve from the sky to the earth, from the starry sky to a field of wheat—when exactly did that emerge in making the film? Was it in the screenplay?*

DL: That's not important. A script, you might say, is a skeleton. You have to give it flesh and blood. And a director is an interpreter. He translates the images that he receives from the screenplay. This is true of all ideas, whether they come from a script or a book. The idea doesn't belong to you. You've received it—including the images, the sounds, the atmosphere that emanates from the material. You try to translate that into film, and sometimes that gives you a lot of latitude, and sometimes very little. Then there are variables that come into play: the shoot locations, the choices of actors, etc. If you try hard to remain faithful to the first impression, everything will work out right.

MH: *You shoot the story in the heartland of the countryside, which could lead one to expect satire. But what creates the beauty of the film is the absence of any irony.*

DL: I've always worked at a much more basic level than people think. Still, I have nothing against satire, but it's not the kind of story where you can introduce comic elements. That would be against the nature of things. It's the story that dictates the approach you take. The one in *The Straight Story* is simple, direct, straight. One that doesn't prevent a director from introducing subtleties. I wasn't deprived of anything doing things that way. For me, the question was: How can I weave these elements together to create a beautiful little tapestry, a tapestry-poem?

MH: *The protagonist's past isn't evoked by flashbacks, but by his encountering other people. His past emerges from the course of his conversations; he liberates himself that way, all while inspiring the people he talks to.*

DL: There's reciprocity there, just like in life. When you meet someone, you form an impression of him, but as you talk to him, he becomes transformed, he appears to you in a different light, and you imagine his past, the trials he's gone through. Alvin Straight is not a saint, but he can share something of his own experience. His heart is wide open. That's all he has to give people. He's a man at once simple, innocent, and very strong.

MH: *He belongs to a generation that one hardly ever sees in cinema anymore: the "forgotten men" of the Great Depression and the Second World War. The setting of the reunion at the end of the film suggests the photographs of Walker Evans or Paul Strand.*
DL: Everyone has a father or a grandfather who lived during that period. Sometimes when they start to tell their life story, people have the impression of understanding it, but that's only an impression, a vague notion, because how can you share what haunts you with another generation? What they share is not their experience, but the aftermath of that experience–how it's marked them.

MH: *You yourself retraced the trip that Alvin Straight took.*
DL: Two times. First for the shoot locations, and then for a deeper perspective. My film crew did it again a third time in order to set up various details. The problem was that you were traveling by car and couldn't really get an idea of what it was like for Alvin—even if you drove slowly. A car can't really go five miles per hour without braking all the time. That dawned on me when I began to shoot the film and I found myself on the shoulder of the road with Richard [Farnsworth], where I saw the eighteen-wheelers overtake us at top speed. Alvin had done that every day without a police escort! We followed his route meticulously. And we did the shoot chronologically. At Laurens [Iowa], we were even able to shoot at his house, which was unoccupied. The neighbors helped us a lot, and so did the rest of the townspeople in Laurens.

MH: *Are all the journey's events represented in the film authentic?*
DL: You could say that they're all inspired by the actual events. But we took a few liberties. For example, Alvin didn't meet the woman with the deer, but she did exist. The locals remember her well and they have tons of stories to tell about her.

MH: *You grew up in the countryside in Montana, the state of Washington, and Idaho. Does your interest in country life stem from your childhood?*
DL: It's not a world that in itself really interests me. But childhood is something so powerful that, consciously or not, some of its images come up to the surface and pervade your work. Still, I don't think that it's necessary to have lived in a particular world in order to feel and understand it. When I went to England to shoot *Elephant Man*, I was pretty naïve. I thought I could get up to speed by studying some books and photos. But when I got there, I sensed some resistance: What was this American really going understand about our history? Then I went to walk around

the East London Hospital for the poor. While I was walking, something came over me all of a sudden, a feeling invaded me, and I was transported to the period of the film. I felt it in all my being, and from then on it hardly mattered whether I was a Victorian Englishman or an American from Montana!

MH: *At several points in the story, you show Richard Farnsworth contemplating the beauty of the natural world. Like us, he's a spectator, but inside of the picture.*
DL: In that part of the country, nature's a force that people have to pay attention to. The seasons take on enormous importance there. The farmers can lose everything because of a sudden thunderstorm. So they live hanging on to every update of the weather report. Every season has its beauty, and the same goes for every hour. The farmers must be used to that. But when you travel through the country slowly, you see things differently and become conscious of that beauty. The film unfolds over the course of autumn.

MH: *Compared to your other road movie, which was* Wild at Heart, A Straight Story *seems to proceed at a slower pace.*
DL: That slowness is appropriate for the story. People accept that sort of thing with music. I'm thinking here of certain majestic symphonies that evoke an entire world. There's a place for different sorts of music, slow or fast. Today, speed seems to be in fashion everywhere, but reality itself is created by contrasts.

MH: *You frequently move from the microscopic to the macroscopic in the course of the same scene.*
DL: When you go beyond a certain point, a sudden shift in dimensions reveals a whole new perspective to you. That happened a lot during the trip. You have the impression that you can see yourself moving forward into the countryside. It's the same effect with the stars. Sometimes when you look at them from the ground, you have the sense of floating with them. You can float across the countryside in the same way. The important thing for me was the vast extent of the countryside, and the feeling of floating in nature.

MH: *At one point, you cut from Alvin to a lengthy pan shot of the clouds, and, when you come back to him, he hardly seems to have moved at all since the beginning of the first shot. Is that a way of indicating the place of human beings in nature?*

DL: One feels that effect there. But that doesn't mean that man is insignificant. We can see that man and nature coexist. They coexist in the city, of course, but we tend to forget that.

MH: *Until now, nature has not been a large presence in the world of your films, which is usually urban and industrial.*

DL: It was to some extent in *Twin Peaks*, even if the characters hardly appreciate it. How many of us appreciate the world where we live? When you are raised close to nature, in small country towns, and you go to New York City, like I did when I was little and visited my grandparents in Brooklyn, it's a tremendous shock. A 180-degree turnaround. It's something that you never forget. Not just what you saw, but above all what you felt floating in the air. It's like when someone enters a room, and without even one word being said, you know he's going to raise a ruckus. It's curious, isn't it? It's not written on people's faces. It floats in the air. The air becomes thick with it. If you feel that in a room, there's all the more reason to feel it in the cramped and overpopulated space like a city. They have done experiments with rats. If you stick them all together, their behavior changes and becomes a little bizarre. It must be the same thing for us.

MH: *You have yourself accomplished a 180-degree reversal with this film, where good neighborliness prevails, where the natives are all wonderful, and where human nature presents its best face.*

DL: Mary comes from Madison, Wisconsin, and we have a house there. The first time that I went there with her and would go into the stores, I thought the local people were little practical jokers, laughing at me the whole time, they were *so* polite! Even today, I find them more courteous and more considerate than anywhere else. They're always ready to help you if you have a problem. Probably because they're farmers. Those regions are so sparsely populated that they all depend on one another. If you are in a difficult spot, someone comes right away to give you a hand. And Alvin received a lot of help during his journey.

MH: *You reject the pathos of the lost prairie, of the garden ravaged by machines. In the film, machines are benevolent and powerfully helpful for people.*

DL: They *are* benevolent—that's the word. The environment is not polluted. That suggests to me a Japanese garden. Nature makes the plants grow, but it's the gardeners who make the trees grow in this way or in that by adding some rocks, making the water flow here or there, all according to aesthetic criteria. They guide nature and get a better result. Over there, machines, harvesters, tractors . . . have a reason for being [*raison d'être*]. It's perfectly organized. It's a perfect example of collaboration between man and nature.

MH: *The Hollywood tradition of Americana from John Ford to Henry King—did it matter to during your childhood?*
DL: Not really. The first film that I remember seeing is *Wait Until the Sun Shines, Nellie* [by Henry King]. It happens that the other night, it was broadcast on television, but I realized that too late, and I only saw the credits at the end. It's not supposed to be a good film, but I remember certain scenes and I would really like to see it again. With Ford, I don't associate him with a particular genre. He told a story, and it was the story that determined his approach.

MH: *The family is the most frequently dysfunctional element in your films. Here, you celebrate it with an unexpected lyricism.*
DL: That's the nature of this story. The image of the sticks that become unbreakable when they're tied together comes from Alvin. It was his family that told us about that.

MH: *The characters are all solidly rooted in their physical environment. And this is equally true of their ethics. For them, there is a clear right and wrong.*
DL: Whatever people may say, we all know what the right path is. We know perfectly well the good and the bad of our actions. Even if it's a personal matter. Even if what's good for you isn't necessarily so for everyone else. We can't really judge the morality of others, but we know what applies to our own concerns. But it's often true that we consider that only when we get older, when death is near and we look back on things.

MH: *Was Richard Farnsworth your first choice for the leading role?*
DL: We considered a lot of people, but once he became a possibility, our choice was obvious. His face and eyes impressed me. Every time that I had seen him in a film, I had liked him. There's something that emanates from him. An aura of honesty and innocence. An intense power. He incarnates the myth of the American cowboy. That corresponds to the life he led. Once Richard had signed on, he couldn't quite convince himself that he could get the job done. Because of his hips, he wasn't sure that he could sit on top of the lawnmower the entire time. But not only did he get the job done, he was perfect. No one else could have done it as well as he did.

MH: *In your films sound plays a part in evoking menace, in suggesting evil forces beneath the surface, behind appearances. Here, it suggests instead the forces of life. Even the rumbling of the silo is euphoric.*

DL: During editing, I had the sound in mind, but it was the music, more than the sound effects, that guided us. When I work with Angelo [Badalamenti], it's generally the image that shapes the sound. But the opposite can happen, or the two can emerge at the same time. In this film, we sometimes reworked the sequence of images because we needed more footage here or there in order to let the sound breathe. Each scene has its appropriate tone. And the sound can either amplify or destroy that ambience. Once you get the right sound, it's all about the right level. Finding the right formula was not so simple for *The Straight Story*. No grand events take place. It's a story so simple, so pure, that introducing a new element risks making it distracting and out of place. If you're in a room that's more or less empty, any furniture there leaps out at you. And if someone enters, his presence will be felt all the more. In other words, if the sound is too powerful, you risk ruining the whole thing. But if it's too understated, you risk it going unnoticed.

MH: *What directions for the music did you give your longtime collaborator, Angelo Badalamenti?*

DL: I did things as usual. I sat beside him, in his studio. I start talking to him and he starts playing. Based on how he reacts, I talk some more. Sometimes, one word is all that's needed and he produces something magical, a note or two, and things take off on a good track from there. That's how we composed a first piece, and that led to all the others. It only took a few insignificant words that I don't even remember anymore. What matters is what circulates in the air. Everything is about interaction, and that's true for all the stages of the production and for life itself.

MH: *Did you choose Freddie Francis as director of photography because of* Elephant Man?

DL: In a way, yes. We became close friends then. And we wanted to work together again. It was the ideal project—because of our ages, not the nature of the film. He's eighty years old, just a little older than Alvin. And he's one of the greats in his field. It was good for Richard to see Freddie work all day long, and vice versa. Not to mention all the other older people. It was good for the film, and for everyone involved. It would have been a lot different with a young director of photography.

MH: *The last line of* Elephant Man *was: "Nothing will die." Couldn't that also apply to* The Straight Story?
DL: Absolutely.

MH: *The scene with the cyclists also evokes* The Elephant Man. *After watching Alvin and his lawnmower, the cyclists' speed seems incongruous, just as the so-called normal people seem grotesque who mock John Merrick as a freak. There is, once again, a reversal of perspective, a 180-degree turn-around.*
DL: Exactly. I don't know how we got that scene! The first time that I did the route in a car, I realized that I hadn't seen much of anything. It was different during the shooting, and that lasted almost as long as Alvin's trip. When you shoot at an outdoor location for relatively long periods, time becomes crucial. You become like a farmer. You begin to see things. You notice details. You adopt a certain kind of rhythm. So it was a surprise to see the cyclists go by at top speed! That led me to shoot the scene a little differently. The same thing happens with the passing trucks. Or at the end of the film, when the tractor seems enormous next to the lawnmower.

MH: *Everything in the film is a question of scale: man in relation to the cosmos.*
DL: Relativity! Yes, but isn't that the theme of all films?!

MH: *This time, however, it's not a source of anxiety.*
DL: No, relativity is a beautiful notion. We're very well situated. The human being, you might say, is situated at the center of things. There's as much above as below us. As much outside as on the inside. Man is in a beautiful place.

MH: *How far along are you with the pilot of the television series* Mulholland Drive?
DL: I shot it while we finished the editing of *The Straight Story*. The two films were mixed in succession. But for *Mulholland Drive*, it's a temporary sound mix. It's not quite right and I am nowhere near completely satisfied with the editing. ABC hated the pilot and refused to pursue the series. For the pilot, ABC has the rights to two broadcasts. In other countries, Disney will sell it as a film for television. I'm not sure that it can be shown in theaters because it has an open-ended conclusion, which was conceived for television. What kills me is that the series was created as a story that's constantly evolving. For me, that's the beauty of television: being able to tell a story that carries on from one night to the next. But

the company executives say that they analyzed the public's viewing habits, and that they frequently skip over episodes. They insist that the episodes should be self-contained. As if the public isn't smart enough to pick up on the story as it goes along. They're so obsessed with market testing that they forget the magic of an ongoing story. In fact they hated what they saw—and that's all there is to it!

MH: *Is it worse than what happened with* Twin Peaks?

DL: I don't understand anything about television. I know too little to understand the executives' way of seeing things. Still, I have the feeling that network television is a thing of the past. On cable, there are fewer constraints, you can create adult projects for it. And soon with the internet everyone will have their own television station—everything will be possible.

MH: *Do you have any other projects?*

DL: No, but I'd certainly like to.

Getting Lost Is Beautiful

JOHN POWERS/2001

DAVID LYNCH AND I are sitting high up in his aerielike studio talking about one of his favorite topics.

"I love concrete," he says. "Concrete is very strong. It can be very smooth and make beautiful, minimal shapes."

He's just launching into a story about the genius of his concrete trowler, Renaldo, who can give a wall a burnished surface full of marvelous shapes and shades, when the phone rings. It's his nine-year-old son, Riley.

"You want to do *what?*" Lynch barks. "Ride your skateboard into the swimming pool? Of course you can't." He shakes his head. "What did you think I'd say?"

As they talk, I think about how weird it would be to have David Lynch as your dad.

To talk seriously about Lynch is to begin with his enthusiasms.

"Look at this," he says one hot August morning. He shows me a photograph of a dilapidated industrial building. "I took it last December in Lodz, Poland. I was at this film festival, Camerimage, and it was so much fun. In the daytime we'd shoot factories, and at night we'd shoot nudes."

Factories and nudes, nudes and factories—of such strange oppositions is Lynch's imagination made. His movies are torn between light and dark, blonde and brunette, goofy and primal, avant-garde and retro, the radiantly transcendent and the downright icky. And this sense of duality carries into his daily existence: Lynch jealously guards his privacy but parades his innermost kinks onscreen for the whole world to

---

From *LA Weekly* (October 19-25, 2001). Reprinted by permission of John Powers and *LA Weekly*.

see. He invariably talks poor—"David's so goddamned *cheap*," his late friend Jack Nance once laughingly told me—but has a three-house compound in the Hollywood Hills. Although his twisted style subverts traditional American values, his political attitudes are profoundly conservative: "She's a wonderful woman," he once snapped when I made fun of Nancy Reagan. Where many are swallowed by their contradictions, Lynch gobbles them down like amphetamines. They're his goad, his fuel, his shivering thrill.

When we first met in the mid-1980s, his big, soft face was immaculately shaven, his hair neatly combed, his crisp white shirt carefully buttoned all the way to the top. He exuded a corn-fed adolescent enthusiasm—did anyone else, even then, still say "Jeepers"?—and I understood why he was often compared to Jimmy Stewart. Now, at fifty-five, he still uses the same cracker-barrel lingo, but time has left its handwriting upon him. His eyes are bloodshot, the white shirt looks a tad worn, and bits of gray stubble elude his razor. He still reminds me of Jimmy Stewart, not the Mr. Smith who goes to Washington but the grizzled obsessive from *Vertigo*. His beaming smile has lost its innocence.

Yet sitting in his studio high above the family bunker (all three houses are made of concrete), he's in fine spirits. After years in the artistic wilderness, David Lynch is back with a vengeance. He's about to launch a pay Web site, DavidLynch.com, and his new movie, *Mulholland Drive*, has proven an unexpected triumph. A rejected TV pilot that Lynch reshot, recut and reconceived, *Mulholland Drive* isn't merely his best work in a decade, it may be the best movie set in Hollywood since *Sunset Boulevard*.

In an essay written around the time of *Lost Highway*, David Foster Wallace neatly explained why Lynch's work is so unsettling: Unlike a normal film, a Lynch film gets under your skin because *you don't know what it wants from you*. It enters you like a dream.

This is certainly true of *Mulholland Drive*, a corrosively beautiful fairy tale that's as mysterious as the inky shadows that lie just beyond the throw of our headlights. It centers on the apache dance of two wildly different women, one dark and one fair. There's the hard-faced brunette sexpot known as Rita (Laura Elena Harring), who is suffering from amnesia, and there's innocent, blond Betty Elms, played by Naomi Watts, whose breathtaking performance takes her from wide-eyed wonder to a lacerating awareness of human emptiness. Wildly ambitious and wantonly intuitive, the movie is at once a touching love story, a portrait of L.A. illusions, a pomo slice of film noir, a clubfooted satire of the movie business and a radical vision of the human psyche—not to mention another Lynchian riff on *The Wizard of Oz*, complete with tiny people. Call it a tale about nudes caught in the Dream Factory.

Like nearly all of Lynch's work, the movie began not with a plot line but with a mood, an image, a title, a place—in this case, Mulholland Drive.

"I picture Mulholland Drive at night," Lynch says, lighting up an American Spirit cigarette. "Anybody who's driven on that road knows that there's not a lot of traffic, and it's filled with coyotes and owls and who knows what. You hear *stories* about things that happen on Mulholland Drive. It's a road of mystery and danger. And it's riding on top of the world, looking down on the Valley and Los Angeles. You get these incredible vistas, so it's pretty dreamy as well as mysterious."

The most instinctive of artists, Lynch has never liked discussing his work and grows instantly leery when you bring up questions of meaning. When I ask how he sees the difference between blondes and brunettes, a classic dichotomy that he returns to fetishistically, his answer's so deliberately vague that both of us smile—we know I'll never be able to use it. Like a good Middle American (he was born in Montana), he views all manner of analysis with mortal suspicion. He once went to a psychiatrist, and after the first session asked if therapy might damage his creativity. The shrink said yes, and Lynch never went back.

The first time I interviewed him, in 1986, I spent hours peppering him with questions, all of which he deflected with cheery aplomb. I felt like a high school kid parked with a perky virgin who politely removed my hand each time I put it on her thigh. Today, we're both too old for that song and dance, and we race through our paces like blasé divorcees.

"You feel warier than you used to be?"

"Uh-huh."

"Less good-humored?"

"Uh-huh."

He leans back in his Aeron chair. I look around his atelier, which is studded with Lynchiana. A coffee cup, a big kit of Brookestone tools, a gorgeous, unfinished painting that contains the words *Bob's Anti-Gravity Factory*. In a touch so talismanic that it feels art-directed, his small portable stereo is adorned with the husk of a dead fly.

He lights up another cigarette, and I ask about his smoking. He says that twenty-two years after quitting cold turkey, he started up again in 1992.

"What happened in 1992?"

He laughs mirthlessly. "Don't get funny with me, Powers."

I originally wondered if his fabled obsessiveness was a sly shtick, a way of giving reporters something droll to write about while throwing them off the scent. No doubt this is partly true. But in 1989, I spent a week interviewing Lynch for a French documentary and saw firsthand how thoroughly his obsessions shaped his life. Back then he wouldn't allow any food in the house (he hated the smell) and ate exactly the same thing every day (as I recall, a tuna sandwich for lunch). Since then, the menu has changed but not the obsession:

"I'll have the same thing every day for six months maybe, or even longer," he says. "And then one day I just can't face it anymore.

"Now, I have cappuccino in the morning, many coffees during the day, and salad that's put in a Cuisinart so each bite tastes the same. No meat. This has got nuts and eggs and some lettuce and different kinds of greens. So it's a little bowl of Cuisinart salad with Parmesan cheese on top. And then at night I have a block of Parmesan cheese, maybe a two-inch cube, and red wine. Mary [Sweeney, with whom he lives] cuts it up for me into little chunks and gives it to me in a napkin."

When I ask *why* he wants to stick to this redundant diet, he tells me that it's "reassuring . . . there are no surprises there." Lynch's inner life is obviously so fertile and turbulent—a steaming Amazon of run-amok impulses—that his culinary routine provides a kind of sanctuary. Like the concrete walls that house him, his dietary rituals help him fend off the outer world so he can devote all his time to work.

For Lynch loves working more than anything in the world. Tireless as a silkworm, he just can't stop creating: He paints, makes movies, produces TV shows, takes photographs, and plays guitar for a heavy-metal band called Blue Bob. Creativity is the one topic he never tires of talking about. He'll tell you how some ideas come from deep inside you, and how other ideas come from places so much deeper inside that they seem to be coming from *outside* you. And he'll tell you how still others trickle into your mind like water and pool there until you finally notice them and fall in love with their possibilities. Just don't ask him what they mean.

"Once you fall in love with the ideas," he exults, "that is so thrilling. There's not much more to think about except trying to go as deep into that world as you can and being true to those ideas. You kind of get lost. And getting lost is *beautiful*."

Of course, some ways of getting lost are not so lovely, and for most of the last decade, Lynch seemed to have dropped off the cultural map.

It hardly seemed possible. From the moment he made the definitive midnight movie, *Eraserhead*, in 1976, he was a guy on the rise. True, *Dune* was a megabudget flop, but Lynch had already landed a Best Director Oscar nomination for *The Elephant Man*, and his next picture, *Blue Velvet*, quickly became one of the cinematic touchstones of the last quarter-century. By the summer of 1990, his trademark blend of irony, grotesquery, and visceral emotionalism had made him the heppest cat around. *Wild at Heart* had just won the Palme d'Or at Cannes, *Twin Peaks* was an international craze, and Lynch himself gazed out from the cover of *Time*, which dubbed him the "Czar of Bizarre." He had turned a common Irish surname into a resonant adjective—the word *Lynchian* was every bit as evocative as *Kafkaesque*—and his eccentric sensibility seeded the clouds of the '90s, influencing TV programs like *Northern Exposure* and cartoonists like Daniel Clowes, and injecting his artistic DNA into the work of Tarantino, Egoyan, and the brothers Coen (what is *Fargo* if not a more anodyne *Twin Peaks*?).

But just when Lynch seemed to have it made, this oddball Icarus flew too close to mass culture's klieg lights. Despite a shattering climax, *Twin Peaks* guttered and died, and the public never warmed to *Wild at Heart* (which I still think is his worst film). By the time *Twin Peaks: Fire Walk with Me* was released in 1992 (and yes, that's the year he began smoking again), he had fallen sadly out of favor. Although his account of Laura Palmer's last week is one of that decade's bravest and most harrowing films, it died in a blizzard of nasty, uncomprehending reviews (*The Washington Post* termed it a "psychic autopsy, a weirdly fundamentalist cogitation on the intersection of Heaven, Hell and Washington state").

When I ask about this fall from grace, he shrugs and replies in the primitivist terms you might expect: "They warned me if you're on the cover of *Time*, you've got two years' bad luck coming. And a black cloud did come over me, and when the black cloud comes over, there's nothing you can do about it. Nothing. And you look out and you wonder, 'How come these things are happening and people are saying these things?' It's just the way it is. It's just part of the deal. And then you wonder, 'How long will the cloud be there?'"

Lynch didn't make another film for five years, and you heard industry types muttering that he was "over." But his own faith in himself was unshaken. "If you don't believe in the work and you get bad reviews, then it's really devastating. But if you believe in it, then the bad reviews, at most, are confusing—you can still live. With *Dune* it was the first example, and with *Fire Walk with Me* it was the second."

Because his work never relies on formula, Lynch has a narrower margin for error than most filmmakers: If a scene or two goes kerflooey, he completely loses the audience. That's pretty much what happened with the patchy *Lost Highway* (1997), whose Möbius-strip structure was miles from Hollywood's three-act cliché—Bill Pullman transforms into Balthazar Getty *with no explanation.* People just didn't get it. That may be one reason he played it so linear in *The Straight Story*, a lawn-mower-powered 1999 road movie that was as square as Grandma's favorite doily. Although the movie was guilty of romanticizing small-town life (no Wal-Mart in Lynch's Iowa), it also marked a heartfelt stab at a new emotional maturity. Lynch genuinely believed what he was saying about family and reconciliation. The movie had a tenderness largely missing since *The Elephant Man.*

That tenderness has carried over into *Mulholland Drive*, which finds Lynch up to his customary trick of dropping light and dark into the Cuisinart. Although this is the crookedest story he's ever told, Lynch never loses sight of his heroines' frailty amid all the hallucinations, mistaken identities, performances within performances, dreams within dreams within dreams. The film's vision is bleak, for Lynch no longer seems to believe in any kind of solid, stable psyche. He portrays the self as a series of trap doors through which we tumble, or perhaps as an onion—peel off its layers and there's nothing left but silence. In a pivotal scene, Rita and Betty go to a downtown theater and watch a Latina singer belt out a song with wrenching passion. It's a dazzling star turn—until we discover that she's merely lip-synching. *Mulholland Drive* suggests that each of our lives is a performance in which we're never quite sure whose voice we're really hearing, or who's writing the lines.

It's not that Lynch has no idea of how he'd like the world to be. For all his dark, perverse imaginings, his social values are rooted in the sunlit credo of the American West: *Don't tread on me.* Nothing matters to him more than his freedom to do whatever he thinks up. I first saw this side of him one afternoon in 1989 when he began railing about the city government: It wouldn't let him put razor wire around his property to keep itinerants from cutting across his property. He shook his head:

"You know, John, this country's in pretty bad shape when human scum can walk across your lawn, and they put *you* in jail if you shoot 'em."

While Lynch doesn't seem like the sort of man who's packing heat, he was drawn to Ronald Reagan because of his "cowboy image" and laments that L.A.'s wonderland of individual freedom is being hedged in by rules and regulations. He takes building-code restrictions personally. "People," he says, "should be able to build *what* they want to build, *when* they want to build it, *how* they want to build it."

Although he claims to know nothing of politics, in last year's election he backed the Natural Law Party, whose philosophy is that an ideal government mirrors the natural order. While this may sound slightly wacko, the party's platform is perfectly sensible—libertarianism with a human face. As part of the campaign, Lynch produced a campaign video for the party's presidential candidate, John Hagelin, an acclaimed quantum physicist. This tape is an extremely strange document for Lynch has no great knack for doing normal. He interviews the candidate in front of creepy golden curtains and punctuates the questions with ominous pulsing music. The superbrainy Hagelin winds up seeming like an off-kilter, B-movie version of a real politician—the presidential hopeful from Twin Peaks.

Lynch's picture of the world was formed in the 1950s, and he clearly adores the mythologized version, that fabulous decade of jukeboxes and sneaky-perverse movies like *Rear Window*.

"It was a feeling in the air that anything was possible. People were enthusiastically inventing things that thrilled them. And there was a happiness in the air. There was plenty going on beneath the surface, but it wasn't as dark a time because there was that other thing going along with it. The '50s was a time when people seemed to be going crazy with design. And the cars were just incredible. I mean, you look at them, and it's like you start to fall in love. That changed, you know, in the '60s and '70s. The cars were pitiful. I mean *pitiful*. It made you ashamed. You'd wanna hang your head and go in a corner. It was sickening."

We're talking a couple of days before September 11, but Lynch is already gloomy about the state of the world:

"You just get the feeling that you're sort of powerless in the big picture. And it's not like 'I better get mine,' but I'm gonna burrow in and concentrate and enjoy doing that. Not try to put my head in the sand, but for my own protection let as little of that outside negativity affect me."

He lights another American Spirit.

Far more than when we first met, Lynch appears to be isolating himself from the outside world. And there's more to this than just surrounding himself with concrete walls. Where he once waxed lyrical about tooling around L.A., he now says he doesn't drive very much anymore. People have gotten too crazy and the cars too hideous. "If the cars were more beautiful," he says about driving, "somehow I think people would take care and enjoy it more."

At the moment, he seems settled in a domesticity I wouldn't have believed possible in the early '90s. Back then he was known for squiring around actresses, from ex-flame Isabella Rossellini to *Twin Peaks* hotty

Sherilyn Fenn. (In life, anyway, he prefers his women dark rather than fair.) He's currently into his tenth year with companion Mary Sweeney, a multitalented brunette who produced his last three films, edited all his work since *Fire Walk with Me* and co-wrote *The Straight Story*. She's also the mother of nine-year-old Riley.

I ask Lynch: "Do you like being a father?"

His smile falters slightly. "What does *that* have to do with anything?"

When the airplanes flattened the World Trade Center, the composer Karlheinz Stockhausen caused a scandal by calling it a great work of art. Lynch is not so cut off from humanity as to say anything like that, but far more than anyone I've met, he does view life through the prism of aesthetics. He's so preternaturally attuned to design that it's sometimes hard to believe he's not kidding.

I've been told that Lynch likes to hang around the vintage modern furniture shop Skank World, and one morning, I ask if he cares about furniture. He instantly sits up.

"*Caring*," he says, giving it a little spin. "Every word has, you know, its spread of power. You could care a little bit or you could care a lot. But if you put this word *caring* at the maximum-level intensity, it wouldn't begin to be enough to say how much I love furniture.

"And I have been *sick* lately. I'm not seeing any furniture that thrills my soul. I look around, I look at stuff, and a lot of times it's close but no cigar. A piece of furniture can completely destroy a whole room." He pauses to sip his coffee. "You know, unless the environment is a certain way, you really do yourself a disservice."

Lynch himself has designed furniture, and though he finds none of it "thrilling"—the highest term of praise in his lexicon—I ask if we can look at what he's come up with. We step carefully down the narrow pathway and wind up in house number three, which is less a home than a gigantic grown-up playhouse.

We pass through a room filled with gorgeous, sinister paintings devoted to the further misadventures of Bob, then move down a dark hallway to a door. It opens to reveal a full-fledged motion-picture mixing studio, with a big silver screen, two 35mm projectors, huge Marshall amps, and technicians sipping coffee. They're working on the sound for the forthcoming *The Elephant Man* DVD, and Lynch promises me that the remix is going to be "pretty tasty." From there, he leads me to a room filled with the equipment that runs the studio, and an Epson 9500 photo printer that uses rolls of paper up to forty-four inches wide. Lynch fondly calls it the "Bad Boy."

All this must have cost you a fortune, I say, and he nods.

"It was not pretty."

Eventually we find our way to his office, where I'm shown a group of tables that he designed—an asymmetrical espresso table, a club table with a special slot for cigarettes, and a "floating beam" table, whose thick underlying beam appears to hang in the air. They were built by a Swiss company called Casanostra, which subsequently went out of business. Lynch insists that his tables weren't the reason why, though it's hard to imagine anyone buying one with the intention of using it—they're fabulous Magritte-style curios rather than practical home furnishings.

Even as he dutifully shows me a bed he designed (the headboard was made, he says, by "Raoul, the upholsterer to the stars"), he's eager to get me over to the computer, a relatively new obsession. Lynch's tastes may run to retro in cars and lamps, but he's not one of those Luddites who find Flash animation as incomprehensible as Sanskrit or hate digital video (he's thought of making a silly DV comedy titled *The Dream of the Bovine*). Lynch happily embraces what he calls the "beautiful world" of the Internet, which he sees as a new frontier of staggering freedom. "The whole world is made of little bits," he says, "and now we've been given little bits that we can manipulate. The sky is the limit."

Predictably, Lynch has no discernible interest in using computers the way most of us do. He rarely surfs the Net, doesn't play video games. Instead, he has spent much of the last two years designing DavidLynch.com, which was optimistically scheduled to launch October 12 (it didn't make it) and should be open for business any day now. The site will showcase all manner of new Lynchiana, from still photographs and music to DV serials. Once his computer's booted up, he clicks his mouse. Up pops a set of surreal teeth that open and close. Very spooky.

Click! We're looking at a seedy apartment occupied by three characters, all of whom have human bodies topped with big-eared bunny heads.

Click! An extraordinary close-up of bees.

Click! A naked woman in a jar.

Click! A butchered pig that's been reassembled and now stands on its back legs ("I'm going to make the pig walk").

Click! To my shock, there's a picture of Lynch bending over and pointing his finger at his backside (covered, thank heavens), which is aimed straight at the camera.

Lynch laughs. "I did this one for a guy who said I hadn't paid him some money."

We spend a long time perusing a still photo of the elevator lobby from *Eraserhead*. Using PhotoShop, Lynch has been able to make the elevator doors slide open to reveal what's inside—light spills out onto the carpet in the foreground.

He stares at it intently. "There was a period when I could get lost in this world for weeks at a time."

My allotted time has run out, and I keep preparing to leave. But looking at all this material, Lynch is getting excited. He keeps offering to show me one more thing. He shows me two nudes. He shows me another Polish factory. He shows me the lovely prototype image for his Web site's chat room, which looks like some unholy hybrid of a steam engine and a film projector.

As the images keep coming (even more bees!), I find myself getting caught up in his boyish enthusiasm. His stuff really *is* cool! And I'm reminded why, though some folks think him dark or nasty, I've always found Lynch inspiring. A true romantic, he believes in the transcendent power of imagination, the possibility of creating wondrous new worlds.

Computers, I say, must be a real boon to obsessives like him.

He tells me that, for the upcoming DVD of *Eraserhead*, a man named Arash has spent four months digitally tweaking all the images.

"You know, like, when you're watching a film on TV, you see little white specks? That's negative dirt. On *Eraserhead*, the dirt was built in. There was no way to get rid of it. Every print had the same dirt. And you know how when you're on your computer and you've got your magnifying glass, you can go to the next magnification and see large? And on the next magnification you'll see billions of pieces of dirt and so on? Well, Arash has cleaned this thing."

"Cleaned it?"

"Frame by frame." He beams triumphantly. "It will be the cleanest film in cinema history."

Mulholland Drive, Dreams, and Wrangling with the Hollywood Corral

RICHARD A. BARNEY/2001

ON A VERY SUNNY DAY at his office complex in Los Angeles, David Lynch is in an understandably buoyant and emphatic mood. After nearly two years of difficulties, his feature *Mulholland Drive* has finally come out—in May at the Cannes Film Festival, where Lynch won Best Director, and in early October in the U.S., about two weeks before our conversation. The American response, in both critical and popular terms, has been nothing less than excited. J. Hoberman, writing for the *Village Voice*, has called the film "a voluptuous phantasmagoria" and "certainly Lynch's strongest movie since *Blue Velvet* and maybe *Eraserhead*." *New York Times* critic Stephen Holden, who saw the film screened at the New York Film Festival, exudes that it "conveys the maniacal thrill of an imagistic brainstorm," and that it offers "a fascinating example of how a great film can evolve out of adversity."

This is a welcome outcome—perhaps even a relief—for a film in trouble for some time: after Lynch pitched it as a pilot to ABC executives for a *Twin Peaks*-like television series, he delivered an early cut that he was not entirely satisfied with, only then to have ABC drop the project altogether. During the ensuing months, Lynch had to be patient and persistent by reformulating the story's elements, scrambling for new funding (the French, again, came to the rescue in the form of Canal Plus), shooting new scenes, and working diligently to integrate everything in postproduction.

Six months before this interview, Lynch and I had a preliminary conversation about *Mulholland Drive*, but since he was still in the last stages

---

Interview conducted on 26 October 2001. Previously unpublished.

of editing—Lynch will discuss no film before it is finished—we postponed a full discussion until after its U.S. premiere. In that earlier conversation, Lynch also talked about a number of his earlier movies during the 1980s and '90s, including *Dune*, whose failure was due in part, he explained, to his being "corralled" by being unable to exercise final cut—a lesson that he never forgot, and that comes up again here in a different context.

Sitting now in his art studio, which is perched high above Lynch's main complex for the purpose of creative retreat when he may need it, I glance around at paintings in various stages of completion, brushes and cans strewn about, a three-foot plastic doll lying on the floor with a missing limb, and various other kinds of debris from previous efforts that, knowing Lynch, could become part of a new project any minute. While clearly pleased at the film's reception, Lynch also remains stalwartly philosophical.

RICHARD BARNEY: *As you know very well, the reviews of* Mulholland Drive *have been predominantly great. Given what it took to finish the film, how has that felt—like a little bit of vindication?*
DL: No. You never know what's going to happen when you finish a film. I've seen it go both ways, so I always say, if you believe in what you did, and like what you did, then that's the main thing. And then you just take whatever comes along.

RB: *When we talked last spring, you were putting the last touches on the film. You said that there were a couple bits of editing and sound you were still toying with; otherwise, you thought that it was a couple days away.*
DL: Right after I saw you, then, in March, we were getting ready to go to Cannes. Mary [Sweeney] flew to France with the print so it could be screened, and it was accepted into the Cannes festival. And then the people at Canal Plus saw it on the same trip. They really liked it, and everything had a good feeling from then on.

RB: *Later on, at the New York Film Festival this fall, did you feel the response was different in terms of emphasis or interest by comparison with the French?*
DL: No. You know, all festivals are so beautiful because they are a celebration of film. But it's also films going back to back, so I have to wonder how the film journalists know when one film ends and another begins, because scenes from one film could almost float right into another. So I've the feeling that all festivals are very full and can't kill time.

RB. *There are of a number of people playing parts in the film who have had longstanding working relationships with you in other capacities: Angelo Badalamenti, the composer, who plays Luigi Castigliane, and Monty Montgomery, who among other things was the producer for* Wild at Heart—*he's the Cowboy in* Mulholland Drive. *How did their character roles come about?*

DL: With Angelo, from knowing him since 1986, and from hearing stories, the character of Luigi Castigliane just grew, and Angelo was destined to play that role. And I always thought that Dan Hedaya and Angelo looked like brothers, and so I had this dream of getting them together, and that happened, and that was really beautiful. They get along great. They are from the same neighborhood in Brooklyn. It was a very good experience, it was just fantastic. Now Angelo has just become impossible, and he's already bugging me about the next role. And I wouldn't be surprised if he's already got an agent, you know, for acting. And it's just pretty bizarre [laugh] what's happened with Angelo.

With Monty, I got the idea for the Cowboy during a session when I was dictating things to Gay Pope [an assistant], and all of a sudden the Cowboy appears, and the Cowboy starts talking, and I start telling Gay what the Cowboy is saying, and pretty soon the guy married up with Monty, or Monty married up with the Cowboy. Earlier, when we made the short film *The Cowboy and the Frenchman*, Monty was part of the film's production company, Propaganda Films. Monty was on the set when I first met him. I may have met him before that, I can't remember the sequence, but I always thought Monty was pretty shy and that he probably couldn't even think about going in front of the camera. When we were in postproduction on *Cowboy and the Frenchman*, doing the sound mixing for this character named Howdy, who was in a scene bulldogging a bull, you couldn't understand any of his dialogue because there was so much noise. The guy [Rick Guillory] who played Howdy was a real bulldogger, but he'd gone back to Colorado, I think, where he's from. So Monty said, "David, I'll do that for you." And I said, "Oh my God"—you know, I'm kidding. And I said, "Okay, Monty, give it a shot." And Monty stepped into the booth and nailed it on the first take—perfect. So I remembered that. And when this role came up for the Cowboy, I knew that Monty could do it, and that it was just a question whether he *would* do it. And he said he would.

RB: *He's a very disturbing, but amazing character.*
DL: Uh huh.

RB: *He's both an enforcer and also a moral teacher.*
DL: [Hearty laugh] Exactly.

RB: *He reminded me a little bit of the Mystery Man from* Lost Highway, *a figure who appears and disappears when he wishes, who has contact with another world, and who can have serious effects on the day to day of human existence.*

DL: If he wants to . . .

RB: *Yes, when he wants to. He's not quite as scary to look at, perhaps, as the Mystery Man, but he has a lot of the same functions. Does that seem right to you?*

DL: Yes, that's okay, yeah.

RB: *I was struck by the similarity. Now there's another person I think you've been a fan of for some time, Ann Miller, who ends up . . .*

DL: Sure, I'm a fan of hers, but I've never said, "I have to work with Ann Miller." Gay was at a tribute for someone at the Academy or someplace, and she was sitting in a row behind Ann Miller and some of her friends. And she was looking at Ann Miller and listening to her and came back and said, "This Ann Miller's so fantastic, she looks so great, and seems so full of life." That was just when we were casting *Mulholland Drive*, and I said, "Well, I've got to meet her, it's a great idea." So Ann came up to the house, and that was the end of it. We just hit it off, and she's a great human being.

RB: *As with your other actors, you didn't have her read at all.*

DL: No, no.

RB: *It was really just based on conversation and . . .*

DL: Yeah, just meeting her, looking at her, and getting a feel.

RB: *Someone else, Robert Forster, playing detective Harry McKnight, made a relatively brief appearance, almost a cameo. Did that happen because of the changes between the pilot and the film?*

DL: Yes.

RB: *Was there going to be a whole story line about an investigation?*

DL: Well, the thing is, what *would* have been wasn't even known at that time. I've always liked Robert Forster, and he's got a strong presence, and even though he's only in that one scene, I feel that his presence carries through the film. When detectives are mentioned, he is the one that comes forward.

RB: *Do you regret a little bit that he had to come out of the story, given the changes?*

DL: Well, he had a great scene later on, that didn't work into the film, but he and his partner [Brent Briscoe, as Detective Domgaard] were great together.

RB: *For your money now, what are biggest changes that happened between the pilot and the final feature-length version?*
DL: Wow—it was a whole new ballgame. The feature utilized much of what had gone before, but seen from a different angle. And the ideas that came later to form it into a feature were golden ideas to me. They were like gifts. And I didn't know whether they would happen, I didn't know what was going to happen, I didn't have any ideas to make it into a feature—nothing. And then I sat down one night at 6:30, and at 7 o'clock, there they were.

RB: *You have characterized that early state as a kind of panic.*
DL: It was panic, but it was quiet panic. It wasn't an outright insane panic, it was just a quiet panic, because people were spending a lot of money to give me the opportunity to turn it into a feature . . .

RB: *Because the new deal had been struck by that point.*
DL: Yes. So the ideas came in maybe two weeks after the deal was . . . —well no, that's not true. The ideas came in before the final thing was set, as I remember. It wasn't quite set, and I was having big doubts about whether or not I should pull the plug on it.

RB: *I guess in a way this brings up your old metaphor of fishing—it happened again.*
DL: Yeah, and I think that when you have a desire for something, it doesn't mean you're going to get it, but if you have no desire for something, you're probably definitely *not* going to get it. If you don't have a desire for it, you don't even know what it is you want. So you kind of have to know what it is you want, in a general sense, and then you have to have a desire for it, and then that desire, I think, pulls that thing out of the ocean of ideas.

RB: *Let me ask you about that, because desire is very important to* Mulholland Drive, *especially Diane Selwyn's desire. And it's related to that little catch phrase you have for the film, "A love story in the city of dreams." So desire and dreaming seem crucial.*
DL: But then again, every actress and actor have huge—well, it's all relative, some have more desire than others, but you have to figure they all have a desire, and the desire they have is to do what they do, to act, and then part of that desire is wrapped up in all that can happen, you know,

if you are successful at what you love to do. And so it's a beautiful gamble, packed with all kinds of dreams and desires, but their life is a life where you can really see fate working, and if it's not in their destiny to get that golden ring, it isn't going to happen. They can be pumped with talent and looks, but it just doesn't happen. And you just can't figure it.

RB: *Diane Selwyn's story is painful and tortuous, as far as her ending goes, given what is ultimately a suicide, and so her dreams come to a bad end. On the other hand, at other times when you talk about dreams, you talk about them as a necessary positive, as when you said to the* Village Voice *some time back about this movie: "Endings are terrible things. They can have great beauty, but only if they leave room to dream."*
DL: Right.

RB: *So on the one hand, dreams have a positive element of catching ideas, but they can also go very . . .*
DL: Bad. Well, it's not the dreams that make it go bad. I guess it's the frustration, and all the negatives—jealousy, and just a whole bunch of things that are just misery and negative—that can cause you to do some things that aren't so good, and when you do that, then you suffer the consequences, and then those consequences can grow like a bad dream.

RB: *Like letting Irene and her companion out of the blue box at the movie's end. Things start small and get rather large by the end.*
DL: Yes.

RB: *In* Mulholland Drive *there are two different movies in progress that illustrate the loonyness of moviemaking as a process. One is Wally Brown's melodrama, which seems rather worn, and Betty auditions for that film; then there's the one that Adam Kesher is attempting to get going in his bewildering struggle to keep control of the production, although even he has to capitulate. Is there some satisfaction for you now in those parts of the film, given the painful way you had to get to the final product?*
DL: No, they are separate for me. If it was that way, I would say so, but it isn't. But I can see how people could see that, and I can identify with that and Adam's trials there, but for me, it was just being with the wrong people. So it's all, really, a beautiful blessing that it worked out this way.

RB: *When I was watching the scene where Kesher meets the Cowboy, I couldn't help remembering a thing you said to me in our last conversation. When you were talking about the painful feeling you had after* Dune *came out, you said that you felt "corralled." And in this scene, it's like a play on* words because Kesher finds himself literally corralled in Beachwood Canyon, and earlier he also hears Castigliane say the chilling words, "It's no longer your film." The sense is that this scenario must have a lot of resonance for you.

DL: Oh yes, like I said, I can identify with him. And I always use the analogy of a corral as either a big corral in terms of not so many restrictions, or a small corral with more restrictions and less room to move. You know, corrals, even small corrals—this is sort of off the subject—are restrictions, and restrictions are mostly just that, but sometimes really good things can come out of restrictions.

RB: *You had restrictions in first imagining this as a television production. Did those actually pay off, even though you had to shift the scope of the project?*

DL: Everything was a payoff. And I don't know all the ways it was a payoff, but because the project started as an open-ended pilot—and I've said this too many times before, sorry—you think in a certain way. And even though you are shooting on film, you're thinking in at least two ways: instead of just thinking of film, you're thinking of the television screen, and you're also thinking—because we were shooting in 16:9 aspect ratio—of the wide screen, simultaneously. You know that you are working in the medium of television on a continuing story, where this is a pilot and it's open ended, and then, suddenly, it's right next door to being killed. It's like you see a corpse, and you are positive that that person is dead, and then you get real close, and there's a flicker of life in there. And it's kind of *fanstastic*, and that thing comes back to life, but in a different form, and now it's a feature. So the ideas that are required for going from open-ended to close-ended feature are particular kinds of ideas, and they have to go back into the open-ended story, and connect, and come to a conclusion at the same time. They have to be ideas that do all those things. And those ideas wouldn't be required if you were working in a feature form from the beginning. So it's a trick of the mind, and I think that tricking a mind can sometimes lead to good things. And I've talked before about how the Surrealists would try to trick themselves: they'd throw up random words in the air and then see how they fell, and see if something could come out of that random act and lead to a new direction or a new thing for them. So those kind of things are good to do as an exercise, but this was a thing that wasn't set out to be an exercise, but it ended up being that—a trick of the mind.

RB: *There's an interesting link there, because when you mention a corpse that's going to come back to life, that corpse in Diane Selwyn's bed in fact be-*

comes the source of all kinds of projects, dreams, and desires, so that it's not really a dead body after all.
DL: Well, it . . . [long pause] you could . . . if you . . . [longer pause] you've got to . . .

RB: *I gave you a tough one.*
DL: No, I don't want to say too much. [Pause] If you look at . . . you see where it is, and, you know, what follows then can make some sense.

RB: *Here's one way I was thinking about this: you've often said that* Sunset Boulevard *is one of your favorite movies, the film you had everyone watch while you were making* Eraserhead, *things like that. I was struck by a similarity there, because even though we don't have a narrating corpse, like we do in* Sunset Boulevard, *we do have a dead body that seems to be the beginning of a whole series of dream-like events or memories—which struck me as very much like Billy Wilder's setup.*
DL: I never thought about that. In *Mulholland Drive*, there's the Sunset Boulevard street sign, there's the car from *Sunset Boulevard* in the Paramount Lot, almost fifty years to the day that that car was there in Wilder's film. It doesn't matter if anybody knows that, but it's kind of a strange thing how the world of film is connected with things like that, and the whole inside world of film is just as alive as this world is.

RB: *I was very struck by that scene, because I went back to rewatch it in* Sunset Boulevard, *but in* Mulholland Drive *there's the same wrought-iron gates, the archway, everything but "Paramount Pictures."*
DL: Yeah, because you can't show that—they won't let you show that. It's one of life's many absurdities. I always say that I love absurdities, so there's another one.

RB: *Does that connection suggest any similarities between Norma Desmond and Betty?*
DL: Well, they're both actresses, and they're both actresses that are— they're completely different, but they're both experiencing some of the negative sides of acting.

RB: *True. Norma Desmond wants to go back to an earlier age in order to be creative, except that she . . .*
DL: She still thinks that she has it. But that's a trick of the mind, and we all do this to one degree or another: you look at someone, you hear them talk, and you say, "This person has got to be crazy. They're living in a dream world. It's *not* the way they think it is." And then you look in the mirror, and you wonder if you're doing the same thing. And we all do it,

because we have to, just to stay alive. You've got to hold on to something or you'll just fly apart sometimes.

RB: *So in that sense Diane Selwyn's possible second persona in Betty is important, like it is for Norma, for having a sense of coherence.*
DL: Yes.

RB: *I was struck by something else, because I watched it carefully: as you may remember, Norma Desmond has many images of herself all over her dilapidated mansion.*
DL: It's a beautiful mansion—it's not so dilapidated.

RB: *In the film we do get the feeling that it's just barely . . .*
DL: Well, yeah, some parts of the outside are deteriorating, but the inside, to me, is pretty solid.

RB: *Similarly, in* Mulholland Drive, *it's striking how there keep appearing all these new versions of Betty / Diane: we have the waitress at Winkies, we have the prostitute at Pinks with the blonde hair and a slight resemblance, and then we have Rita herself with the blonde wig suddenly taking on a very Betty-like look. I was struck by these two actresses, each of them with multiple images . . .*
DL: For actors, that's their life, taking on different people, so it's a world where these things are kind of natural, whether it's real or imagined, in a film, or here and there. They're all different people.

RB: *In the scene where Betty remakes Rita's appearance, there was a sense of a Hitchcockian moment, like in* Vertigo, *where you recreate someone into something that you wish because you've lost the original in some way. I was amazed that Betty would make Rita look like herself, and yet that scene is not unlike Scottie's desire to regain what he'd otherwise lost by transforming Judy Barton into Madeleine Elster. Does that make sense to you?*
DL: Sure.

RB: *Do you want to go anywhere with that?*
DL: No.

RB: [Laugh] *In the first part of the film, there's a marvelous energy in the dancing montage. Then that's followed by a very intriguing sequence: a shot of the floor in Diane Selwyn's bedroom, then a tracking shot over to her pillow, a dolly-in collapsing into the pillow—all suggesting that there's a kind of circularity in the film as a whole when, at the end of the story, we come back to her on the bed and she shoots herself. Is that a kind of circle that you find useful for holding things together in the film?*

DL: It's not to hold things together, it's to tell the story, and in the dancing there are certain things that occur there that are critical to understanding what is happening. So even before the credits start, there are some important clues that people should see and remember, because they help in understanding things.

RB: *One thing that's happening there is that many of the same figures are replicating right, left, and center, appearing in larger and smaller versions of themselves, like dancers. Is that one of the things?*

DL: No, that's not one of the things I was referring to.

RB: *Could you name a couple?*

DL: No [small laugh]. Just look at the thing before the credits, and see a couple of clues.

RB: *Okay. I've mentioned circularity here is because it reminded me a little of the way in which* Lost Highway *has a similar circle, where "Dick Laurent is dead" is a message that comes over the intercom [to the character Fred Madison, played by Bill Pullman], suggesting he could go through everything all over again. And if Diane's despair is about her own desire, which can be rejolted back to life, if you will, then there seems to be the possibility that this movie could also cycle, as a dream might.*

DL: All movies could, and there can be variations on a theme, like in jazz. You start in one melody, and there are all kind of possibilities. But feature films have a form, and even though you can play with that form, the possibilities come to an end.

RB: *There are a number of visual things I wanted to talk to you about. To start with color: as always, there's a rich palette of color here, but I was struck by the warm browns, greens, and yellows in Aunt Ruth's old Hollywood apartment, which gives it a kind of distinction from the rest of the environments that we see in the film. It feels almost organic, with a kind of safety that Aunt Ruth herself might represent. What were you after with all those warm colors?*

DL: Like you say, it's a place where, because it feels safe, many things can happen, and certain *types* of things can happen. And because it's wrapped inside a courtyard, which is even more protection, characters like Rita and Betty have that feeling there.

RB: *There are other strong colors that run throughout the film, appearing in all sorts of places—pink, red, and blue—pink, for instance, in Betty's sweater, the paint that Kesher pours on his wife's jewelry, and so on. How did you work out those color schemes?*

DL: Every single thing in the film is based on the ideas. If you could get the whole film as an idea at once, you'd be watching the film from start to finish. But unfortunately ideas come in fragments. Each fragment, though, is full, and it plays in your mind as it comes into you. But it comes in fast, like a spark, and then you start to see it after the light of the spark settles down— there's the idea. And it's known to you: it plays way too fast, but it seems the right speed. You sort of know it, you just know it, and it's there. A millisecond before it wasn't there, now it sparks in and you know it. The rest of the job is staying true to those ideas. And that seems to be the trick, to translate those ideas to film and stay true to them. It's just as simple as that.

RB: *How did the color pink first show up with the ideas that arrived?*

DL: The pink—there wasn't any conscious pink-thought. But there's the place called Pink's, and that scene came complete with the pink color, and Betty's blouse could have been a happy accident. I don't remember, I don't remember my choices. And a lot of clothes are talked about, but [pause] it's one area—if something is really wrong, you see it right away. But there's something about costumes so that it's the one area where I really like to be surprised. And you get a lot of fuel from the way people look. More often than not, I've worked with people like Penny Norris [costume designer for several Lynch films] and many others, who were really tuned in at the beginning, and brought fantastic things.

RB: *Did you have any specific surprises in the making of* Mulholland Drive?

DL: Well, let's see. You mean bad surprises or good surprises?—they're all good surprises, I think. For instance, Ann Miller in real life likes to dress up, so Coco was a perfect character for her. And what she would come out looking like was pretty fantastic, and it fit in her world so beautifully. You know, the costumes have to marry to the character and can't go against that, and that all comes from the ideas. So if they are marrying to the character, you go happily forward.

RB: *The camera work in this movie felt like it had a lot more moving shots than I can remember in your previous films.*

DL: Yes, maybe so. There's a thing we got into which was this "floating" camera, and this was pretty important at the scene at Winkie's [when Dan and Herb discuss a dream]. And again, based on the ideas, this floating camera adds to the fear.

RB: *It often felt as though the camera took on a mind of its own.*

DL: Yeah, it's a third person.

RB: There's another thing I noticed, not quite the same thing, but there are moments when the moving camera will join up and then separate from a third point of view or perspective.
DL: Give me an example of that.

RB: When Betty is on the phone talking to her Aunt Ruth in the living room of the apartment, the camera shows her there lying on the couch, and while she is still speaking, the camera then tracks away and leaves her behind, going up the hallway to the bedroom door. But strangely, when the camera reaches the door, suddenly Betty is actually right there, melded, in a way, with the camera . . .
DL: That's exactly right.

RB: So the camera separates off from characters and then rejoins them in very intriguing ways, and there are other instances like that in the film.
DL: You know, a lot of film is action and reaction. So when you have action, and then you react to that action, you learn things, and you find that a lot of film is experimenting. It's experimenting at the same time that you are being true to the original ideas. The reason that you are experimenting is so that you don't leave a golden possibility uncaptured. And so every rehearsal is a kind of experiment and in the editing there's a lot of experimenting. With all the stages or elements, there's an element of experimentation in order to get things to feel correct. And it goes like that.

RB: My thought was that this camera technique feels right to you because it's similar to the performances in Club Silencio, where singers or players are actually singing or playing an instrument, and then suddenly they're not, and yet the performance continues. It's as if there's a disjunction between the technology or instrument and the person attached to it, so that things can go on of their own accord. The camerawork, then, reflects that theme so powerfully brought out in the scene with the magician. Does that fit?
DL: That fits, but—if you arbitrarily said, "Okay, we're going to shoot this with this one thing in mind," it may kill or it may hurt things. So you can't just say, arbitrarily, "We're going to do this because of something coming up, or because our theme dictates it." That's going to another place, where it's just an arbitrary overlay, and a false thing. So you've got to go scene by scene and bit by bit, and keep checking back to the original idea. I've said this before too, but if the idea is like a seed, the whole tree is in the seed, but if you dick around with the seed, it's going to be a strange tree, and it's not going to be the tree that it really wants to be. So if you

stay true to the seed, chances are you're going to get a good tree. And if you get a good tree, then the tree is going to be appreciated as a tree by different people, and they're each going to get something from that tree, and they're going to get a correct thing from that tree. But if you fiddle around, they'll smell a false tree, and they won't even appreciate it.

RB: *So working with an idea is different than working on a theme...*

DL: If you find themes *in* a series of ideas—peachy keen—but if you take a theme and say, "I'm going to make the film with this theme," then, to me, that's working backwards.

RB: *I wanted to ask you about the music. The Latina singer Rebekah del Rio plays herself in an arresting Spanish version of Roy Orbison's "Crying." How did she become part of the film?*

DL: By a happy accident. I have a friend who is also my music agent named Brian Loucks. And I have a recording studio, and I love music. I always say that Angelo [Badalamenti], bless his heart, was the one who got me really into the world of music. So I'm in the world of music to a certain degree, and Brian sometimes calls and wants to bring people over for me to meet, or we have a project going together. He called up and said he wanted me to meet someone who was really great, and so they came up to the house. When they got here I said, "Rebekah, why don't you go into the booth and sing into the microphone?" And she said, "Fine." So she went into the booth, and what she sang is the exact track that we used for the film. At first, before she sang, there was no thought that Rebekah del Rio or the song would be in the film—it was just so beautiful. And I started thinking about it, and it became part of [Club] Silencio. One thing leads to another that way sometimes. So it was a happy accident.

RB: *So Spanish wasn't originally conceived as an important part...*

DL: Well, you know, there was another happy accident: Laura Harring is half Spanish, and L.A. is half Spanish, and so Spanish started working its way into the film. It just happened. There are feelings with words, and a lot of times, even when you don't understand a word, you get this feeling, and it's almost better sometimes if you don't understand a word, in a strange way. It's the feeling, or the mystery, or just—a thing.

RB: *The critics have liked the movie overwhelmingly, but even many who liked it have said that it creates a lot of loose ends, and that you'll never know what they mean. My own experience—I've seen the film three times—was not that at all. The first time, I was dazzled. I wasn't quite sure all that I'd seen, and I knew I'd seen something that had impressed me emotionally and visu-*

ally, but I didn't quite know how it all fit. The second time, I had a kind of intellectual exhilaration, since I saw pieces falling into place. And the third time, since that had happened, I felt the film more. Do you now just count on the probability that your viewers will re-view your films?

DL: It would be a beautiful world if people liked the world inside the film so much that they would want to go back and be in it again. That's the way it is for me with a film like *Sunset Boulevard*. We all have favorite films. For me, it's just a world that I like to visit again and again. It seems real and I like being inside that world. And I think a lot of times we rely on a film to explain itself completely, and so a part of us is—not asleep, exactly, but we are not *heightened*. We do not realize that there may be clues there that are important. It's a sort of laziness, in a weird way, though seeing a film shouldn't be work. But there are different depths of getting into it. So it's interesting how much I think is missed the first time around, just because you are not aware you are supposed to pay attention to certain things. And intuition, to me, is a thing that goes to work when you watch a film. There are so many clues in all films that we just pick up on, so that you sense things and know them internally as you go. You can still miss things, but I just think that intuition is the key to so many things.

RB: *Do you have any ideas yet about what your next feature will be?*
DL: Not a clue. I'm working on the internet now.

RB: *You've got a November 16 deadline, when davidlynch.com should be up and running.*
DL: [Nods] Should be up and running. I hope it will be.

RB: *And whatever comes, comes after that.*
DL: Yeah. You've got to have ideas, and I haven't had time to sit down and try to . . . I have a desire for it, and I've had some ideas, and that's always the way. Whether it's *the* idea I don't know.

David Lynch and Laura Dern: *Inland Empire*

JOHN ESTHER/2006

BY FAR HIS BEST FILM since *Blue Velvet*, writer-director David Lynch's *Inland Empire* will likely be the most radical film of 2006. Running 179 minutes with much rhyme and very little reason—in the positivist sense—*Inland Empire* debunks nearly every Hollywood trope imaginable.

The primary plot focuses on Nikki Grace (Laura Dern), a rich, kept wife and actor who has just landed a role as Susan Blue in a new film. Her co-star, Devon Berk (Justin Theroux, who played the young film director in Lynch's *Mulholland Drive*), has a reputation for seducing his co-stars and that could be a problem. As Nikki becomes more and more like Susan, the multifaceted films-within-films refuse to offer any simplistic path to follow.

Co-starring Jeremy Irons as film director Kingsley Stewart, Harry Dean Stanton as his assistant, Naomi Watts as a surreal sitcom character, Diane Ladd as a talk show host, William Macy as an announcer, and Julia Ormond as a murderous wife, this is a demanding yet rewarding film that has left many novice filmgoers nonplussed, if not downright angry.

Sitting at a table full of journalists, the usually quiet Lynch and the typically gregarious Dern talked about their film over a slice of banana crème pie.

JOURNALIST: *When did you first start writing the script?*
DAVID LYNCH: I wrote a scene without Laura. But I didn't know it was going to be a big scene with Laura. And shot that as a stand-alone thing.

From *Greencine.com* (15 December 2006). Reprinted by permission of John Esther.

I didn't know anything was going to happen. I kept looking at this scene thinking, "Wait a minute. There's something more. It's holding something." And then I'd get another idea and write that scene and go shoot that. And then I'd get another idea without Laura and I'd shoot that. I didn't know how one would relate to another—if it was going to hold together, or be anything. Then a thing happened five or six scenes down, where I see a story coming out that unites these scenes. Then it went faster. I'd write more and more and more and then we'd shoot more traditionally after that. But in the beginning, it was a long time; wait, another scene; wait, another scene.

JOURNALIST: *Which scene [was the first]?*
DL: That doesn't matter. Because I always think if you're watching a movie and that scene comes up, somebody will go [he nudges Dern], "This is the shot." It putrefies the thing.

JOHN ESTHER: *To counteract the first question, how did you know when you were done writing?*
DL: There's a thing—it happens in painting, music, and other things—a moment where the whole thing feels correct and it's done. When you shoot a film, there's all these stages; so it's not until the very end that you start dealing with the whole. Toward the very end, you think you got the whole thing corralled and then you have a screening, some other people are there, and you say, "Wait a minute." You've got huge problems. And you go to work, get closer, have another [screening], get closer, and then there is a moment where it happens. It's done. It feels correct as a whole.

JOURNALIST: *David, this movie explodes in different directions—horizontally, vertically, and it's asymmetrical in that sense, to me. Also the naturalness of everyday life is there. I found that to be the structure. Was that something that you thought of?*
DL: No. It's the ideas. An idea comes. You get an idea and the idea tells you everything. I understand the idea enough to translate it to cinema and stay true to that and try to get everybody to tune into that idea that's driving the boat. Sometimes, if you're true to the idea, these ideas have "harmonics" and someone may pick up a harmonic like you—some kind of angle—and, if you've been true to the idea, then the harmonics are true. You see what I mean? I can go back on a film that I made a long time ago—if I was true to the ideas—and get a whole different thing out of it. Because I was true to this idea, this idea is true. See what I mean? Stay true to the idea. Stay true to the idea.

JOURNALIST: *How difficult is that?*

DL: It's not so difficult. It's just that you can't let up, because every element is critical. Every element has got to feel correct before you walk away, correct in terms of the idea. You just have to do your work until things feel correct. Then you've done that day's work. The next day you come in, you've got all these unfinished things looking at you, bit by bit by bit by bit. All elements you try to get to 100 percent feeling correct based on the original idea. That's your job.

JOURNALIST: *Laura, you've obviously worked with David before—Blue Velvet, Wild at Heart. Was it that much different of an experience of working this particular way?*

LAURA DERN: Yes. There are obviously things that stay true to the unique experience of working with David. And interestingly, they weren't in the area of working scene by scene, not having a script. It was more in the area of working with digital film: the ease with which you can shoot your day; the ease with which David can shoot alone and move the camera around and get the scene; to—which is unheard of on a traditional 35mm movie set—have a working day and have filmed ten of our twelve hours. We got to work and we'd start working. We had the luxury, because forty minutes is in the camera, of shooting an entire scene without cutting. It gives you a great deal of freedom as an actor to truly be in the moment as opposed to being in the moment, holding it, and [laughs] trying to go back to that moment and replicating it.

Then comes the fact that he gave me several characters to play. It was just pure bliss. To have someone who I've admired my whole life to trust me enough to say, "Let's work this way and you're going to explore these different people, or aspects of a person, let's just go." If David could impart anything to other filmmakers, one thing that I think would be so helpful in the area of working with actors is that actually actors will be what you want them to be and feel brave and daring and be as good as you want them to be. Believe in them. And you can't fake that. He so believes in actors. He is so specific and detailed about what he wants. Because the film is abstract one thinks that his expression of what he wants to you would be vague or surreal and it's not.

JOURNALIST: *Laura, you're a producer on this film. What did you see, the script or the author?*

LD: This is question for David, really. I can't even speak as to what that means.

DL: I don't understand that question.

LD: Well, as an actor, what I always see first is the author, the filmmaker, and that's who I go to work with. When this David calls, I show up. I don't need a script. As a producer, I think that's a very gracious token of esteem from David for going along for our three-year ride

JOURNALIST: *Is the Jeremy Irons character sort of a surrogate of yours?*

DL: No. Kingsley Stewart always came from the idea that he's British. And there's Jeremy Irons all over it. I was very fortunate to get Jeremy because he, in my mind, was the guy.

JOURNALIST: *You used the quite famous Japanese actor Nae Yuuki in your film.*

DL: I can't say enough good things about Nae.

JOURNALIST: *Although she speaks English you used subtitles?*

DL: Yes, she's saying many things that are critical and with her accent, many people couldn't understand everything. So it's better to go with subtitles.

JOURNALIST: *What role did music play in your creative process?*

DL: Music is huge. It's huge because sometimes you get ideas from listening to music. Sometimes a scene comes right out of music, or a mood. It's inspiring and sometimes marries to a scene. It's a magical ingredient.

JOURNALIST: *Was there any specific music?*

DL: All the music that you hear is music that I found married to the place in the film where it exists. A lot of things were tried. If it doesn't work you know it doesn't work. So then you got to start again.

JE: *What are your political intentions with the film?*

DL: Political intentions. Zero. Some people are very political [Dern raises her hand to indicate she is one of those people] and they'll see politics in everything. This is a world on its own and you just go into this world. When there are abstractions, people have varying interpretations, thoughts, about it. But it's the same with all film. It's so beautiful when the lights go down, the curtains open, and we get to go into a different world.

LD: The mere existence of this film is political. It is rare people are using their voice and doing what they want to do. David isn't trying to redefine cinema; he's defining his own voice. And we need more of that. So I think it's a highly political film.

JOURNALIST: *Well, you're a brave actor.*
LD: Oh, no, I just feel lucky.

JOURNALIST: *Can you tell us a little about your Oscar campaign?*
DL: Laura should be at least nominated. But we don't have any money and we're not connected with a giant studio. So I had this idea, because Academy members love show business, that I would go out on the street with signs for Laura, along with a cow and a piano player. It was beautiful. It was to make people aware a film was coming that had a great performance by Laura.

JOURNALIST: *What is the main thing about your relationship that makes it work?*
DL: Pure love.
LD: Love.
DL: Seriously, it's love, trust. Laura's a great talent. If someone you love is right for the part, you're very happy because you're going to get to go down the road for a long time with this person. There was so much happiness seeing her nail these things.

JOURNALIST: *Could you talk about the Polish theme?*
DL: I fell in love with the city of Lodz, Poland, a city so beautiful and old, filled with factories and great giant electrical plants and these low hanging gray clouds and a Polish rain or cold and mood, and ideas started coming.

JE: *Fellow Academy nominee and filmmaker Robert Altman recently passed away. Could you comment on what his work, and he as a person, meant to you?*
DL: [A wave of sadness crosses his face]. I felt so happy that he respected me. We had a bond. I respect his work, his talent, and his strength to stand up against all the studios through the years, and stick to his voice and make sure he stuck to his voice. I don't think there's anybody stronger than Robert Altman out there for getting the job done the way he wanted to get it done. I kind of loved Robert Altman, really respected him, and I'm sorry to see him go.
LD: I just want to add, the purist, greatest times I ever had on movies were with David and Robert Altman. Because they both demand that it's a family having a good time together. And it is a complete party 100 percent of the time because they believe in it being fun. Unfortunately, it's a very rare experience.

Inland Empire, Transcendental Meditation, and the "Swim" of Ideas

RICHARD A. BARNEY/2008

SINCE OUR LAST interview in 2001, a lot has happened for David Lynch: the popularity of *Mulholland Drive* has stirred new interest in his work, he has launched his website davidlynch.com, created the David Lynch Foundation for Consciousness-Based Education and Peace, turned sixty years old, published *The Big Fish*, released *Inland Empire*, and announced that digital video will be his main filmic medium for the foreseeable future. He has multiplied the already diverse venues, media, and projects that have preoccupied him, and as he comments at the end of this interview, he has even ventured into singing and recording. Although he claims to be "joking" about it, in fact he has already issued "Ghost of Love," the song he sang for the opening of *Inland Empire*, as a CD single, and he is earnestly working on a complete album.

In good sidewinder fashion, our conversation begins by straying in several directions—from his cross-country drive with Jack Fisk and his brother when he moved from Philadelphia to Los Angeles, to the geography of the American southwest and a road sign I had seen in the Texas panhandle declaring, in almost Lynchian fashion: "Rattlesnakes: Exit Now." We then come back to his films, his relation to interviews, and what's happened in the year and a half since *Inland Empire* had its world premiere. It becomes dramatically clear that his relatively new public role as spokesperson for transcendental meditation, combined with a recent lecture tour on the subject in the U.S., sparks an uncharacteristic expansiveness in his responses to questions. And Lynch's answers

Interview conducted on 16 January 2008. Previously unpublished.

also underscore a number of intriguing, though enigmatic, connections among his enthusiasm for meditation, his process-oriented approach to filmmaking, and the specific themes of *Inland Empire*.

RICHARD BARNEY: *I have found what is one of the first interviews you ever did, in* The East Village Eye.

DAVID LYNCH: Yeah, and that was with . . . [pause]

RB: *Gary Indiana. Do you remember that?*

DL: Oh yeah, and, it was at a time, well, for a long time, I didn't understand the concept, really, of speaking about a thing. So I didn't say very much. And I didn't say very much for a long time. But that was one of the first interviews. And what was good about what he did—he just wrote it the way it came out. I remember it, for sure, my first interview for *Eraserhead*. It was probably my first interview ever. I think that *Eraserhead* had just been publicly released. There was kind of a—I guess you'd call it a press screening one night. And that was pretty well attended. Then it opened to the public at Cinema Village [in Greenwich Village] on Friday and Saturday night. And I think it was midnight. The first night, as I always say, twenty-six people came, and then Saturday night, twenty-four people came. [Laugh]

RB: *And you're thinking: we're going down, rather than up.*

DL: Oh yeah, and Ben [Barenholtz, who distributed the film], bless his heart, he said: "David, do *not* worry. It's a word of mouth thing, and there will be lines around the block in two months." And that's what happened. So it was kind of incredible.

RB: *Indiana liked it.*

DL: Yeah, yeah, yeah. It was a love-hate thing, though, I tell you. It screened first at Filmex, the L.A. film festival, and there was an article that I think I still have from *Variety*, and it was pretty, really . . . [pause]—the guy, whoever wrote it, was the wrong person.

RB: *There were a couple pieces like that that came out about* Inland Empire . . .

DL: [Laugh] Yes, probably . . .

RB: *People who said "I don't know what happened," those kind of remarks. You didn't really notice them, didn't pay attention?*

DL: No.

RB: *Let me track this a little bit, because there have been some people who have remarked that this most recent movie,* Inland Empire, *which was re-*

leased almost a year and a half ago now, was the closest, they think, to the kind of experimentalism you were doing with Eraserhead.

DL: But it wasn't experimentalism, that's the thing. There are these terms like *cult films, experimental films*, and to me, an experimental film is a film where you don't know what you're doing, you're just shooting anything, you have no idea, and you're just shooting. You may call it experimenting, but that's not what it is. There are very specific ideas, and there's a script, and a job to do to translate those ideas, to be true to those ideas. And that's the thing. But what people really mean is that it's more abstract, or it's nonlinear, or whatever—but it's not experimental.

RB: *Are there other ways in which working on* Inland Empire *or looking back on now that it resonates with* Eraserhead *for you?*

DL: Not really. Every film resonates, because it's the same kind of process. But the thing that makes it a little closer is that it was a smaller crew and it went over a long period of time.

RB: Eraserhead *took five years . . .*

DL: Five years, but obviously I wasn't working every day. I worked every day for one year, and then we ran out of money. And we were down for almost a year. I didn't know what I was going to do. It just seemed like, I didn't know where the time went, and suddenly it was a year, and we hadn't shot anything. And then I think I got a job, I'm not positive, and started saving up to shoot a scene, saving up to shoot a scene, like that. And then it got finished that way, except that Mary Fisk, my second wife, got her friend to invest, and that was the finishing money.

RB: Inland Empire *took two and a half years, correct?*

DL: Well, two and a half to three. But it depends . . . the start of it, I don't know what started it, but it took a long time.

RB: *You've always talked about ideas that are pivotal in moving a movie forward or developing things one step further. What were the first ones about* Inland Empire *that you can remember that did that?*

DL: Well [long pause], in a way I never really. . . . See, it's tricky to talk about stuff, because, now obviously, the film's been out, but . . . [pause] let's just say there was this scene. . . . [Pause again] Like I always say—I've said the same thing a million times—in the beginning, there was no *Inland Empire*, there was no idea of a feature. All there was was an idea for a scene, that's it. So I always say I wrote out the scene, and then shot the scene. Then that was going to be the end of it.

RB: *This is the scene where Laura Dern, as Susan Blue, talks to Mr. K in a starkly lit room . . .*

DL: Maybe, yeah, could be. Let's just say it *was* that one. So I'm looking at it, and I say, "No, this isn't just a scene, this holds something more." And I think about it. In the meantime, though, I got another idea, and I wrote it down, and shot that. And that was actually two different scenes. And those scenes did not relate to the scene we were talking about. . . . Then, I got another idea, and I wrote it out, and shot that scene, and it didn't relate at all to what had gone before, not a bit. It did in a way, because it was the same character, but it didn't really. But there was something—I was still thinking about the previous scenes, but they did not relate, *at all*.

RB: *Were you ever tempted to write a script that might link them together?*

DL: Well, what you just said was, "Were you ever tempted to write a feature script?" But in order to do that, you need to have ideas. You can't sit down and start writing—I guess the Surrealists did, they'd just start writing anything: you, know, "The kiln is silver, and it has red." Or whatever you see, you write down, or whatever just starts flowing. But when it starts flowing, that's the flow of ideas, just a flow, but it may be total baloney. So, yeah, you can write pages of baloney, but you need ideas, and so you're waiting, and I always say that, once you have something, if you focus on it, it's like bait that will pull in those other ideas. That's sort of what I was doing, but it was throughout the day, here or there, focus on this thing, and think about it, think about it—and then suddenly more stuff, more ideas, came in. Now those new ideas that came in were the ideas that related to what had gone before, but it took those [earlier] ideas. And a whole other thing started coming out, and that was what led to it showing itself to be a feature. And it went like that.

RB: *When in the three years did StudioCanal become officially involved?*

DL: Frederic Sichler [the director of StudioCanal] was the only guy I was talking to, and he had come to visit twice before, and each time he came to visit, there was nothing really to talk about. But I liked his face. And so when this thing started to look like it was going to be a feature, I called him, and he said, "Oh, I am going to be in Los Angeles." I said, "Okay, come by for a coffee." And when he came by for coffee, I said, "Frederic, I don't know what I'm doing, and I'm shooting in low-res DV. Are you in?" And he said: "Yes." So it was low budget, but I had the money to keep going. And I could look him in the eye and pretty much guarantee him that it would be a feature.

RB: *Maybe with a little winking, but not too much . . .*
DL: Yeah, I didn't *really* know, even then, but I felt it was going to happen.

RB: *And they didn't want a script, so you never really had to think about that.*
DL: No, no. . . .

RB: *I have read some comments you've made about the pleasure of working that way. Can you talk about that and whether it was a horror at other times?*
DL: There's no horror. The horror, if there is a horror, is the lack of ideas. But that's all the time. You're just waiting. And I always say, it's like fishing: some days you just don't catch any fish. The next day, it's another story—they just swim in. It's such a great process. Once you get going down a road, it's that first idea—the Rosetta Stone idea, that's what you're looking for—and if you're focused on it, more will come in, in time, in time.

RB: *Were there points when you wanted to make it go longer than three years?*
DL: No, no, no, no. You don't say, "Oh, I want to spend fifteen years." [Laugh] It's absurd. It would be great if they all just swam in, the ideas, and you were rolling. But there's one more connection, this thing of how fast you work. I always say that if you are doing more of a traditional shoot, the whole thing is to get geared up: once you've got your cast, the script, a schedule, then you are geared up to start and not stop until you've shot all the scenes. And the schedule is built to be as short as possible because of cost, so you have to stay on schedule. That kind of pressure and thinking is mostly fine, if you've been involved in the scheduling and picturing yourself doing those things. But I am sort of an optimist and I say, "Oh yeah, I can do that easy," but it's never really that way. And then you get somebody who says, "David, let's get real, you're going need more time than that." So you get a schedule you think you can do. But that kind of speed isn't really so deeply pleasurable as a slower speed, where you have down times, when you are on the sets or on the locations, dreaming away and can catch a deeper thing, and it becomes another level of "realer." I think it kind of feeds things. Anyway, it's very pleasurable. A lot of times on *Eraserhead*, there was nothing going on, I would just be on the set, and imagine the whole world around there. It was so pleasurable—like that. I think it just makes it more real,

and certain little, tiny choices might be altered and be better because of that time in that world. It's nice.

RB: *You've often talked about the world that a film creates, but with Inland Empire, it seemed to have upped the ante, it felt like many worlds colliding, interchanging, intermingling in ways that were much more multiplied than what I've seen in your movies in the past. Does that feel right as a description?*

DL: Yeah, it does. It's no different, though, than just being a human being on earth. You know what I mean? [Laugh]

RB: *I read somewhere that you said you were meditating when the idea of dancing to the song "Locomotion" with the prostitutes came up for Smithy's house . . .*

DL: Smithy's house . . .

RB: *The house that Susan [Blue, played by Laura Dern] lives in.*

DL: Oh yeah, uh huh.

RB: *Is that right—you were meditating when that idea came to you to try that?*

DL: I don't know. I don't remember how that idea came.

RB: *Were there any other meditative moments when you were doing your transcendental meditation and something "popped" for the movie?*

DL: Okay, I always say, transcendental meditation is a mental technique that opens the door to the transcendent, the deepest level of life, the unified field. So when you meditate, you are transcending many times in your meditation, and when you experience that deepest level, you enliven it, and you literally and honestly and truly expand your ball of consciousness. Then, after meditation, you've got tons of energy, more awareness, consciousness, I-amness, more intelligence, more understanding, more appreciation, more happiness, more energy, and you're more apt to catch an idea and understand it.

Most of the idea-catching is outside meditation, although many times in meditation, thoughts will come—and thoughts *are* part of this process—but when you transcend, you're beyond thought, you are experiencing the source of thought, source of the universe, source of anything that is a thing. That's what the unified field is—it is unmanifest, it is no-thing. But all things come from it. *Very cool.* Vedic science has always said that, and now modern science says it, that every thing that's a thing has emerged from this unified field. They say it emerges in a process they call "spontaneous sequential symmetry-breaking." This is a field of total, pure symmetry, absolute balance between infinite silence and infinite dynamism, pure consciousness. How can something come from no-thing, just consciousness? Unbelievable! Vedic science will tell you how it happens. Incredible! The unified field a home to total knowledge. And the whole story really is the self knowing the self. Unbelievable story, we're involved in.

So yes, sometimes you'll get ideas in meditation, things will bubble up, but you don't use your meditation to get ideas, you use it to transcend thought—go to the source, experience *that*. That unified field will do everything for you when you experience it. When you experience it, you infuse it, and you grow in that, and that field in Vedic science is called "atma," meaning the self. Know thyself. This is the thing—and so many things get better when you experience that and grow that. And it's just incredible. It's not a religion, it's not a cult, it's a human being thing. The human being—unbelievable beings, we are. And we have a full potential, and it's called enlightenment, and we can unfold that enlightenment. It doesn't happen overnight, it happens in time, but you've got to unfold it.

RB: *Then were there any unintentional things, you think, that emerged from a meditative session?*
DL: It's like this: you don't use meditation to get ideas. You use it to expand consciousness, and all the qualities of consciousness, which are all positive, and when you expand consciousness, you expand intelligence, because it's a field of infinite intelligence. It's like all the intelligence that there is is there, and it's fullness, infinite—infinite energy, infinite happiness, infinite love. So it's this field. And like I always say, you have consciousness, everybody has consciousness. And if you want to know what it is, take it away, and then you realize that without consciousness, you don't exist, and if you *did* exist, you wouldn't know it. I've been saying this on this tour for a long time. Without consciousness we don't exist. We can only say "I am" because of consciousness. And there it is: everybody has consciousness, but not everybody has the same amount. And as Maharishi [Mahesh Yogi] says, there are a lot of people who have more consciousness than the people who are meditating. . . . Consciousness is a real thing, that's the reality, and you can expand it, but only by experiencing the big ocean of it. So get yourself there for that experience.

And one more thing: like I always say, before brain research, we knew about all different kinds of meditation. Say six people get together and each one is doing a different kind of meditation. And they're all saying, "Man, oh, man, that was such a beautiful meditation, so deep, so sublime, so powerful, [I] came out so refreshed." But were they all talking about the *same thing*? How much of it was imagination, how much of it was—you know, whatever? It's the old thing—are we all seeing the same color when we say "red"? It's weird. So, with brain research, they now can show you—and it was, like, surprising—when someone truly transcends and experiences this deepest level of life, *boom*—automatically, there, right in front of them, total brain coherence, the only experience in life that lights up the full brain. We've always heard that we only use five or ten percent of our brain. Here is an experience that uses the full brain. *Full brain*. So you say, "Wait a minute, that *is* interesting."

RB: *I ask about this also because in the documentary film called* Lynch, *which was released last fall, there's a scene in which you tell two of your assistants that you need a young, twenty-something, edgy male actor for a particular role in* Inland Empire, *and that you want them to meditate in order to come up with suggestions.*

DL: What I meant by that was this: You fellows go meditate, and then afterwards come talk to me, because when you come out [of meditation], you are so clear that that's when things can come to you. . . . I was telling them: Go meditate, meditate great, as per usual, come out, then focus on that thing, and maybe then you'll bring the name to me that I want.

RB: *It suggests that there's a group effort of meditation in making your movies, at times, and not just you.*

DL: When you talk about groups, there's transcendental meditation and there's the TM city program [in Los Angeles], and one of those things is yogic flying. And when a group does their yogic flying together, they say that the effect is quadratically [sic] more powerful than the same number scattered about. Yogic flying basically looks like hopping on foam rubber. So people say, "What in the world is going on? How in the world could this bring peace? How in the *world*?" And then I always say, if you were riding on a zoom lens, and you could ride closer and closer and closer to the yogic flyer, and then go inside and experience what that person is experiencing, you wouldn't ask any more questions. "Bubbling bliss" is what they call it, and when you catch it, what drives you up on that hop is intense bliss, *huge*, like electric happiness. And it's so powerful. And when they're together this makes a huge wave. They're enlivening the unified field in huge waves, and it radiates out. And it affects collective consciousness.

For the past twenty years, they've been testing these groups who are hopping and telling people that's going to affect collective consciousness, and reduce crime and violence in the area of the test. How big an area, they were actually experimenting to see what the results were. And the yogic groups said, "We know this is very strange looking, and so we can't run the tests ourselves. These tests have got to be independently verified." I think the first one was done by Yale University, which looked at everything that was going on in this city where the groups were. And they analyzed the results: every time the groups came together, they'd looked at the crime stats before they started and they'd look at them during the thing and they'd look at them after they stopped, and—there it was—crime and violence went down. All the police reports showed it, all the FBI data, and all the other things people were using to measure this, went down: trips to the hospital went down, road accidents went down, and so on. They independently verified all this, but people said, "No, it's a fluke, a coincidence. It cannot be true." Even so, others said, "This certainly did happen," but the skeptics insisted, "You've got to test it again. It can't be true." So, long story short, fifty-two tests, and out of all these experiments, [it turns out that] the square root of one percent of a population is the minimum number of people it takes to create huge—HUGE—peace, harmony, coherence, and collective consciousness. So it's the unified field, which is a field eternal, unbounded, infinite, always been there—it's the enlivening of that that does it. This enlivened field is peace—and there it is.

RB: *I've often wondered about this because when I've read your descriptions like that, they sound in some ways, some ways—up to a point—similar to Nikki Grace's going down into some other dimension, and . . .*
DL: I don't know Nikki Grace—oh, Nikki Grace, sure . . .

RB: *Laura Dern's character, the actress, in* Inland Empire. *She has to go down into some other dimension . . .*
DL: Okay, here's another thing. What is kind of incredible is that there are, like quantum physics now says, ten dimensions of space and one dimension of time—that's what they've come up with. Ten dimensions of space—what does that mean? There's a field of relativity, it has a surface, and it has depths. There are, like they say, worlds within worlds within worlds, just unbelievable stuff going on in the field of relativity. And, that's all real interesting, but as Maharishi says, that's only "the marketplace." You go through the marketplace, and it's real interesting, but there are lots and lots of chances to get waylaid and even go backwards and get

lost, get in trouble. Maharishi always says, capture the fort, and then all the territories are yours—so get to the palace, get to the palace—and then you own all that you survey. "Get to the palace" means transcend, get to the deepest level, and Nikki Grace isn't getting *there*. Nikki Grace is somewhere else, and she does experience different kinds of things.

RB: *She does sound a lot like what you said in terms of worlds within worlds, where you get lost and get into plenty of trouble . . .*
DL: For sure.

RB: *The only thing that feels—the feeling of it, without it being explained entirely why—like this deeper thing Maharishi talks about, is the ending of* Inland Empire . . .
DL: For sure . . .

RB: *. . . when she simply sits on the couch, in that blue dress, . . .*
DL: Yeah . . .

RB: *. . . and she says nothing, her face doesn't change very much, but there's a feeling of a kind of stillness that's finally arrived, it seems . . .*
DL: Beautiful, yeah, that's very beautiful.

RB: *There's such a quietness there, of course, that she hasn't had at all in whatever various manifestations she's had . . .*
DL: Right.

RB: *. . . earlier on. Let me ask you, then: there's a lot in what you're describing in this movie, and probably in your other movies as well, about breaking out of boundaries and moving outside of limitations. I really had that sense in the credits of the movie, because the feeling of it was that the celebration was about* Laura Dern's *success, not necessarily Nikki Grace's, the character's. It was about the crew and the pleasure of the film as a film, because you have references going on to your other movies: you've got a lumberjack with logs . . .*
DL: That's the only one . . .

RB: *. . . alluding to* Blue Velvet *and* Twin Peaks, *we've got Laura Haring there who's from* Mulholland Drive. *There seemed to be a kind of unification . . .*
DL: That's a nice word . . .

RB: *. . . being suggested about the cast, the actors, the people making the movie, and in terms of the kinds of movies you've made. This is a riff I'm offering here, but I'm curious whether you have any thoughts about it.*
DL: Well, let's just say that's a good way to think.

RB: [Quick laugh] *You've brought up time, and that's very interesting in the movie too, because there are moments when the movie makes you feel like this could be an unending experience of pain for various characters, especially Laura Dern's characters, and then at other times you get the feeling that time may not really have passed at all. For me, the moment like that is when we reach almost the very end of the film, and we see Laura Dern looking across her living room again, as Nikki Grace, with Grace Zabriskie there, and she's already looked across the room to see herself get the role, but now she looks across the room to see herself finally quiet and still—almost as though she may not have gone through all that other stuff at all.*

DL: That's interesting. You know, you could say, when you think about this, as Maharishi says, it's "the pathless path." We don't go from *here* to *there*, we go from *here* to *here*. And, it's like this trip that we're on, human beings, from *here* to *here*. It doesn't make any sense, but somewhere inside it makes sense. And much of this is like that. And there's another thing: the world is as *you* are. And so, we see the world: the analogy is, if you have dark green dirty glasses and you look out, that's the world you see, that's the world you experience, but if you clean those glasses, or change those glasses to rose-colored glasses, there's a different thing you see, a different way that you experience it. With these stages that we go through, you just start seeing a different thing, and a different thing, and a different thing, and then you see that enlightenment is seeing it the way it really is. And that's interesting to think about.

RB: *There are several director-like figures in* Inland Empire: *there's Kingsley Stewart, played by Jeremy Irons, but then there's what could be called your voice cameo as Bucky Jay, a lighting grip having trouble that day, and apparently by your description on the DVD, Bucky Jay had a really bad time. He's a kind of director figure, but in this case he's just not getting anything quite done. And then there's another character who could be a maneuverer or manipulator, the Phantom, who could have his hands in possibly everything. Can you say something about that range of possibilities for a director?*

DL: Well, I don't think that there's . . . [pause]—that's *your* thing. Bucky Jay is not a director. Bucky Jay is a character, but I sort of . . . I like Bucky Jay. The other people you are talking about are—one of them is a director, Kingston. [Pause] I don't know what else to say . . .

RB: *Where did Bucky Jay come from?*

DL: Okay, I'll tell you. John Churchill—I call him "Churchie"— he's assistant director [Chuck Ross in *Inland Empire*], and Churchie's been my friend for a long time. Churchie—you know, different people bring out different things—Church started this because he used to drive me when we were shooting. He used to say, "David, those people over there, what's their story?" And I would just start riffing, and so I think that Bucky Jay came out of this thing. We were shooting Justin [Theroux], and I don't even know why we were shooting him; he was just smoking, and I was on the floor shooting up at him, and we were talking. It wasn't part of a scene—I forget what it was we were doing, we were testing something. And so we start riffing, and Churchie's asking me these questions, and anyway, Bucky Jay was born. And then the scene with Jeremy [Irons, as director Kingsley Stewart,] came out of that.

RB: *And you had a continued fondness for him, apparently.*
DL: For Bucky Jay? Yeah, yeah, yeah. I think there's more there, but I don't know for sure, but I like Bucky Jay and I like to think about what happened to him the night before and what the consequences are for the future.

RB: *Switching to the DVD, that seems like a real departure for you, because rather than the very stripped-down, "Here's-the-movie" approach, a lot more happens now, which seems like a shift in either your willingness or your enjoyment about those kind of things. You've got stories, you've got your cooking show [laugh from Lynch], you've got "More Things that Happened," as you call it, and you even put in little sections without labels. Did that feel like a big change?*
DL: I know what you're talking about. Always, the film is the thing, but if you don't hurt the film, other things are possible. And even with these things they call "extras," I worked for three years and I haven't made a nickel on *Inland Empire*. So it's a strange story. I wouldn't have put anything in there that would have hurt the film, and in some ways, "More Things that Happened" gives you more room to dream and to wonder about certain things. I like that idea. And the cooking was sort of a joke, but then the story came out and it had a mood, and so I kind of liked that kind of format. I don't cook [laugh], so it was fun to do that...

RB: *I had an intriguing thought about "More Things that Happened," because the feeling that I get is that that's like the relation you had to* Fire Walk with Me, *because you couldn't quite leave that world, you wanted to put it out there a little bit more. And the sense I have—here is what I wrote down—is that "Lynch seems to be saying, 'These things really happened in the world of the film,' rather than, 'These are the things I decided to leave out.'"*
DL: Uh huh.

RB: *And it seemed to be an expansion of that world, even though it's not officially a part . . .*
DL: That's very, very right. That's very, very good, because they *did* happen. And so, there it is.

RB: *Was it hard getting the movie down to its ultimate length?*
DL: Every film goes through that same thing. And I always say, when you work at the end of every film, you're now seeing it as a whole thing, and making the whole feel correct is the trick. And with every film, that's why time limits, arbitrary time limits, are so absurd. The thing wants to be a certain way—when it feels correct, that's a certain length. It just is. And that's the length. So it's unfortunate, in a way, if it feels correct and it's three hours long; you could say I would be a little more fortunate if it felt correct at two hours and seven minutes.

RB: *Was StudioCanal ever concerned about that?*
DL: Oh sure. You know, it's the kiss of death. [Laugh] But they made the money, and I didn't, so that's the way it goes sometimes.

RB: *There's another part of the extras that surprised me. There's a bit called "Lynch 2," where there are moments when you are barking at a couple of people, or you are saying "This is unacceptable," or you're cross, and I wondered [laugh from Lynch]—first of all, why you put that in, and second, whether this long a process was perhaps more frustrating than you wished.*
DL: No, no—it's funny, when you look at it, you know, . . . [pause] Well, my friend who made "Lynch 1" and "Lynch 2" [and who, as the director of *Lynch*, has wished to remain anonymous] followed me for close to a year, maybe nine or ten months, and I just got used to him being around. But at the same time, you always know that someone is there, and so it's a strange thing. But when you get real comfortable, you get more of a real thing of the making of a thing, or maybe seeing a time when an idea got caught, or seeing a thing go somewhere. And seeing it from the very beginning. And that was the idea. A lot of times people say, "We want to come in and shoot you for a day" or whatever, and it doesn't catch anything, and it seems false. It's not really, but it's false. As soon as a camera is there, no matter how comfortable, it's always part of what you know, but when you get used to it more and more and more, it gets closer to being something. And that was the experiment. And then, I bark out stuff, but it's really, if you look, it's all like I'm not really mad [laugh], it's just part of the thing. And I think that people know that I'm not really mad at them. It's part of the story.

RB: *Did you watch the documentary* Lynch in toto *once it was finished?*
DL: Oh sure.

RB: *What did you think of it?*
DL: I liked it. I have to give the same kind of freedom that I want to other people. And it's his film, and I like it okay. I like "Lynch 2." "Lynch 2" is more compact and faster, and it catches a feel of working, so I like it.

RB: *He decided to stick with kind of a pen-director's name, "Black and White." Do you know why he decided to do that?*
DL: You would have to talk to him sometime . . .

RB: *I have not seen that kind of thing in a long time. It was almost like a nineteenth-century novelist who doesn't want to be identified.*
DL: [Laugh]

RB: *Here you are about a year and a half since* Inland Empire *was released, and you've been through the reviews, the festivals, and all the rest. Are you feeling like something else is germinating?*
DL: I'm making a documentary of this tour that I was on for the past two months. We traveled with two guys who weren't professional cameramen, but each place we went, film students came, a couple other cameras came—so it's a lot of footage. And I'm just going to put it together as a documentary. After that, we'll see what comes. I've got to do this documentary. But the other night, I was driving and I passed a scene that inspired me. So, you know, I think about that since I saw it, and something could come from that.

RB: *You were driving in Los Angeles?*
DL: Yeah. . . . I love L.A., and every place has a million, trillion stories, but I like the possibilities in Los Angeles. . . .

RB: *The documentary you are working on is about your tour about meditation.*
DL: Yes, meditation and peace.

RB: *The way I would put it, you are now an official spokesperson.*
DL: Well, I don't how I got there, but I heard long ago that Maharishi had this technology for peace-creating groups. And I always say the same thing—"Oh, we're going to have peace right away." Then no one believed it, and it didn't happen. I thought, "The next time I go out, I'm going to tell people about it." And that's how that happened.

RB: *You are much more in the spotlight now doing that. Do you like that?*
DL: No, I don't like going in front of people.

RB: *But you feel it's kind of a calling?*
DL: Well [laugh], how do you say it?—yeah, I guess. I know that there are so many people who strongly believe in one thing or another, and to everyone else they sound like a nutcase, you know, and a lot of them sound like nutcases to me. It's very, you might think, dangerous to commit to anything. You put yourself on the line. But I just come back to what Maharishi has always said: water the root and enjoy the fruit. This unified field, if you enliven it, that's watering the root. For the individual, the fruit of that enlivening is enlightenment. In the world, watering the root is enlivening that unity with peace-creating groups, and the fruit of that is peace on earth. Peace. I created the David Lynch Foundation to give meditation to students, and you can't believe the horror stories. What happens when you give students TM—it just transforms things. And with school after school after school, student after student after student, there's so many stories of it being real dark, real stressful, and students next to wanting to commit suicide, and you give them this, and they open the door to infinite bliss, and intelligence, and all this stuff that's really just the self, and *boom*, they are cooking, and grades go up, they start getting along with their fellow students, they start appreciating the teacher—automatic. It's just a real thing . . .

RB: *Coming back to* Inland Empire, *was your company Absurda born with the need to distribute the movie, or had it been in existence before?*
DL: It had been in existence before, because we started distributing *Eraserhead* and the *Short Films*, and *Dumbland*. When *Inland Empire* came along, it was a risk, but it seemed a risk worth taking to go on our own for distribution. And I think it would have worked out if there had been more desire to see *Inland Empire*. But, you know, the good news is that films, some films, seem to come and go—even if they were popular for their time, they disappear. But even those will never disappear, really, because of digital; there will always be a way to see pretty much everything. But some films, even if they might not have been so popular, they have a way of continuing, and I am hoping that is *Inland Empire*—that over time, it will kind of keep going, and then, I think, I will be okay. It doesn't really matter, it's just that in order to do things, unfortunately, it takes money. It takes money. I always think it doesn't, but it does. [Hearty laugh]

RB: *Were you disappointed, then, with the way things went when* Inland Empire *was released?*

DL: No! No, no, no—we were in one hundred twenty theaters, and for a three-hour picture that no one understands, that's damn good—*really* good. And then, even though there's no money in theatrical distribution, it's back in theaters right now. They're booking theaters. DVDs are the thing where you have a chance of making some money, but DVD sales have been going down. And I think this is the first year when they're going up again. So there's hope, there's hope out there. There *is* hope.

RB: *The continued life of a film you talk about—that happened with* Fire Walk with Me.

DL: *Fire Walk with Me*—there's also this thing of fate, and, you know, in astrology, you can chart the highs and lows of our lives, and you can see that this is going to be a tough period. And that happened to me after around 1992: *Fire Walk with Me* was just crucified, and yet, over time, it got more and more acceptance, and appreciated more. So, yeah, that's all good news. And I'm starting to sing now, anyway, so that may be the next thing.

RB: *You're starting to sing?*

DL: [Laugh] I'm partly joking you, but I started singing, and it's kind of opened up another world.

RB: *Have you been doing public venues?*

DL: No, no. It's been totally a studio thing, and . . . I'm not a musician, so the problem is that to play something once is one thing, but to play it twice is another. And so, I don't see how I could tour, and now the music business is in such strange shape. They say that the only chance musicians have is through touring, and even that's tricky.

RB: *Are you writing all the songs yourself?*

DL: Yeah.

RB: *Are you collaborating with other people?*

DL: Well, Dean Hurley, who is the engineer in the studio here, is a killer bass player, and Dean is really helping me a lot. So Dean and I are doing it. I just love—I always say, Angelo Badalamenti brought me into the world of music, and so I love working with Angelo, but he lives in New Jersey. And so little by little, I am getting into it.

INDEX

ABC Television, 51, 53, 116, 220–21, 232
Alien, 9
Allen, Woody, xi
Altered States, 171
Altman, Robert, 250
Anderson, Laurie, 51
Anderson, Michael J., 119, 139
Arbus, Diane, 125
Arquette, Patricia, 159
Austin Powers: International Man of Mystery, 171

Bacon, Francis, 128, 175
Badalamenti, Angelo, 51, 61, 109, 122, 137, 138, 139, 140, 154–55, 158–59, 163–64, 192, 219, 234, 244, 266; "And Still," 158–59; "Mysteries of Love," 155; "Up in Flames," 109
Badlands, 209
Baecque, Antoine de, 202; *François Truffaut: A Biography*, 202
Barenholtz, Ben, 252
Basinger, Kim, 195
Bates, Jeanne, 5, 14
Bauhaus School, 168
Beach Boys, The, 40
Béhar, Henri, 134, 135–36, 139–40, 142; *Hollywood on the Riviera: The Inside Story of the Cannes Film Festival*, 134

Bergman, Ingmar, 114, 148; *Hour of the Wolf*, 202; *Wild Strawberries*, 4
Bergman, Ingrid, 44, 45, 198
Bergren, Eric, 19–20
Beymer, Richard, 57
B-films, 5, 14, 110
Blake, Robert, 159
Body Heat, 171
Bonanza, 5
Bonnie and Clyde, 110
Boorman, John, 115; *Zardoz*, 114
Bosch, Heironymous, 36, 47
Boston Museum School, 47, 53, 60, 120, 185
Bowie, David, 151, 155
Brakhage, Stan, 187
Brooklyn Academy of Music, 51
Brooks, Mel, xi, 19–20, 51, 56, 72, 180, 189–90; Brooksfilms, 19, 56, 189
Buñuel, Luis, 51, 69, 114; *An Andalusian Dog*, 69, 114
Burns, George, 133
Burroughs, William, 39

Cage, Nicolas, 49, 110
Camerimage, 222
Camus, Albert, 99
CanalPlus, 232, 233
Cannes Film Festival, 61, 134–44, 145, 180, 192, 195, 206, 226, 232, 233; Palme d'Or, xiv, 61, 180, 195, 226
Capra, Frank, 35, 119

268   INDEX

Casablanca, 44
Castelli, Leo, 121
Chaplin, Charlie, 13
Chareau, Pierre, 168
Churchill, John, 261-62
CIBY 2000, 135, 193
Citizen Kane, 10
Clowes, Daniel, 226
Cocteau, Jean, 51
Cohen brothers, 226
Columbia Pictures, 14
Connor, Bruce, 187
Coppola, Francis, 119; *The Godfather*, 202; Zoetrope, 119
Corcoran, James, 121
Corcoran School of Art, 47, 60, 184
Cornfeld, Stuart, 19, 189-90
Coulson, Catherine, 92
Cousteau, Jacques, 87
Cruise, Julee, 51, 122

Dafoe, Willem, 112
Dali, Salvador, 69; *An Andalusian Dog*, 69
Dallas, 57, 117
Daniel, Frank, 54, 84, 108, 122
Dead of Night, 4
Dee, Sandra, 123
De Laurentiis, Dino, 32, 51, 56, 71, 89, 93, 119, 190-91
De Laurentiis, Raffaella, 71
De Laurentiis Entertainment Group (DEG), 29, 51, 191
Deming, Peter, 171, 173-79
Dern, Laura, xii, 37, 49, 57, 110, 111, 181, 246-50, 260
De Vore, Christopher, 19-20
Diller, Barry, 190
Disney Pictures, 220
Donahue, Troy, 123
Dr. Jekyll and Mr. Hyde, 210
Drop Dead Fred, 171
Duchamp, Marcel, 90; *Given 1) The Waterfall 2) The Illuminating Gas*, 90
Dunham, Duwayne, 107, 108
Durbin, Deanna, 9
Dynasty, 116

Eames, Charles, 168
Eames, Ray, 168
East Village Eye, The, 252

Ebert, Roger, 41, 96
Egoyan, Atom, 226
Eisner, Michael, 190
Elmes, Frederick, 31, 55, 57, 115, 208
Engels, Robert, 137-38, 142, 144, 192, 193
Escher, M. C., 151
Evans, Walker, 215
Evil Dead 2, 171
Exorcist, The, 42

Farnsworth, Richard, 201, 203, 204, 207, 208, 215, 218
Fellini, Federico, 114; *8½*, 202; *La Strada*, 47
Fenn, Sherilyn, 229
Figaro, Le, 87
film noir, 29, 111, 172, 198, 223
Filmex, 252
Fireworks, 4
Fisk, Jack, 53, 54, 57, 121, 185, 209-10, 251
Fisk, Mary, 3, 5, 7, 55, 121, 189, 253
Fleury, Jean-Claude, 134, 135-36
Ford, John, 218
Forster, Robert, 235-36
Francis, Freddie, 22-28, 207-8, 219; *The Doctor and the Devils*, 22, 24
Freeman, J. E., 112
Frost, Mark, 57, 58, 61, 86-87, 116, 153, 180

Getty, Balthazar, 159, 176-77, 178
Gifford, Barry, 59, 94, 106, 150, 198; *Night People*, 150; *Wild at Heart: The Story of Sailor and Sula*, 59, 78-79, 94, 106, 114, 150, 198
Goldwyn, Samuel, 95, 107
Good Times on Our Street, 115
Great Depression, 215
Guns of Navarone, The, 192

Hagelin, John, 228
Hardy Boys, The, 34, 56
Harring, Laura, 244
Harris, Thomas, 85; *Silence of the Lambs*, 85; *Red Dragon*, 85
HBO, 173
Hedaya, Dan, 234
Henri, Robert, 128, 185; *The Art Spirit*, 128, 185
Herbert, Frank, 51; *Dune*, 51

Hill Street Blues, 116
Hitchcock, Alfred, 47, 114, 202; *Rear Window*, 123, 202, 228; *Vertigo*, 223, 240
Hoberman, J., 232
Holden, Stephen, 232
Hollywood Shuffle, 171
Hopper, Dennis, xii, 31, 37, 43, 112, 170, 181, 191
Horse, Michael, 88, 122
House Party, 171
Hurley, Dean, 266
Hurt, John, 19, 20–21

Independent Spirit Awards, xii
Indiana, Gary, 252
It's a Mad, Mad, Mad, Mad World, 86

Jeanneret, Pierre, 168
Joseph, Allen, 14
Jung, Carl, 7

Kael, Pauline, 50, 57
Kafka, Franz, 38, 47; *The Trial*, 38
Kagan, Vladimir, 168
Keaton, Buster, 13
Keeler, Bushnell, 120, 128, 184–85
Keeler, Toby, 120, 128, 181, 184, 187
King, Henry, 123, 218; *Wait Till the Sun Shines, Nellie*, 123, 218
Kokoschka, Oskar, 53, 185
Krantz, Tony, 116
Kubrick, Stanley, 47, 52, 114, 123, 202; *Lolita*, 47, 202

Ladd, Diane, 111–12
Lansbury, Angela, 111
Le Corbusier, 168
Lee, Sheryl, 142
Levine, Gary S., 53
Lipton, Peggy, 57
Little House on the Prairie, 14
Loucks, Brian, 244
Lovecraft, H. P., 37; *The Color Out of Space*, 37
Lynch, David: on abstraction, viii, 8, 33, 39, 52, 69, 70, 74, 75, 76, 77–78, 81, 84, 85, 119, 135, 148, 157, 179, 200, 202, 203, 249, 253; on the absurd, 13, 29, 30, 33, 36–37, 48, 54, 85, 88, 90–91, 119, 239; Absurda, 265; on accidents in filmmaking, 151, 152, 157, 177, 244; on acting, 88–89; on actors, 11–12, 20–21, 32, 35, 88, 92, 107, 110, 111–12, 119, 122, 124, 140, 142, 143, 159, 177, 198–99, 203, 204, 206, 207, 208, 209–10, 215, 218, 234, 235–37, 239–40, 244, 249, 250; on adaptation, 94–95, 106–7, 114; adolescence, 47, 53, 60, 66–67, 120, 123–24, 128, 153; on Americana/American life, 35, 62, 115–16, 130–31, 212, 218; at the American Film Institute, 5, 15, 19, 54, 60, 71, 108, 121, 122–23, 168, 199, 201; on his anger, 99, 263; animation, 13, 26, 121; on ants, 62, 183; appearance and dress, 10, 43, 51, 145, 200, 223; on architecture, 166–68; on the "Art Life," 67–69, 184; art school study, 5, 47, 53, 60, 120, 183, 184–85, 201; on art vs. reality, 96–97, 136–37; Asymmetrical Productions, 170; on audience response, 17, 82–84, 148, 233, 244–45, 252–53; on autobiographical elements in his films, 32, 35, 56–57, 119; on the "baby" in *Eraserhead*, 6; on "balance," as aesthetic principle, 37, 109, 126, 128, 130, 136, 137, 141, 257; on the "beautiful," as aesthetic, 5, 12, 31, 75, 77, 86, 97, 104, 128, 129, 130, 131, 152, 157, 160, 161, 167, 172, 178, 186, 192, 197, 200, 209, 210, 211, 220, 225, 230, 237, 244, 249, 250, 258, 260; on being "detectives," 58, 153, 209; and being enigmatic, vii, 47, 138; on B-films, 14, 110, 141; *The Big Fish* (book), 251; on the body/body functions, 65, 68, 76, 96, 105, 123, 127, 238–39; *The Bride* (painting), 185–86; *A Bug Dreams* (painting), 129; Nicolas Cage, on resembling, 119; on cars, 146, 204, 228; casting, 43, 44, 119, 140, 235, 258; Center for Advanced Film Studies, 54, 60, 84; childhood, 16, 35, 47, 53, 60, 62–64, 119–20, 123–24, 127–28, 132–33, 153, 182–84, 203–4, 215,

Lynch, David (*continued*)
218; cinematography, 16, 22, 28, 57, 107, 110, 115, 118, 122, 173–79, 208–9, 214, 216–17, 240–41, 242–43; on city traumas, 62, 64, 65, 68–69, 101, 186, 217; on color, 241–42; color vs. black and white, 26–27; on comedy, 33, 86, 88, 119; on commercials, 90–91; on concrete, virtues of, 222; consciousness, states of, xii–xiii, 68, 133, 257, 258–59; on contrast as aesthetic principle, 34, 74–75, 111, 128, 137, 141, 143, 181–82; costumes, 31, 177, 210, 242; on creativity, 98, 99–100; David Lynch Foundation for Consciousness-Based Education and Peace, xiii, 251, 265; DavidLynch.com, 223, 230, 245, 251; on death, 75, 133, 197, 220; on decay, 47, 65, 66, 101, 127, 186; on directing, 8, 21, 38, 106, 115, 124, 137–38, 146, 157, 158, 205, 213, 214, 263; on director figures in his films, 249, 261; directors he admires, 36, 47, 52, 114, 123, 148, 202, 239, 250; on "disease," 39, 77–78, 99; on the disgusting, 40; distribution of films, 265–66; dreamlike quality of films, ix, 4, 6–7, 39, 74, 97, 113, 115, 144, 153, 172, 178, 223, 227, 241; on dreams/dreaming, 40, 63, 68, 123, 126, 136, 148, 150, 168, 202, 236–37, 262; on the duck as aesthetic principle, 71, 160–61; on DVD extras, 262, 263–64; as Eagle Scout, 180–81; editing, 107, 108, 124, 138, 166, 178, 203, 219, 243; electricity, interest in, 48, 189; endings of his films, 14, 48, 88, 95–96, 106–7, 111, 117, 214, 237, 260–61; on Europe, 68–69; exhibitions of his artwork and furniture, 120–21, 160, 164, 165, 199; on experimentalism, 253; on factories, 31–32, 74, 222, 231; family, representations in his films of, 9–10, 13, 111, 119, 137, 172, 210, 218, 227; on fatherhood, 69, 76, 188, 195, 229; on fear, 37, 47, 62, 99, 109, 126, 127–28, 130, 132, 153; on feeling things "in the air," 63, 101, 122–23, 141, 153, 205–6, 215–16, 217, 219, 228; on film favorites, 47, 114, 123, 148, 202, 210, 223, 239; on film festivals, 142, 233; on film noir, 29, 111, 172; on final cut, importance of, 30, 56, 71, 192, 233; "fishing" for ideas, x, 13, 30, 53, 97, 198, 236, 254, 255; food and eating habits, 52, 55–56, 189, 195, 225; French interest/support for his films, xiii–xiv, 233, 254; on furniture design, 164–66, 168–69, 229–30; on Great Depression, generation of the, 215; on the grotesque, 17, 29, 31; on horror, 35, 64, 67, 73, 100, 103–4, 109, 113; on humor, 13, 37, 72–73, 86–87, 91–92, 109, 111, 144, 148; on "ideas," 8, 13, 30, 40, 48, 58, 77, 80, 93, 97, 100, 102, 112, 149, 150–52, 157, 158, 159, 161, 164, 171, 177, 179, 190, 205, 214, 225, 238, 242, 245, 247–48, 253; on "ideas" vs. "themes," x, 76, 81, 243–44; imagination, the, 47, 80, 96, 100, 126, 148, 177, 182, 213, 258; improvisation, 14, 111–12, 177, 243; incest in his films, 79–80, 140; influence from other filmmakers, 5, 28, 30, 47; influence on other filmmakers, 142, 226; on interpretations, divergent, 8, 138, 179, 247, 249; intuition, x, 6, 26–27, 70, 75, 76, 81, 82, 97, 144, 149, 151–53, 172, 196, 206, 211, 244, 245; on irony, 111, 214; *I See Myself* (painting), 182; Kafka, Franz, admiration for, 38; "kits" of animals, 32, 89, 160; on the "Log Lady," 92; on Los Angeles, 206, 224, 227, 264; *Lynch* (documentary), 258, 264; "Lynchian" as descriptor, xi, 33, 57, 226; on machines, 31, 204–5, 217–18; Kyle MacLachlan, on resembling, 32, 35, 56–57, 119; on the "magical," 47, 58, 98, 113, 121, 127, 141, 142, 148, 249; on midnight screenings of his films, 3, 12, 17–18, 19,

252; on the Midwest, 212, 217; on money, 89, 98–99, 131, 265, 266; on "mood," ix, 10, 28, 29, 66, 141, 152, 156, 166, 171, 172, 209, 249, 262; on the movie business, 237–38; on music, interest in, 123, 154–55, 158–59, 172, 202, 266; music in his films, 3, 36, 88, 109–10, 116, 122, 125, 137, 138, 140, 157, 159, 166, 171, 172, 176–77, 192, 209, 219, 249, 266; on the mysterious, vii, 8, 30, 39, 48, 68, 70, 76, 78, 86, 98, 104, 109, 114, 126, 147, 153, 224, 244; on mystery stories, 74; Jack Nance, on resembling, 32; on nature/the natural, 52, 66, 71, 74, 101, 126, 127, 129, 161, 204, 205, 209, 216–18; on his obsessions, 72–74, 97–99; on originality, 123–24, 139, 154, 184, 185; "painterly" effects in his films, 38, 70; on painters, 36, 47, 90, 120, 128, 184–85; his painting, x, 5, 6–7, 12, 26, 28, 30, 32, 66, 72, 74, 84, 99, 120–21, 123, 126, 127, 128–30, 154, 160, 163–64, 184–86, 202; on painting vs. filmmaking, 32, 70–71, 115, 186; on Philadelphia, 5, 16, 27, 47–48, 53–54, 64, 66, 69, 121, 124, 154, 186; photography, 72, 125, 231; on politics, 74, 101–3, 143–44, 223, 227–28, 249; popularity, 131, 226; on "power" in his films, 34, 40; his "preverbal stage," vii–viii, 187; on producing, 116; Propaganda Films, 234; on props, importance of, 108; on the psyche, instability of, 227, 256; and psychiatry, 73, 74, 83, 97–98, 142, 224; on "psychogenic fugue," 172; on psycho-killers, 93; on realism, 113; rehearsal, 14, 159, 243; on reincarnation, 197; on relativity, 220; on religious experience, 132; reluctance to explain the meaning of his films, viii–x, 3, 6, 8, 18, 26–27, 28, 29, 30, 31, 103, 138, 187, 196, 224, 239, 253; sadomasochism in his films, xii, 41, 43, 45, 78, 141; on science fiction and fantasy, 30; on screenwriting, 20, 28, 106–8, 116, 122, 124, 137–38, 144, 150–51, 166, 246–47, 254, 255; on scripts, translating into film, 214, 253; on Second World War, men of the, 211, 215; on secrets, 64, 67, 103–4, 113–14; on set design, 108, 166–67, 169, 241; on sex/sexuality, 38–39, 43, 68, 72–74, 76, 79, 94–95, 118; *She Wasn't Fooling Anyone, She Was Hurt Bad* (painting), 129; on shooting, process of, 107–8, 110; singing, 251, 266; on "sickness," 35, 36, 38, 39, 40, 58, 77, 85–86, 93, 100, 103, 198, 229; on smoking, 68, 224–25; soap operas/melodrama, 38, 111, 116, 117, 123; songwriting, 61, 158–59, 251; *So This Is Love* (painting), 127; sound design, 157–58; sound effects, 4, 6, 10–11, 14–15, 37, 141, 158, 218; sound mixing, 110, 116, 117, 138, 152, 158, 220, 229, 234; on soundtracks, 109–10, 138, 152, 154–55, 219, 244; speaking style, 43, 51, 52, 62, 134, 170, 194, 223; story structure, 3, 39, 71, 74, 107, 179, 215, 227, 241, 247; on the subconscious, 3, 7, 36, 197; on surface/depth relations, 31, 46, 147, 183, 228, 259; on the surreal, 209; on Surrealism, 69–70, 238, 254; on technology, 167; on television, 130, 131; on television, working in, 116, 118, 136, 137–39, 144, 146, 220, 235–36, 238; on television vs. film technical quality, 90, 117–18; on temporality, 261; on test screenings, 82–84, 203; on "texture," ix, 12, 27, 28, 31, 68, 71; on Transcendental Meditation (TM), 70, 99, 161–62, 256–60, 264–65; on violence, 58, 64, 68, 86, 126, 186; violence in his films and paintings, xii, 16, 43, 72–73, 94–95, 106–7, 108–9, 111, 118, 129, 137, 140–41, 164; on *The Wizard of Oz*, importance of, 94–95, 107, 114–15, 210; women, his representations of, xii, 7, 9, 31, 38, 42–43,

Lynch, David (*continued*)
45, 50, 76–80, 198, 199; on wood as aesthetic principle, 165–66; on words, difficulty with, vii–viii, 103, 187, 252; on world-making, 65, 74, 116, 118, 157, 163, 242, 245, 249, 255–56, 262–63
  Projects (unproduced): *Dream of the Bovine*, 193, 230; *Gardenback*, 84; *Goddess*, 86; *The Lemurians*, 87; *One Saliva Bubble*, 86–87, 89, 119, 138–39; *Ronnie Rocket*, 19, 33, 37, 48, 85, 89, 119, 138–39, 189; *Up at the Lake*, 89
  Works: *The Alphabet*, 54, 75, 96, 121, 187; *The Amputee*, 92; "The Angriest Dog in the World," 61, 99, 160; *Blue Velvet*, 26, 28, 29–33, 34–40, 41–48, 50, 51, 53, 56–57, 61, 72, 76–78, 79, 88, 89, 93–94, 96, 109, 113, 115, 135, 143, 154–55, 170, 181, 191, 196–97, 198; *The Cowboy and the Frenchman*, 87–88, 122, 234; *Dune*, 22, 29, 30, 32, 51, 56, 61, 71–72, 89, 102, 187, 190–91, 207–8, 226; *The Elephant Man*, xi, 19–21, 22, 24–27, 31, 45, 56, 60–61, 72, 75, 77, 112, 166, 189–90, 207–8, 213–14, 215–16, 219–20; *Eraserhead*, xiii, 3–8, 9–18, 19, 26–27, 30–31, 32, 38, 46, 48, 54–55, 56, 60, 65–66, 69, 70, 79, 84, 88, 92, 122, 123, 156, 166, 167, 170, 187–89, 195, 208, 209, 231, 239, 252–53, 255; *The Grandmother*, 7, 10, 26, 54, 60, 75, 84, 96, 121, 158, 187; *Hotel Room*, 173; *Industrial Symphony No. 1*, 51, 61; *Inland Empire*, xiii, xiv, 246–50, 251–64; *Lost Highway*, x, xiii, xiv, 155–56, 159, 165, 166, 167, 171–79, 182, 183, 195–99, 202, 235, 241; *Mulholland Drive* (film), x, xiv, 223–24, 227, 232–45; *Mulholland Drive* (television), 202, 220–21, 223, 232; *On the Air*, 146, 195; *Six Men Getting Sick*, 54, 96, 121, 186; *The Straight Story*, 201, 202–12, 213–20, 227; *Twin Peaks*, xi, 51–52, 53, 57–58, 61, 77, 79, 89, 91–93, 116–18, 131, 138–39, 153, 166, 192, 197, 217, 226; *Twin Peaks: Fire Walk With Me*, xi, 61, 134–44, 145–47, 150, 170–71, 193, 195, 197, 221, 226, 262, 266; *Wild at Heart*, xii, 49–52, 55, 59, 61, 75, 77–79, 82–83, 93–96, 103, 106–14, 140, 150, 195, 216

Lynch, Jennifer, 55, 64, 76, 132, 187, 188, 195; *Boxing Helena*, 55, 195
Lynch, Mary. *See* Fisk, Mary
Lynch, Peggy. *See* Reavey, Peggy

MacLachlan, Kyle, 31, 32, 56–57, 58, 143, 191, 196
Mailer, Norman, 46; *Tough Guys Don't Dance*, 46
Malick, Terrence, 121, 122
Mancini, Henry, 123
Manhunter, 86
Manson, Marilyn, 155; "I Put a Spell on You," 155
Martin, Steve, 86–87, 119
McKenna, Christine, 120
Miller, Ann, 235, 242
Missing, 39
Mod Squad, The, 57
Monroe, Marilyn, 86
Montgomery, Monty, 234
Morricone, Ennio, 139
My Cousin Vinny, 171

Nance, Jack (John), 4, 11, 32, 55, 88, 94, 104, 187
Natural Law Party, 228
NBC Television, 87
Neff, John, 202
Neutra, Richard, 168
Newsweek, 10, 41
New Yorker, The, 50
New York Film Festival, 41, 232, 233
New York Times Magazine, The, 181
Norris, Patricia, 108, 115, 169, 173, 175, 210, 242
Northern Exposure, 226

O'Neal, Ryan, 46
Orbison, Roy, 50, 244; "Crying," 244

Paramount Pictures, 19, 239
Parker, Alan, 189
Pennsylvania Academy of Fine Arts, 5, 47, 53, 60, 120, 183, 185, 201

Perkins, Tony, 43
Perriand, Charlotte, 168
Petticoat Junction, 42
Philadelphia Story, 187
Piano, The, 191
Polemisis, Estelle, 158–59; "And Still," 158–59
Power Mad, 110; "Slaughterhouse," 110
Pullman, Bill, 159, 175–76, 178

Rathborne, Tina, 88–89; *Zelly and Me*, 88–89
Ray, Johanna, 140
Reagan, Nancy, 223
Reagan, Ronald, 101, 227
Reavey, Peggy, 55, 64, 76, 132, 183, 185–86, 188–89, 191, 193
Reed, Rex, 44
Reznor, Trent, 153, 155
Right to Live, The, 110
Rio, Rebekah del, 244
Roach, John, 205, 210, 213
Roberts, Judith Anna, 5
Roberts, Pernell, 5
Robie, Wendy, 86
Rockwell, Norman, 36, 47, 50, 171
Rohe, Ludwig Mies van de, 168
Rosselini, Isabella, vii, 31, 35, 38, 41, 43–48, 52–53, 87, 88, 102, 119, 181, 187, 190, 191, 193, 197, 198–99, 228
Rossellini, Roberto, 45

Sade, Marquis de, 35
Salvador, 39
Sanger, Jonathan, 19–20
Schindler, Rudolph Michael, 168
School of the Museum of Fine Arts, Boston. See Boston Museum School
Scorsese, Martin, 52, 114–15, 123; *Alice Doesn't Live Here Anymore*, 114–15
Second World War, 215
Shepherd, Morgan, 112
Short, Martin, 86
Sichler, Frederic, 254
Silverman, Freddie, 189–90
Siskel, Gene, 41, 96
Smith, Jack, 17; *Flaming Creatures*, 17
Sontag, Susan, 17

Spacek, Sissy, 209–10
Splet, Alan, 4, 10–11, 158, 201
Stanton, Harry Dean, 50, 88, 110, 112, 122
Stewart, Charlotte, 5, 14
Stewart, Jimmy, xi, 51, 61, 180, 187, 223
Stockhausen, Karlheinz, 229
Straight, Alvin, 201, 205, 213, 215
Strand, Paul, 215
Strauss, Richard, 110; *Four Last Songs*, 110
StudioCanal, 254, 263
Summer Place, 123
Summers, Anthony, 86; *Goddess: The Secret Life of Marilyn Monroe*, 86
Surrealism/surrealist effects, 6, 29, 50, 51, 69–70, 177
Sweeney, Mary, 179, 182, 190, 191, 193, 201, 205, 210, 212, 213, 217, 225, 229

Tamblyn, Russ, 57
Tarantino, Quentin, 226
Tati, Jacques, 47, 114, 123, 202; *Mr. Hulot's Holiday*, 202; *My Uncle*, 202
Taylor, Koko, 109
Theroux, Justin, 261
They Live by Night, 110
This Mortal Coil, 154; "Song to the Siren," 154
Thomas, Ross, 36
Thompson, David, 191; *Biographical Dictionary of Film*, 191
Tibetan Book of the Dead, 7–8
Time, 181, 182, 226
Toubiana, Serge, 202; *François Truffaut: A Biography*, 202
Trading Places, 119
Transcendental Meditation (TM), xii–xiii, 52, 55, 70, 190, 191, 251
Truffaut, François, 202

Under Fire, 39
Updike, John, 39; *The Witches of Eastwick*, 39

Visconti, Luchino, 37

Wagner, Natasha Gregson, 199
Waits, Tom, 161

Wallace, David Foster, 223
Wall Street Journal, The, 55
Walter, Tracy, 88, 122
Wasserman, H. Barton, 186–87
Waters, John, 36–37, 189
Watts, Naomi, 223
Weidemann, Jon, 47
West, Jocelyn, 158–59; "And Still," 158–59
West Side Story, 57
White Noise, 121
Wilder, Billy, 239; *Sunset Boulevard*, 47, 57, 123, 202, 223, 239
Winters, Shelley, 111

Wittgenstein, Ludwig, 9
Wizard of Oz, The, 94–95, 107, 114–15, 210, 224
Wood, Natalie, 199
Wright, Eric, 167, 168
Wright, Frank Lloyd, 167, 168
Wright, Lloyd, 167, 168; Beverly Johnson House, 167

X Files, The, 194

Yogi, Maharishi Mahesh, 257, 259–60, 261, 264, 265
Yuuki, Nae, 249

www.ingramcontent.com/pod-product-compliance
Lightning Source LLC
Chambersburg PA
CBHW021834220426
43663CB00005B/238